STRENGTH TRAINING
FOR CYCLING
PERFORMANCE

THE *VORTEX METHOD'S* ULTIMATE TRAINING PROGRAM

STRENGTH TRAINING FOR CYCLING PERFORMANCE

MENACHEM M. BRODIE

NSCA-Certified Strength & Conditioning Specialist, USA Cycling Expert Coach

FOREWORD BY SELENE YEAGER

CONTENTS

FOREWORD

ENTER THE VORTEX

By Selene Yeager

When I picked up bike racing in the mid-90s, cyclists were often told not to strength train. Lifting weights was deemed mostly counterproductive. As a mountain bike racer, personal trainer, coach, *Bicycling* magazine contributor, and woman, I have always believed resistance training was time well spent. But the resources were sorely lacking . . . and contradictory.

I fumbled my way through—learning, growing, experimenting, and dishing out advice the best I could—as core training, foam rolling, functional training, body weight workouts, mobility and stability work, and more all entered the scene.

Today we have more information than ever on all of these methods, right at our fingertips. We also have more *misinformation* than ever. And sometimes that misinformation looks really good with the right lighting and perfect pictures on Instagram.

How the heck do you sieve through it all and come up with a cohesive, comprehensive plan that benefits you and your cycling clients most? Read this book. Seriously.

PULLING IT ALL TOGETHER

Menachem Brodie's Human Vortex Training workshops are among the most sought out in continuing education circles for a reason: He has done the hard work of living, breathing, and synthesizing all the components of getting stronger—truly stronger— in the sport of cycling. And now he's pulled them together in an easy-to-use resource.

Strength Training for Cycling Performance is a user's manual for your human frame. Much like your bike, you want your frame to be stiff where you need it to be stiff and fluid where it needs to be fluid so you can produce power and speed that doesn't waste energy or, worse, create undue wear and tear.

This program includes soft tissue work, breath work, dynamic exercises, and, of course, intelligently programmed resistance training. It's all there, and then some. Honestly, this book could have been four or five books. But the beauty is that it is not. If you're anything like me, you already have books and articles on core and mobility and strength and breath and training. And so we're left with a stack of books and a blank schedule to fill in while still trying to leave spare time for clients and ourselves—not to mention a day job and family life.

Brodie beautifully explains each essential exercise component, each fundamental movement, the science behind a healthy spine, why breath work matters, how soft tissue manipulation improves performance, and more, in plain language but also in complete detail. Then he puts it into a framework you can use. With this program, you'll know what soft tissue and body work to do and how long it will take; what your dynamic warm-up should look like; and how it meshes with your plyometrics, strength, posture, stability, and corrective exercises in one 70-minute session. The annual overview provides guidance on strength training you can use year-round.

A PROGRAM FOR EVERYONE

While cycling is recognizing that it hasn't always been the most inclusive space, it's a breath of fresh air that Brodie devotes a chapter to women.

Sports science has caught up to the fact that "women are not small men." Our unique hormones and physiology require understanding, training, and fueling adaptations for optimum performance, especially during menstrual cycles and as we enter perimenopause and menopause. It's refreshing to see that language used and those issues addressed in a strength training for cycling performance book.

THE ONLY BOOK YOU'LL NEED

Spine health, posture correction, programming, metabolic training, on-bike intervals, breath work, in-depth knowledge of the mechanics behind producing power on a bike, bike fit . . . the list of what you'll find in these pages goes on and on. And while there are entire books written on each of these topics, most of us just need to know what we need to know to help ourselves and our clients get and stay strong, improve performance, and enjoy the sport we love injury-free.

For that, this is the only book you'll need.

INTRODUCTION

Since around the year 2010 there has been a significant shift happening in the world of cycling regarding how we, as a community of athletes and enthusiasts, think about and approach our training.

This shift has happened through a few stages:

First, there was a focus on decreasing the total amount of time cyclists spent out on the road while increasing the density of their training. This stage came to the masses in the book *The Time-Crunched Cyclist* by Chris Carmichael, published in 2009.

Next, the focus turned to improving recovery from sport stresses. This stage taught cyclists to expand on the idea of what "recovery" entails and how to get there. This culminated in the book *The Athlete's Guide to Recovery* by Sage Rountree.

The last stage, which builds upon the first two and is where we currently stand, has seen the focus turn to improving our muscles' ability to move us, via the addition of strength training for cyclists—a concept which is now coming together in this very book.

While there have been one or two other books written on the subject, none of them has done as deep of a dive into what *really* boosts your performance, or how to best include strength training in your year-round training regimen, as what you're about to read. In fact, many of them suggest that you include strength training *only* during your transition and base periods. That prior understanding of strength training certainly opened the door for you to be where you are right now, ready to open your eyes to the incredible advantages and improvements that an intelligently built, year-round strength training program has for you.

For decades, poor practices and myths surrounding strength training have been allowed to run free in endurance sports circles, despite there being coaches who knew a better way. Too often, their guidance fell on deaf ears, as athletes wouldn't listen without proof of research to back their coach's claims. I've spoken about it in my courses, presentations, and continuing education classes for coaches from around the world. If you wait to follow the research, you are easily 5–10 years behind what the best in the profession are doing.

Over the last nearly 25 years that I've been studying and practicing in the health and fitness and strength and conditioning fields, I've been able to figure out what exactly endurance athletes, specifically cyclists, need to get from strength training.

My job as a Strength and Conditioning Coach isn't to make my athletes as powerful as possible. Nor is it to make my athletes as lean as possible. My number one job, far and above all else, is, as Frank Velasquez, the former Strength and Conditioning Coach for the Pittsburgh Pirates baseball team once said, "to keep the money on the field."

My job is to keep athletes healthy, balanced, injury free, and able to continue to perform and excel in their specific position or role—and that is where this book comes in. Just by picking up this book and reading it, I know that you are someone who enjoys their chosen endurance sport, who loves the competition it allows for, and who enjoys (perhaps in a sadistic way) the discomfort and even "good" pain associated with training and pushing your boundaries. You're someone who wants that competitive edge and is willing to work hard for it. And while you work hard, you're smart about how you approach and do things. You don't train on a whim; you do things because you know they work. Because you've seen results. Because you know that there is so much more to endurance sports than just going out and spending the time and effort to get miles in.

This book was not written as an "end all, be all," nor is it meant to be used as a Bible for endurance strength training. Rather, it's meant to give you the basic tools necessary for you to truly understand your body—how it moves, its strengths and weaknesses—and to allow you to form a solid battle plan to get it to where you want or need it to be.

I want every individual who picks up this book to understand that strength training can do amazing things for your abilities on the bike. It is the missing link to allowing you to perform at a high level, for a prolonged period of time, and to do so pain free when done correctly.

So how do you use this book?

Take your time, first off. Read through it before jumping into the exercise regimens. I cannot stress how important this is, as there is so much more to strength training than what you've read, learned, or been taught up to this point!

In order to get what you want and need out of this book, I suggest you go through the stages of learning these new, sometimes paradigm-shifting ideas. This will allow you to better understand that *how* you do something is far more important than what you are doing.

"Give a man a fish, and he'll eat for a meal. Teach a man to fish, and he'll feed himself and others for a lifetime."

You'll learn the why's and when's. You'll learn, using today's most cutting-edge science, why breathing and learning to create stiffness and tension in some places while allowing other places to completely relax and be loose—will not only help make you more powerful on the road, but also help protect your body from overuse or malalignment injuries, which have forced so many cyclists to give up the sport that they love.

In order to help you get the most out of this book, I've created a special members area on the Human Vortex Training website. Head over to the Book Bonus Content section on the website (www.HumanVortexTraining.com), and sign up to get free access to the videos for the exercises shown in the book, and other cool bonus content. The access code is: THEVORTEXTRIBE

You'll notice there are lots of photographs to help you better understand the exercises and what's being asked of you. I know from my own experience from the last 15+ years of coaching athletes of all backgrounds and abilities from around the world, that in order for something to be taught best, it has to be taught the way an athlete learns.

Developmental psychologists have identified four predominant ways of learning: reading, seeing, feeling, hearing (or written, visual, tactile, and auditory). *Seeing* and *reading* are completely different. *Hearing* and *feeling* are very different as well. So in an effort to allow as many individuals as possible to learn from this book, I focused on the reading and seeing route here, and the seeing and hearing route on the web. Now, if you learn best by feeling (tactile), you'll have to sign up for one of my hands-on lectures, or schedule an appointment to come work with me.

Each one of us learns best in a very different and unique way, and it's my goal to help you learn the best way for YOU!

THE OTHER MISSING LINK

While this book primarily addresses the physical side of things, and that is a large part of success in cycling, it is far from our only limiting factor. Will improving your physical abilities and prowess alone help you succeed? Absolutely not!

There is another thing, something often neglected in the coaching world, but that you *must* train for success. Yogi Berra said it best: "90% of the game is half mental." Your brain, or your mind, will determine how high you can fly, more so than any of your physical capabilities.

Failure to train your mind to focus or to build mental strength and resilience are non-negotiables if you're serious about performing well in any aspect of life. There are plenty of books written on this topic, and I would encourage you to research this important part of training. Check out some of my recommendations, on this and other topics, in the Additional Resources section at the end of the book.

I'm incredibly proud to share this book with you. Thank you for the opportunity to help you get stronger, fitter, and faster.

Let's get started.

SECTION 1: FUNDAMENTALS

CHAPTER 1
THE IMPORTANCE OF STRENGTH TRAINING FOR CYCLISTS

Strength training is not easy, but then neither is interval training for the bike. Given how many non-endurance athletes incorporate and benefit from strength training in their training programs, I find it rather odd that endurance athletes have not taken to proper strength training en masse.

Interval training, which is incredibly prevalent in the endurance sports world and especially cycling, is so closely related to strength training in how the work and rest periods are designed to get a specific response. Speed, intensity, percentage of maximum effort, and timing of sets and rest in between sets all must be planned for appropriately in order to get the training effect you are after!

These principles are all one and the same, as for any other sport. So why is it that cyclists have resisted strength training for so long?

In part, it has to do with the field of strength and conditioning still being in its relatively early years, and the fact that it has grown as a completely separate field from sport-specific training and skill development. The other reason is that there is no one official governing body, leaving each program or governing agency to set their own rules for what can be considered "strength training" for a given sport and how athletes will operate under the guidance of that organization or its coaches.

As a result, many of the strength training approaches used for cyclists have simply copied common general practices from other sports or used the current trends. Up until the mid-2010s most people thought that strength training for cycling meant light weights with high repetitions and lots of core work. Then, around 2019, the rallying cry swung the other way as "lifting heavy stuff" became the accepted norm.

Let's take a look at a few of the common mistakes for strength training in the cycling world. These mistakes are similar to mistakes made by others training for sports performance, whether for fun or seriously. Similar lists can be seen in books written by top coaches in these other sports, such as Joel Jamieson and his *Ultimate MMA Conditioning*. Then you'll understand some of the problems found in the design of strength training programs, and you will have a sound understanding of what your actual needs are, and can build a foundation to get what you want and need out of your strength training.

SIX COMMON MISTAKES IN STRENGTH TRAINING FOR CYCLISTS

MISTAKE #1: TRAINING LIKE A GENERAL FITNESS ENTHUSIAST/GYM GOER

Over the last 50 or so years, strength training has slowly worked its way into mainstream health and fitness. However, since it became more widely accepted and practiced, much of the knowledge and many of the practices have been based off of bodybuilding approaches and philosophies. Pop icons like Arnold Schwarzenegger made films like *Pumping Iron* that got many into the weight room, as well as Jack LaLanne and a number of other popular folks who wowed audiences with their chiseled physiques and six-pack abs.

However, given how the modern-day cyclist and triathlete are built, adding unnecessary muscle mass is not an outcome that will suit you or help you achieve your goals. There is a huge difference in the training approaches that help you build muscles for performance and those that just build bigger muscles.

Your training must be centered around improving your performance and your ability to move extremely well. If you're following a workout plan that simply mimics cycling movements, or prescribes a bodybuilder workout (e.g., 3 sets of 15, or 5 sets of 5 heavy), odds are that you'll need to redesign and rethink the training approach.

MISTAKE #2: "LIFTING HEAVY SH*T," AKA TRAINING LIKE A POWERLIFTER

"Lift heavy sh*t" has become the rallying cry for cyclists and triathletes, and while it could be perceived as an improvement on mistake #1, it's actually not much better. Sure, it feels really good to lift more weight on a weekly basis, and to turn heads in the gym, but the demands of lifting heavy in this fashion don't carry over well into the sport of cycling. The demands don't match our demands on the bike.

When was the last time you had to move something heavy while riding your bike? The closest most of us come is riding into a stiff headwind, or trying to tackle the famous Rialto Street climb in the Dirty Dozen bicycle ride in Pittsburgh. But even those are a far cry from your actual needs on the bike.

While you do need maximum strength, and it does serve a purpose in the big picture, training only to lift heavier things on a week-to-week or month-to-month basis will take away from your ability to meet the endurance demands on the bike.

MISTAKE #3: GETTING "FUNCTIONAL"

I don't know who coined the term "functional fitness," but it's gotten to the point of being ridiculous. Squat racks and Olympic platforms have been replaced with BOSU balls and battle ropes, leaving many of the basic human movements, or what I call the "FUNdamental 5+1 human movements," hard to load up. The functional training trend has led to an over-programming of corrective exercises and a focus on the slightest movements needing to be corrected, instead of building the strength and athleticism required to be a healthy, powerful, strong cyclist.

If you're following a program that is designed with sound principles to help you perform better in the demands of your chosen activity, while lowering your risk of injury, it's already functional. You don't need a program with that label.

For those who want to jump up and yell, "But functional training prevents injuries!" the response is simple: Injury prevention at its foundation is about using a training strategy that balances out the high repetition movements in a sport and the need for the individual to move better. A strength training program designed around this foundation and done within the individual athlete's capacity to load, adapt, and recover, will prevent far more injuries. The Vortex Method, which you're about to learn, does exactly this.

MISTAKE #4: ONLY DOING STRENGTH TRAINING DURING WINTER OR BASE PERIOD

This is one of the most common mistakes cyclists make—and by far the biggest! It's also exactly the kind of mistake you cannot make if you want strength training to keep you from developing Quasimodo posture, or prevent you from losing the ability to reach up overhead, as many masters cyclists have experienced.

Only training in the winter or in your base period is a mistake that has deep-seated roots in the cycling community, and it ties into mistakes #5 and #6, due in large part to marketing and what cyclists in the past used to do. Well, cyclists back in the 1930s and '40s used to smoke cigarettes to "open their lungs," but we don't see anyone doing that anymore!

In order for strength training to have its desired and best effect on your abilities, it needs to be done consistently year-round. You can have fantastic cardio fitness and strong energy systems, but if your motor patterns and strength are poor, you won't be able to express your fitness on the bike fully. This will leave you frustrated or even cramped up on the side of the road.

Add to this that the very adaptations that you're in need of from strength training will disappear, almost completely, if you stop strength training for 6+ months in a row, and the argument is now irrelevant for the 99% of cyclists who are not world tour or pro-continental pro cyclists.

MISTAKE #5: BELIEVING THAT SORENESS FROM STRENGTH TRAINING IS A SIGN OF A GOOD PROGRAM

Thanks to mass media and CrossFit, images of exhausted individuals lying on the ground after a workout and claiming it was a great workout while they pant, have misrepresented what makes a good strength program.

In fact, soreness, especially the kind that hits you harder the second day after a workout, is a huge, flashing sign that your body is telling you that you did way more than it can handle. Performing your strength training with soreness as a guiding principle leaves you unable to complete your training on the bike, and it reprograms how your body moves, due to muscle fatigue and tissue damage. Not only that, but instead of adapting to the new challenges, your body has to repair the immense damage you've caused, sapping energy from progression.

If you're looking for a surefire way to say you tried strength training to help your riding and it did nothing but make you slower, then this would be your go-to. If you want to improve your performance on the bike, then following a program that keeps you working just enough on your strength to improve it and keeps you fresh enough to complete your rides with quality, is the way to go.

MISTAKE #6: NOT COORDINATING YOUR ON-BIKE AND STRENGTH TRAINING

No matter what sport you look at, the most effective training programs are those that coordinate strength training with in-sport conditioning and skill development. Unfortunately, many cycling and triathlon coaches and athletes simply stick strength training into their program for a few months a year without thinking about or understanding how to tie them together.

When you strength train or perform an on-bike training session, the effects don't just happen to one part of the body. Every and any type of training that you do has an effect on all of the systems of your body. If you fail to recognize this and train appropriately, you'll be designing a program that may be working against the very adaptations you're trying so hard to build! Using a structured system that allows your strength training to complement and work alongside your on-bike training is one of the fastest ways to significantly and swiftly improve your performance.

THE EVOLUTION OF STRENGTH TRAINING FOR SPORTS PERFORMANCE

Cyclists and endurance athletes seem to be inherently afraid of the weight room and strength training.

Basketball went through a strength revolution thanks to Michael Jordan, and now we are able to watch an incredible game full of athletes who are faster, stronger, and arguably more athletically capable than their predecessors. Swimmers? Same thing! Coach Loren Landow told me he made Missy Franklin globally stronger, so that she could get into the water and do her thing with more strength. Michael Phelps also spent time in the weight room, just like every other Olympic athlete, regardless of what sport they play.

What effect does strength training have on an athlete's ability to perform in their sport? Strength training, when done as *strength* training, not merely weight lifting, is one of the biggest legal "performance enhancers" there is. Note that when I refer to weight lifting, I mean general weight lifting, where you go to the weight room, lift things up, and put them down—*not* Olympic weight lifting. Those guys are serious athletes!

One of the major issues that Americans have is taking the mainstream bodybuilder approach: Lift things up, put them down, take rest periods as you like. Occasionally, there's some thought—or more precisely, mindfulness—as to how fast to perform a lift, or how much to rest in between sets in order to get results. But overall, people think that going to the gym and just lifting things up and putting them down is the way you strength train.

However, that is primarily a bodybuilder approach, where the goal is to lift heavier weights on a continuous basis, and thus get stronger. Oh, and don't forget the marketing messages that we are inundated with day in and day out that tell us that in order to be strong, men need to put on lots of lean muscle mass and lose body fat, and that women need to be very slender and perform lots of cardio.

Due to this mindset and approach, the weight room and strength training have gotten bad reputations in the bicycling world. Cyclists tend to respond to requests to get them into the weight room with one of four answers:

"I don't want to put on unnecessary weight."

"Weight lifting makes you slow."

"I just need to ride more, that's all. I'll do more . . . hills/speed work/low cadence work/endurance/strength work on the bike."

"I just need to activate my glutes and do core work."

The fact is, that when you learn the important interrelated pieces of a sound strength training program and how they affect the desired outcome—that is, you have thought through *all* of the following variables and properly adjusted to bring about the results you both want and need—you will enter a whole new stratosphere of understanding, and you will see results.

The key variables to strength training are:

- **Set and repetition** scheme to bring about desired response
- **Weight** (as a % of *estimated* 1 rep max)
- **Tempo** (speed) of each part of a repetition
- **Rest periods** in between sets (neuromuscular or metabolic)
- **Consistency and length of time** between training sessions (tissue and hormonal adaptations)
- **Type of training sessions** (movement, stimulation, development)

For it is only with *all* of these variables, applied correctly, that you are truly strength training. If you go into a gym and follow the mainstream method of 3 sets of 10, build up to 3 sets of 15, then go up in weight, you *will* put on unnecessary weight/bulk and be slower.

Why? Because that is, by definition, a hypertrophy program—the very same kind of program that bodybuilder types are doing to grow the size of their muscles!

You see, everything we do, especially in our everyday lives, is creating movement patterns and adaptation. With every motion and posture, such as sitting for long periods of time with our shoulders slouched forward and backs rounded, we are refining the neural system to be able to do that motion and hold that position easier, faster, and with less effort.

If you've taken my "Strength Training for Triathlon Success" course with Training-Peaks University, the first thing that may come to mind is what I repeat regularly throughout the course: Joint position dictates muscle function!

When we are strength training correctly, especially to boost performance in sport, we must ensure that we are putting the joints into positions where the muscles

Great posture and correct positions are vital in unlocking your potential.

MUSCULAR HYPERTROPHY: An increase in size of the skeletal muscle through a growth in size of its component cells. Two types of hypertrophy: sarcoplasmic hypertrophy, which focuses more on increased muscle glycogen storage; and myofibrillar hypertrophy, which focuses more on increased myofibril size.[1]

are getting better at performing the job they were designed and intended to do. That is, we need to make sure we are doing the exercise with proper technique, with the correct weight, at the correct tempo (speed), and with our rest intervals executed within the correct time frames for the response we want (neuromuscular vs. metabolic, which I'll cover in Chapter 3).

THE RIGHT RECIPE FOR THE DESIRED OUTCOME

This may sound overwhelming. But the thing is, having all of these ingredients and in the right amounts allows us to "make the right cake," so to speak. You cannot add some of the components and leave out others, or you'll wind up with a dud.

Have you ever wanted to make pancakes in the morning, only to realize that you don't have any baking soda? Yeah . . . you might choke down the results, but they won't be satisfying.

It's the same with strength training. If you leave out any one of the key ingredients, you may see *some* effect from the training, but it won't be the desired result. And that, my friends, is the exact problem we face with endurance sports and strength training.

PERFORMANCE ESSENTIALS

In order to see performance increases on the bike, there are a few essential things that can and should be addressed:

1. Breathing patterns
2. Learning & practicing bike handling and the skill of riding
3. Getting a quality bike fit
4. Strength training with a program that builds performance on the bike, not in the gym

While the first two are not thought of or practiced by most, they have a huge effect on your riding power, speed, and recovery. You'll learn about breathing patterns later on in this book.

If you want to really maximize your results, find an experienced bike fitter who can dial the bike in to you and your needs, and start practicing your bike handling for 5–10 minutes every day that you ride.

The nervous system is a complex, multidimensional, and fascinating thing. It learns whatever it is that we do most and will adapt to do so with less effort. That's why it is important that we do things correctly from the beginning. Every time we perform a movement, the nervous system remembers this movement and responds accordingly while we sleep. It creates a thicker myelination (insulation around the nerves used for that movement) to allow us to be more precise with the motion, as well as perform it with much less effort.

And this is why it is imperative to have a proper bike fit, to learn how to sit on your bike properly, to learn how to ride in a group, and to have general biking skills such as braking, cornering, and bike handling. Yet many riders feel that they don't need to hone these skills because they aren't competitive racers (or worse, because they are so good at them already).

As your strength training progresses and you begin to have better balance at the joints, specifically referring here to your hips and lower back, and your shoulders and upper back—you will begin to notice that you feel "different" on the bike. This will not happen overnight, though. It will take a few weeks, possibly even a few months (depending on how far gone down the road of imbalance you were), but you *will* start to notice. Not only will you feel different on the bike, but you'll also notice that you are able to maintain your power in a steadier fashion, and maybe even see a little more speed on your surges and attacks.

As you begin the program and start holding yourself to a higher level of training, you will undoubtedly see progress and improvements in your abilities in a rather short amount of time. That's because the program begins by first grooving proper movement patterns, and then adds more technical difficulty after a few weeks.

Earlier I mentioned the nervous system, and how everything we do with strength training is primarily done by the nervous system. As we go through each movement, we are causing the nervous system to recruit and use muscle groups and motor units to refine and increase their abilities in these patterns.

This leads to a stark difference between the Vortex Method Strength Training programs and any others out there: Instead of relying on just weights, we want to utilize your body in various positions to supply the challenge. Unsurprisingly, the group that has the most to gain from this, and which has the biggest challenge with these initial positions, are cyclists.

Due in large part to the crammed-up, bent-over position most cyclists are in for long periods of time, their bodies adapt to that position and start to change the length and strength of the different muscles around joints, especially the spine, hips, and shoulders. This can, and usually does, create significant problems for most cyclists.

What has surprised me is how such a large percentage of the cycling community has accepted this as being a normal change that happens if you're a serious rider! The fact that many longtime cyclists suffer from limited shoulder flexion (overhead reaching), chronic or frequent acute back pain, neck pain, and shoulder pain, but fail to do anything about these problems until the pain limits their riding abilities, or causes a serious injury, baffles me.

How did this become accepted as part of the lifestyle?

Many cyclists enjoy the bike because it gives them the ability to get away from things, to tackle large obstacles (mountains), to belong to an exclusive group (how many people that you know think you are crazy for riding your bike so much?), and to feel the wind in your face and the freedom of the open road.

So, naturally, doing anything that's *not* on the bike, especially in a room with fluorescent lighting and intimidating-looking individuals, in order to improve your riding abilities, is not a part of the cycling mindset. If anything, it goes *against* this mindset!

However, this mindset must change . . . and *is* changing.

BUILDING THE FUTURE RANKS OF CYCLISTS EVERYWHERE

Riding your way to dysfunction and pain should not be accepted as inevitable. If anything, there needs to be a large push, from the Juniors (kids) levels and the collegiate teams on up, to learn the right way to strength train. As a feeder system for professional cycling in the USA, I can think of no greater underestimated and underappreciated system, than collegiate cycling. Building a robust strength training mindset in these young athletes is one of the best things we can do for professional cycling. The future will be made of those who have learned and practiced strength training as a part of a regular training regimen, thus changing the future of cycling, perhaps as much as the invention of the drivetrain and gears!

In 2007 I began coaching the University of Pittsburgh Cycling team. From 2007–2014, I coached over 10 riders from that club to the USA Cycling Collegiate National Championships, with one of them eventually racing for Kelly-Benefit Strategies' Category 1 domestic professional team.

The majority of collegiate riders fall into cycling as a competitive sport for one of these two reasons: They either enjoy commuting on their bikes and want to try pushing their limits, or they played other sports in high school and are looking for a competitive sport to join at the collegiate level.

No matter how they find their way into cycling, these collegiate riders not only enjoy riding but also pushing themselves. And because many of them understand the importance of doing things other than their sport in high school, they are open to, or actively looking for, how to implement strength training for cycling.

Juniors, on the other hand, don't have any idea as to what training is or should be. They trust their coaches and mentors to show them the right way to train. Many of their coaches and mentors have been riding for many years, and while they enjoy riding, they are not necessarily open to strength training year-round.

These two groups, collegiate cycling and Juniors, are ideal places to start teaching strength training, as they are likely to accept it as a part of their normal training regimen and see it as a valuable part of their training.

A real change will come from riders like you, who understand or feel that there is something to this strength training thing, and who recognize that the information and current samples out there are falling short and missing something.

LEARNING TO CREATE PROXIMAL STIFFNESS FOR DISTAL MOVEMENT

If you want to improve your power and strength out on the road, you need to learn how to create stiffness and control at different parts of the body. One of the best things you can do is learn to create proximal stiffness at the spine, ribs, and hips, while the limbs move distally, or away from the center of the body.

In other words: Learn to lock your rib cage and hips together to decrease movement between them and at your spine in order to allow the arms or legs to produce more power that moves you forward. I'll discuss this in more detail in the chapter focusing on the spine (Chapter 5). This concept is a cornerstone for building quality strength training programs for cycling, let alone any sport.

Unfortunately, too many athletes lose sight of proximal stiffness, and thus wind up neglecting any significantly meaningful strength training that has a direct impact on their performance. Yes, there are "core workouts" and holding planks for as long as possible, and doing those exercises is very similar to the movements we do in our chosen sport of cycling.

However, you could miss the bigger, much more important picture. The big picture is that the trunk—the muscles that run from the base of your skull to your rib cage, from your elbows to your rib cage, from your knees to your pelvis, *and everything in between*—must be strong *in proportion to* its different parts for true peak performance to be possible.

The core doesn't just mean what you can see in the mirror, but also the muscles on your backside:

- glutes (of which there are three)
- quadratus lumborum
- erector spinae
- the pelvic floor
- the diaphragm
- and more!

A STRENGTH TRAINING APPROACH THAT WORKS SMARTER, NOT JUST HARDER

We are finally beginning to see a change in the culture of endurance sports, as top athletes seek out the best "secret weapon" for performance and figure out ways to refine and progress their bodies to be able to handle more.

Well, my friends, here comes the Vortex Method into the picture!

Professional athletes in a variety of sports have come to realize the importance of the role of an intelligently designed strength and conditioning program built by a professional Strength and Conditioning Coach as a part of the sports medicine and performance team.

Unfortunately, the strength and conditioning field is still relatively new, and is just now being understood as to its importance in the role of sports performance and injury prevention. And years ago, as mentioned in the Introduction, many athletes actively avoided lifting.

Today, *every* player at the professional level lifts in some form. If they don't, they are seen as putting themselves at a performance disadvantage, as well as a higher risk for injury. And chances are, if they slacked off in the strength training department during their collegiate years, word would get around and their value (and draft number) would fall.

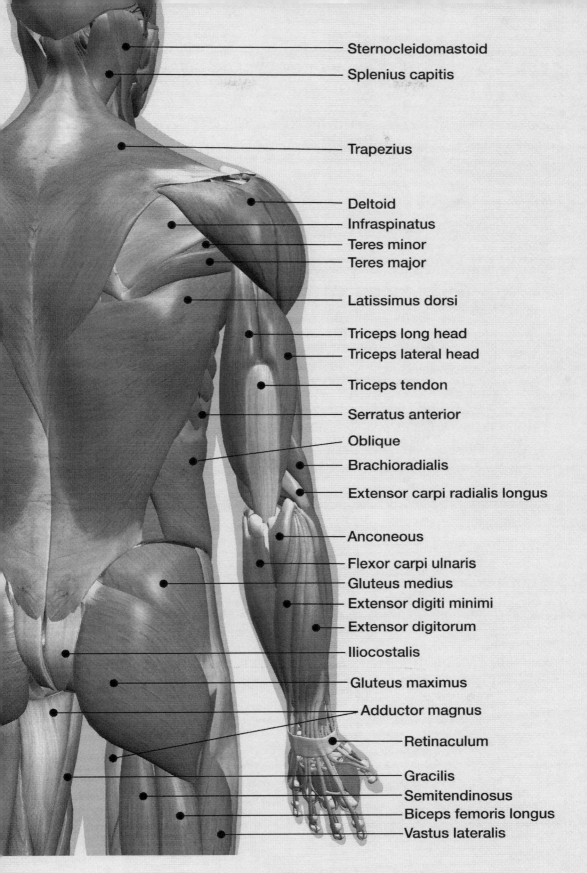

Sternocleidomastoid

Splenius capitis

Trapezius

Deltoid

Infraspinatus

Teres minor

Teres major

Latissimus dorsi

Triceps long head

Triceps lateral head

Triceps tendon

Serratus anterior

Oblique

Brachioradialis

Extensor carpi radialis longus

Anconeous

Flexor carpi ulnaris

Gluteus medius

Extensor digiti minimi

Extensor digitorum

Iliocostalis

Gluteus maximus

Adductor magnus

Retinaculum

Gracilis

Semitendinosus

Biceps femoris longus

Vastus lateralis

Image Source: Grebe, Hank. Labeled Anatomy Chart of Male Back Muscles, Shutterstock.

Cycling and triathlon are pretty much the last holdouts when it comes to not including sound strength training programs in their training regimens. And that's a huge part of why I've written this book.

As you read this book, you'll quickly realize that it is not like any other strength training for cyclists book out there. In fact, I haven't seen another book on strength training for cycling or triathlon come close to what we're going to cover. Most of the information out there is outdated, watered down to the very basics, or takes general exercises that work muscles in a similar function to endurance sports and labels them as "sport specific."

Any professional strength coach worth their salt will tell you that simply mimicking sports movements in strength training is a recipe for injury, disappointment, and disaster.

You want to become a better cyclist? Demand a variation of movements that: 1) help improve your body's balance of strength at each joint, and 2) help you learn how to hold better positions and postures that allow you to be more efficient and economical.

Programming set and repetition schemes *must* allow you to build not just strength, but better tissue qualities and a more efficient connection between your brain and your muscles.

Your work and rest periods need to be programmed properly to allow you to either improve your neuromuscular abilities (stronger, more forceful muscle contractions), or your metabolic abilities (energy production at the local muscles used in a movement).

And all of this absolutely must be built into a year-round strength training program that complements your on-bike training to ensure you're building all 4 pillars of athletic development:

- **Cardiovascular** (heart and lungs)
- **Hormonal** (drugs we produce in our bodies that affect how we respond and build)
- **Neuromuscular** (nerves and muscles)
- **Metabolic** (energy systems)

KNOW YOUR TRAINING TERMINOLOGY!

Set: A group of repetitions of a movement completed without rest. For cyclists, a set is usually in the range of 3–25 repetitions.

Repetition: A single full cycle of a movement. For example, one repetition of a squat would be going from standing, to touching your butt to a chair as if you're sitting, to standing again.

It's not just about mimicking sports movements. An intelligently designed strength training program is about maintaining balance, working carefully to gain strength and balance for the working joints (shoulders, pelvis, spine), and challenging the nervous system and energy systems, so that you are getting the best response possible to allow you success in your sport.

KNOW YOUR ADAPTATIONS!

Neuromuscular adaptations: The ability of the muscle to get stronger and to better coordinate the body's abilities to put more force out in the desired direction.

In order for these adaptations to be the main results from strength training, you need rest periods between 3–6 minutes in between sets, depending on what changes you are trying to make happen, and where in the cycling season you are.

Metabolic adaptations: The ability of the local muscles to more effectively produce and maintain energy necessary to perform a specific movement or movements for a given period of time.

In order for these adaptations to be the main results from strength training, you need rest periods between 30–90 seconds in between sets, depending on what changes you are trying to make happen, and where in the cycling season you are.

This includes movements that aren't in your sport, which will help you maintain great positions and postures, establish great breathing patterns, and maintain a happy balance at the joints.

And it's important to not push yourself to the max every single workout. That won't get you where you want to be. In fact, as Tony Gentilcore and I speak about in episodes 6 and 7 on my podcast *The Strong Savvy Cyclist & Triathlete,* building up your strength and on-bike abilities happens through consistency in your strength training and in practicing moderation.

For 95% of your strength training sessions, you will want perceived exertions (also known as "RPE" for "Rating of Perceived Exertion") of 5, 6, and 7 on a scale of 1 to 10. This means that many days you'll be walking out of the gym thinking, "Did I work hard enough? I feel like I can do more!"

A NOTE ON INJURIES AND TRAINING INJURED

There are a few common issues that run throughout the sport of cycling:

- generally weak muscles
- low back pain
- neck pain
- hip pain
- knee pain
- poor posture
- increased risk of osteoporosis and broken bones

Injuries, especially overuse and posture-related injuries, are all too common. They are most often the result of not performing any kind of training outside of riding bicycles.

Since 2005, the cycling world has done a complete about-face in its attitude towards strength training and how it can help improve performance. One of the major benefits of strength training is to decrease the occurrence of injuries. So why is it that the prevalence of injuries is still unacceptably high amongst riders?

All too often, I have heard cyclists brag about what injury they are currently training through and how much ibuprofen or ice they need after a workout just to get back to, or through, daily life.

I have also seen the same trend among runners, although presented differently:

Runner #1 to Runner #2: "IT band syndrome, huh? Yeah, that's what you get for being a runner! When I had it, I bumped my mileage down to less than 10 per week for two weeks and then slowly ramped back up. Do the same and you'll be fine."

Cyclists have unique and different issues. In addition to overuse injuries, they suffer postural imbalances and bike-fit issues. Most commonly, cyclists develop an anterior tilt to their pelvis, due to extremely strong quadriceps, shortened hip flexors (psoas, in particular), along with elongated hamstrings and soleus muscles from the rolled-hip position on the bike. Combine this with the shoulders rounding forward due to sitting on the hoods of the handlebars, an elongated spine with the natural curves of the spine being compromised in some fashion, due to adaptations to weak and tight muscles, and you have an individual who has an increase in their thoracic and lumbar curvature in their spine.

These factors can lead to an increased risk of injury due to faulty mechanics. Think about your bones as being the beams of an Erector Set and the muscles being a series of pulleys and levers that help move the pieces. When those beams are out of alignment, the stresses placed on the pulleys and levers change, and they can no longer work as designed. This (aside from a trauma injury) is one of the prime factors in cycling injuries. There is increased demand on the tissues of the body from training and racing, and while the body is incredibly adaptable, over time the imbalance and malalignment takes its toll, and tissues break, tear, and rupture.

This can all lead to big shifts in the alignment of the diaphragm and pelvic floor, which leaves us in a really poor position to enforce great breathing patterns. This doesn't just affect our on-bike performance; it can greatly decrease our body's ability to get into a parasympathetic (recovery) state.

Unfortunately, it seems that today cyclists view training injured as a rite of passage. Training injured is not okay! Even professional or semi-pro athletes have to carefully weigh the risk and reward of playing injured, and determine if it's worth it to keep going.

I once worked with a retired professional baseball player. He had worked his ass off his whole career, and had landed in the top minor league system in the U.S., definitely in the top 5% of baseball players in the world. He shared a story with me about the time he had a really bad ankle sprain, to the point he could barely walk, but unless he suited up and played, he would lose his position on the roster to someone who could. He was playing for his livelihood and a chance to get to the big leagues.

There are countless stories of NCAA collegiate athletes playing injured as well, for their livelihood, or at least a chance to play professionally in the future. These athletes really don't have much of a choice: Either suit up, play injured, and *slightly* hurt your chances of making the pros, or sit out and risk someone else taking your spot and your one shot.

People like you and me? We aren't participating in our sports for livelihood. If anything, we train to push our limits in our off time from our full-time jobs. Whether it's because we are goal-oriented and need or want something to work towards, or because we have always been an athlete and need to be doing something athletic, the bottom line is that we are doing this for our enjoyment and entertainment. So let's be good to our bodies, listen to them, and not train while injured.

PUTTING ON UNNECESSARY WEIGHT FROM STRENGTH TRAINING

All too often, cyclists—and endurance athletes in general—are afraid of gaining unwanted weight. Because they want to have the highest Watts per kilogram, or the leanest body. . . . And that's good, right?

Well, as it turns out, not necessarily. It all comes down to what your body mass is comprised of, and if you optimize to put the most power to the pedals or power to the pavement in the most effective manner. If you want to improve your power and strength out on the road, you need to learn how to create stiffness and control at different parts of the body—not necessarily focus on your weight.

A fear of putting on unnecessary weight is one of the main reasons I hear cyclists say they don't want to lift. Perhaps you've heard this at some point or another. Someone on your team or group is trying to get their weight down so that their Watts per kilogram or power-to-weight ratio is higher. That's a nice thought, but neglecting the muscles that support and move you on the bike will only lead you to slower progress. It may, perhaps, get you lower in weight, but it could open you up to a myriad of other issues, including illness and poor recovery, which would erase much, or all, of the fitness you've been working so hard to gain.

So how do we address the issue of not wanting to gain weight? Let's look at Olympic weight lifters. You know, the guys and gals you see during the Summer Olympics in singlets with knee wraps and a support belt, who heave barbells with weights that are as heavy as a Mini Cooper over their heads in a deep squat, and then stand up with them. Yeah, those crazy guys.

Why them? Because they're all about power-to-weight as well. And very few of them put on meaningful amounts of weight from competition to competition, unless they are trying to go up a weight class.

How is it possible that these incredibly strong athletes can do this? Don't they have to gain weight to get stronger? Not necessarily! It depends on the forces that are being placed on the body, and how it needs to respond.

GOOD INTENTIONS, WRONG TOOL

One of my favorite stories about strength training and cyclists involved this exchange with an athlete:

Me: "So, let's get started on the strength training ASAP. We need to focus on some trouble areas you've seen this past season."

Athlete: "I don't want to put on weight. I want to stay the same weight and bring my Watts per kilogram up. Can we just do threshold stuff?"

Me: "No, we absolutely must take the time to do targeted biomechanical chain work, posture work, and get you breathing better. We need your systems to be stronger and working better. And I won't set you up for mental and physical burn-out by pushing your Lactate Threshold higher just because you're worried about putting on weight by lifting."

Athlete: "Okay, I hear your point. Can I think about it over the weekend?"

Me: "Absolutely! Let's talk Monday morning."

Monday morning rolls around, and my phone rings:

Athlete: "Hey! I found a solution for the strength training you want me to do!"

Me: "Uh, a solution? I haven't given you a program yet."

Athlete: "Yeah! A solution! I signed up for CrossFit! All my friends are doing it, and they love it. I thought you'd be so excited!"

Me: (audible thud of my head hitting the wall)

I don't share this to knock CrossFit. I've coached at a "Box" for almost 5 years, and I taught Strength Training for Endurance Athletes classes. Like everything else out there, CrossFit is a tool that, when used correctly and for the right goals or sports, can be very good.

1. asking for injury
2. programming the body for unnecessary weight
3. not addressing the issues specific to their sport

As you'll learn in this book, Olympic lifts are important, but they are to be taught by an experienced coach with appropriate credentials (a weekend CrossFit certification doesn't cover it). And while the idea of performing Olympic lifts is good, the vast majority of cyclists just don't have the strength and stable range of motion to get what is needed out of the Olympic lifts.

CrossFit's approach, while really cool and hard, is not the workout you want to be doing if you don't want to put on unnecessary weight! Every experienced and professional CrossFitter has large amounts of muscle mass—and, consequently, many of them also seem to have shoulder and knee issues.

Remember, the whole idea behind strength training is to balance you out and make you stronger on the bike, *not* bulkier and with more issues!

THE BENEFITS OF A GOOD STRENGTH TRAINING PROGRAM

While unnecessary weight gain is the number one concern most cyclists have when it comes to strength training, with a well-designed strength training program like the Vortex Method, your strength training will:

- help significantly boost your performance
- decrease your aches and pains
- decrease your recovery time
- improve your adaptations to your training
- help you feel and look better, on and off the bike

These benefits will happen because of how the Vortex Method addresses the four areas that every athlete in every sport must be certain to address and train— neuromuscular, metabolic, hormonal, and cardiorespiratory—if they want to see improvement in their performance, or simply to wake up every morning feeling better than the day before.

Next, we'll take a look at the basics, and where we need to start.

---

1. Thomas R. Baechle and Roger W. Earle, eds., *Essentials of Strength Training and Conditioning*, 3rd ed. (Champaign, IL: Human Kinetics, 2008).

CHAPTER 1 SUMMARY

- Cyclists have often resisted strength training or approached it incorrectly. When done properly and in conjunction with on-bike skills, it is a game-changer for performance.

- Key variables for strength training are: set and rep scheme, weight, tempo of each rep, rest periods between sets, consistency and length of time between sessions, and type of training session. Having all variables and in the right amount will give the best outcome.

- Work the core in the right way. Power and strength on the road will come with proximal stiffness at the spine while the limbs move.

- Use a smart training plan that helps you improve your body's balance of strength at each joint and helps you learn how to hold better positions and postures.

- Cyclists are prone to specific injuries, especially overuse or posture-related injuries. Training injured is not okay.

- The benefits of a good strength training program will include improved performance, fewer aches and pains, and less recovery time.

CHAPTER 2
STRENGTH TRAINING BASICS

CHOOSING THE RIGHT COACH OR PROGRAM FOR YOU

Unfortunately, much of the information out there on strength training for cyclists has not been vetted properly, with many programs being General Physical Preparation (GPP) programs that have been altered to mimic the common positions and movements in cycling. But it doesn't help cyclists to be strong in the wrong areas, or to be doing the wrong exercises.

To truly improve your strength for cycling, it's imperative to work with a strength coach who really understands the demands of cycling in order to develop specific strength for those demands.

Do not simply pick a coach because they look like a strong cyclist or because they are a highly accomplished rider. Select a strength coach who has not only an understanding of cycling, but who also has a deep understanding of how to determine which exercises to use, and how to program the relative intensities, progressions, volumes, and speeds needed to train. This coach should be able to watch you ride and understand what you do well and what you do poorly. They should be able to determine if what's limiting you is a movement, skills, or a lack of understanding.

Finding a coach like this is not easy—there aren't enough good coaches, and many people don't have the resources or time to find them. Too many cyclists end up just accepting "good enough" advice from a local fitness enthusiast, gym rat, or personal trainer. That's where this book comes in handy. If you really want to really understand what cycling strength training is, this book is for you.

Even though the science of strength training is changing every day as we learn more about the human body, the foundations are more or less the same.

WHY NOT MIMIC CYCLING MOVEMENTS?

When it comes to strength training for performance improvement, what surprises most people is that you don't want to simply copy the same movements you already get in your sport. While it might sound like common sense to do the same movements you're doing in your sport in order to get better and stronger at them, the reality is quite the opposite!

Anatomy is often taught in a muscle-by-muscle approach by the movements that the individual muscle can do. However, this isn't how the body actually works. In order for that one muscle to create movement, other muscles in the body—which are sometimes far away from where the work will be done—have to fire to stabilize the body.

However, when we repeat a movement thousands of times, and stay in relatively static positions for long periods of time, the brain and body begin to change how the muscles work together: Some muscles remain stretched, and others stay tight in an effort to conserve energy used for that task. This may seem like a good thing, but in fact it saps performance from you in a number of ways:

- poor breathing patterns

- more difficulty moving from a "stressed" (training) hormonal state to the rest-and-digest hormonal state

- loss of functionality in the body parts involved

- increased wear and tear on the joints and passive tissues

- changes in how the brain fires the muscles

These are some of the bigger negative effects of continuing to practice the same movements that you already get in your sport. Instead, strength training for performance looks at how the body is functioning and moving all together, embracing and working with the joints and muscles how they were designed to move—and working to keep a balance of strength and movement at each joint.

This means that a training program will involve movements and muscles that are *not* used heavily in your sport. You may already be familiar with this idea as "posterior chain" training, and while this is a small step in the right direction, there are actually six key movement patterns that you'll need to train if you're looking to improve your performance and how you're moving on and off the bike. You'll learn about these FUNdamental 5+1 movements in Chapter 6.

GETTING THE RIGHT MIX OF MOVEMENTS AND EXERCISES

When we think of strength training, most tend to think of big, heavy barbells, large men in gyms, and most of the strength work relying on barbell exercises.

Well, that's not exactly right.

- Women make up a significant amount of cyclists who strength train. And women are just as strong as men when we look at strength relative to body weight.

- There are lots of *extremely* strong human beings who are just a little bit heavier than professional cyclists. You don't have to be large to strength train.

- The Vortex Training Method only uses barbell exercises around 15–20% of the time.

That last point is a *really* important one.

We don't focus a ton on barbell movements, and in fact, because many cyclists just don't have time to get to the gym on top of riding their bikes, we teach movements you can do at home with a pair of kettlebells, your body, and a few bands. For the 15–20% of exercises that use barbells, it will almost always be in the fall or winter, when riding volume is lower. This allows for a lot more time throughout the year to get more riding and other strength work in. Of course it depends, and some may find that a short 30- to 45-minute focused gym routine is just what is needed in the middle of the summer.

Regardless of whether you're using bands, kettlebells, dumbbells, or barbells, one thing remains true: When you want to become a faster, stronger, and more resilient cyclist, you have to be careful not to put on any unnecessary muscle mass.

The key word here is *unnecessary*.

You want to be sure that any muscle you put on is in areas that will improve your on-bike abilities. For most cyclists, these areas are the:

- middle back
- hips
- glutes
- abs and obliques
- spinal erectors
- and even a little in the chest and shoulders

With muscle mass focused in these areas, you will be able to improve:

- the quality of FUNdamental 5+1 movements (discussed in Chapter 6)
- absolute strength
- explosive power
- your ability to put power out for long periods of time

As long as you are out on your bike training and riding for at least 6 hours a week, your body won't blow up like a bodybuilder, especially not if you follow the principles and information in this book.

THE DIFFERENT TYPES OF STRENGTH

Part of the challenge we have when it comes to strength training is that most people (including lots of trainers!) don't know or understand that there are *different types of strength*! While we won't go into detail on each, it is important that you are familiar with the following 6 types of strength in order to train smart and improve your on-bike performance.

1. **Concentric Strength** (muscle shortening)

   This kind of strength requires powerful starting strength. Examples of movements that use concentric strength are dead-stop deadlifts, or the first repetition of a deadlift.

2. **Eccentric Strength** (muscle lengthening)

   This is the strength required to lower a weight. An example of this kind of strength is the first part of a bench press, when you are lowering the weight.

3. **Isometric Strength** (static strength)

   This strength is when you are using a muscle, but its length doesn't change. An example of this kind of strength is a static front plank.

4. **Speed Strength** (maximum force during high speed movement)

   Speed strength is something all cyclists should be familiar with and where, after building a solid foundation of quality movements, your strength training program will move towards. This strength is trained by using lower weights or lower resistance, as the movements must be quick and done with great technique.

5. **Reactive Strength**

   This strength is used for jumping and agility.

6. **Starting Strength**

   This kind of strength is the maximum force you can put out at the beginning of a movement or muscular contraction. An example of this would be a power start on the bicycle, or jumping straight up out of a chair without leaning forward.

Each of these different types of strength need training not only on the movements you are doing and your technique (form), but attention must be paid to *how* you are doing the movement (your speed and intent), and the amount of resistance or weight that you are using.

When you're building a training program, you should focus primarily on one type of strength for a 3–6 week period, depending on your training age in strength training. While the focus will be *primarily* on one type of strength, it does not mean that you are only using one type of strength. For example, during the Anatomical Adaptation weeks in your plan, you'll be focusing on concentric type of strength, but you'll still be doing some isometric and eccentric exercises.

This approach to training is called conjugate training. To those in the weightlifting and powerlifting communities, conjugate training is most often associated with one of the top powerlifting coaches (and gyms) in the U.S., Louie Simmons and his Westside Barbell gym. The origins of the conjugate training method come from a Soviet physical education program in the 1980s, which encouraged the development of a variety of athletic skills for overall better fitness. In regards to strength training, this applies when you introduce separate and specific strengths and combine them sequentially for an overall more effective result.[1]

Sounds simple, but it takes experience to be able to tie together the different moving parts in a way that allows you massive improvements in your sport performance, with as little time and energy spent working out. The Vortex Method does exactly this, and many cyclists regularly say, *"Hey, I just saw X increase in my cycling (FTP/sprint power/ climbing power) from your program, but I never felt tired or really sore for that matter. Am I doing something wrong?"*

No, you did nothing wrong. In fact, that is a sign that you're doing it exactly right. When it's done correctly, it's pretty easy!

WHAT IS YOUR TRAINING AGE?

Understanding where you are in terms of training age is really important, as it will allow you to determine how and what you should be training, in order to match your body's abilities and needs at that particular stage. Training age refers to the number of months or years that you have been training for a specific discipline. In your case, this refers to how long you have consistently been training on the bike, and how long you have consistently been training with resistance (dumbbells, barbells, bands, kettlebells).

However, there is an important caveat here: If you have not been *consistently* strength training throughout the entire training year, your training age will be less. Let's look at an example.

Mary is 47 years old and has been riding a road bike for 12 years. During the 12 winters, she has ridden her bike indoors on the trainer 2–3 days a week, and she has included some Pilates and weight training another 2 days a week. However, Pilates and weights are only included from December until March. From March through December, she only does a few stretches and light Pilates moves as she feels the need throughout the week, in addition to her riding.

Since Mary has been riding consistently and year-round for 12 years, her riding age is 12.

But her strength training age is much lower. Because she has only done Pilates and weight training for 4 months each year, and then mostly skipped it the other 8 months, her strength training age will be a fraction of her riding age, about 12 months old.

The reason her strength training age is so low, even though she has been doing Pilates and weight training for the last 12 winters, is because of her lack of consistency. When you train, you are looking for specific adaptations of the body, which for strength training are mainly:

- nervous system
- muscles
- bones
- connective tissue (cartilage, ligaments, tendons)
- hormones

However, in order for those changes to take effect and build, there *must* be consistency in the frequency of your training sessions.

By taking 8 months out of the year to only do some abs or Pilates or yoga, you will lose much, if not all, of the training effect that strength training had. Consistency is what gains you improvements from strength training, not just putting in the time seasonally or when you feel like it, and it's one of the main reasons why cyclists don't see gains from their strength training.

If you do only strength training in the winter, you won't likely have to start from zero, though. While you've lost muscle, tissue, and hormonal adaptations (a huge loss at that!), you will most likely have kept the coordination (movement patterns) of how to do each exercise from year to year.

Following the Vortex Method allows you to avoid this mistake and keeps you building strength and performance year-round.

TRAINING VELOCITIES (SPEEDS)

One of my favorite parts of strength training programming is when we teach riders about the different training velocities and how to do them properly. This area gives cyclists another big leap forward in their abilities on the bike.

A simple way to apply velocities is through the use of prescribed tempos for each of the different parts of the movement, which are broken down into four parts and written as 1-2-3-4. I'll describe what each part represents in Chapter 11.

As with the different types of strength, we're not going to go into great detail here, but it is important to have a basic understanding of these 3 training velocities.

1. Maximal Effort (the slow grind)

A maximal effort is one in which you are firing 100% of the nervous system to get full voluntary output to the muscle(s). Think about trying to pick up one of those huge 24-inch water main pipes at a construction site, as Dan John talks about on episode 79 of *The Strong Savvy Cyclist & Triathlete Podcast.*

Back in high school when I was playing basketball, I fell in love with powerlifting. The powerlifting style is what many people think of when someone says "strength training," i.e., lifting heavy weights while struggling to keep moving.

As cyclists, we won't do a lot of, or really any, maximal effort lifting for the first few months, especially 1 repetition maximums. This is for a few reasons:

- First, cycling doesn't require pushing a really big gear slowly. . . . We need medium to fast pedaling!

- Second, while some style of maximal effort lifting is used to help us get stronger (at the proper time), riding our bikes doesn't give the kinds of tissue adaptations needed to be able to do this often and without getting hurt. It will take between 8–12 weeks (if you are a true beginner to strength training) before you start working on your ability to lift maximal loads.

- Lastly, when you start doing maximum strength lifts, it will only be through ranges of motion you have great control over, and for sets of 2–4 repetitions for up to 95% of what you can do, not a 1 repetition maximum.

2. Speed Strength

Speed strength is the ability to absorb and transmit forces quickly. It is also one of the 6 types of strength listed above, as the ability to produce maximum contraction and relaxation to create pulses of energy, via speed, requires the skill to be developed. This is where much of your training will need to be focused, *after* you learn how to move well and have built up the tissue qualities your body needs in order to keep you from getting injured. For some riders, this may mean they do not work on speed strength until their second or third year. It all depends on what your postures are, how well you move, and what kind of stress your riding and daily life demands of you.

You'll learn more about this as you go along, but a couple of important things to know about speed strength: 1) when working on it, you're only going to use around 50–70% or less of your estimated 1 repetition maximum, and 2) you'll only train speed strength using major multi-joint movements like the squat, the hinge, or the press. . . . But more on that later!

3. Explosive Strength

Explosive strength is the ability to put out the maximal amount of force in the shortest time possible. What many people—trainers and athletes alike—get wrong about training true explosive strength, is that they train at weights that are *way* too heavy, or they add explosive strength into a program before the rider has good movement qualities and a good foundation of strength. The foundation of strength and quality of movement cannot be ignored or skipped over, as these are the very things that will keep you healthy, able to recover, and able to perform.

When training for explosive strength (in the strength training setting), you will be using weights that are less than 30% of your estimated 1 repetition maximum for that movement, or you will perform jumping exercises.

THE 1 REPETITION MAXIMUM TEST

This test is often used in the strength training and personal training world to determine the working loads of an individual, for a specific movement. This testing involves a thorough warm-up and the completion of a movement while adding weight to the bar until you cannot perform more than 1 repetition. This repetition should be done with great technique.

But for cyclists, this isn't a great idea. Cyclists place some pretty big demands on their bodies—but holding heavy weights in the hands or on the back is not one of them, as the risk of injury due to tissue or technical failure is extremely high. That means lost riding time, or even a riding or career-ending injury, which could have been easily avoided.

Because of the extremely high risk of injury, the Vortex Method does not perform a 1 repetition maximum test.

WHAT IS HEAVY?

When it comes to strength training, many of us think of heavy weights as having a barbell loaded with at least 3–4 of the big 45 pound (20kg) plates. While this may be heavy to an intermediate-level powerlifting athlete, cyclists shouldn't think of heavy in these terms.

Heavy is relative to you, your movement patterns, how you're loading the movement, and the volume (or total weight moved) in that particular movement.

If a strong, burly powerlifter was asked to perform a heavy set of barbell back squats, sure, they may load up the bar with four 45 pound plates. . . . But if asked to perform 30 barbell squats without a rest, they'd probably choose no more than one 45 pound (20kg) plate on each side, totaling 135 pounds on the bar.

An even bigger determiner of what "heavy" might be is the type of training outcome you're aiming for.

Stop thinking of heavy as adding more weight to the bar, and start thinking of it in relation to the specific exercise and the needed load in order to get the training effect you want and need. When you do this, you'll find that your "heavy" is now very different from week to week and from training cycle to training cycle!

The tissues of the body—the ligaments, tendons, muscles, and bones—adapt to the different kinds of pressures and demands that we put them under. For cyclists, these demands include next to no external loading, except for climbing a mountain, a hill, or riding into a headwind. While gravel riders and mountain bikers have to deal with some more muscular efforts due to terrain, their stressors are still not enough to strengthen the body to be able to meet the continued demands of the sport on the body.

With the #1 rule of strength training being "to keep the athlete healthy and able to compete in their sport," there is zero need for a 1 repetition maximum test. The Vortex Method will test to see what you are capable of, but we will not use weights that have an extremely high potential for injury.

If you'd like to learn more about the unnecessary risk of injury that the 1 repetition maximum testing places on riders, and how most cyclists hurt their backs and spines in the weight room, listen to episodes 8 and 9 of *The Strong Savvy Cyclist & Triathlete Podcast*, where I interview Dr. Stuart McGill.

WHAT'S NEXT?

As you can see, there is a lot more to strength training than deciding on an exercise, picking a weight, and then doing it. By the time we get into programming and you understand the goal of strength training at different times in the year, you'll be able to:

1. Know what changes in the muscles and nervous system you want to get from that day's session
2. Set up for the exercise
3. Do the exercise with great technique, movement, and breathing patterns

All this, without having to think about 15 million things. Yes, you can do it, and YOU WILL!

---

1. Tom Myslinski, "The Development of the Russian Conjugate Sequence System," Elite FTS, December 19, 2016. https://www.elitefts.com/education/the-development-of-the-russian-conjugate-sequence-system/.

CHAPTER 2 SUMMARY

When it comes to strength training basics, there are a number of things to think about:

- Choose a strength training coach or program that understands the demands of cycling and develops the specific strength types needed, and does not just mimic cycling movements.

- Get the right mix of movements and exercises so you aren't doing a ton of barbell movements or putting on unnecessary muscle mass.

- There are six types of strength to train: concentric, eccentric, isometric, speed, reactive, and starting strength. Focus on one type of strength for a 3–6 week period.

- Make sure you are using the correct training velocity for a given exercise: maximal effort, speed strength, or explosive strength.

- The 1 repetition maximum test is not needed for cycling and has a high risk of injury. The Vortex Method does not use the 1 rep max test, as there are safer alternatives to determine training load.

CHAPTER 3
PERFORMANCE LIMITERS & RESPONSES TO TRAINING

Before we get into the nuts and bolts of the Vortex Method and how to build an intelligently designed strength training program, I want to share with you the deeper reasons why strength training is so important for cyclists, and endurance athletes as a whole. And it has very little to do with maximum strength in the weight room.

Competitive cyclists tend to become really focused on power numbers:

"What were your Watts per kilo for that climb?"

"What were her average Watts to take the QOM on that Strava segment?"

"How many Watts did you put out in your sprint?"

Watts are a way to objectively measure and compare abilities, but what if I told you that there are a few ways that most people don't even realize they can improve power output and performance? Would you believe me, or would you think I was just going to tell you some "secret interval" or "pro recovery treatment"?

It's actually just a basic understanding of how the human body works. The topics covered in this chapter will help you better understand not only how strength training improves on-bike performance, but also how to make small changes to your own program to get more out of your training.

I've purposefully kept it short and to the point. This will be the most scientific chapter in the book, but it's well worth it.

HOW DO YOU IMPROVE PERFORMANCE?

When it comes to improving performance, we all tend to get lost down the rabbit holes of:

- sleep
- nutrition and hydration
- interval training

While these are pretty widely accepted as the determinants of performance, there is a bigger and more impactful picture. Yes, these four pieces are important, but you really need to broaden your perspective if you're going to truly achieve top performance.

When you take a step back and look at what determines your performance successes, you actually find there are three main things:

1. **Power Output:** This is the amount of energy you expend or work you perform over time, and it is influenced by your fitness. Power is measured in Watts. You have to have the power to keep up, or to stay away!

2. **Technical Skills:** These are the essential skills you need on the bike, like cornering, braking, descending, climbing, sprinting, and getting out of the saddle. These are also areas that many cyclists completely avoid giving proper attention or time to, which almost always costs them dearly in events.

3. **Tactics and Race Strategy:** Tactics are the strategic use of one's skills, strength, and abilities in combination with a plan to achieve a desired end result, such as winning a race or finishing first on a climb. Race strategy is a well-thought-out plan designed after looking at a course, making use of the individual's or team's strengths and mitigating their weaknesses, in order to have the highest chance of the desired outcome. These are specific to race preparation and even specific courses. When walking around the parking lot before races, I often hear teammates talking race strategy, and they are usually extremely optimistic but rarely focused on real course recon or knowledge aside from a paper map that shows turns and elevation gains.

While we could say more about technique and specific race preparation, we're going to focus in on the fitness side of things, aka power output. However, since many of you want to improve your performance in some kind of race or event, I wanted to at least make you aware of the major considerations for event or race preparation.

With local or regional skills clinics, race strategy clinics or presentations, and other resources to help you buff up on your abilities and knowledge in these additional areas, you'll truly maximize the results you gain from this book and its programs to unleash your full power out on the road!

Speaking of unleashing your full power on the road . . .

WHAT INFLUENCES POWER OUTPUT?

Many riders dive head-first into the waters of increased performance via lighter and stiffer equipment, but this is both a very expensive path and one that should only be taken much later down the road of your development as a rider or athlete.

Yes, you absolutely can buy speed, but it comes at a heavy price . . . and I am not talking about the massive dent it will put in your bank account! Buying speed is essentially cheating yourself out of learning how to tap into your own potential as a rider, and it slows down your learning curve on riding technique, riding skills, and improving your movement patterns.

Let's not kid ourselves. It *is* fun to buy a new set of wheels and to see that speedometer roll up an extra few mph/kph. But these kinds of advantages should be saved for after you've unlocked your full potential with solid, basic equipment, and you've begun to master the six factors that affect power output that you can easily train without spending mucho dinero:

1. **Motor Control:** Good coordination and control of your body allows for better neural connections to the muscles and less energy to create a movement.
2. **Stress Management:** Training stress, and also life stress, have a huge impact on our abilities to perform at our best and to recover well. When we're stressed, our hormonal state is skewed, which leads to more energy being used as we're constantly on high alert.

3. **Movement Qualities:** The more in balance your body's joints are, and the higher the quality of your movement patterns, the better you're going to be able to perform. Loose is fast, and fast is loose. But if your muscles are out of balance at a joint, you're going to hold tension and have to work harder for a given movement.

4. **Energy Systems:** Your training should place demands on all of the energy systems you will need for an event, in how they adapt, improve, and become more efficient.

5. **Skills:** Riding is a skill that must be taught, learned, and practiced often. Yet the vast majority of cyclists never, or rarely, practice the basic skills of braking, cornering, sprinting, bumping, pedaling, or learning how to work the bike in a figure-8 up the climb, just to name a few.

6. **Techniques:** While these are often grouped together with skills, I prefer to separate them, as there are different techniques used for each skill.

While all of these factors greatly affect power output, if you dig a little deeper, you'll recognize that power output really comes down to energy creation and energy use, and how efficiently your body can do both.

Whether you race or not, it's all about energy management.

ENERGY CREATION & ENERGY USE

We can't pedal our bikes without creating and using energy. There are three main components that affect energy creation:

- **Developing/training the energy systems.** This is where the on-bike training does a major part of the work. When you perform specific intervals in particular fashions, you are challenging the specific energy systems to become stronger and more efficient.

- **Muscle type and size.** I could go very deep into detail here, but let's just boil it down to this: Type 2 muscle fibers use shorter energy systems, and thus if you have more Type 2 muscle fibers you'll do much better in short, explosive power sports like basketball or Olympic lifting. But if you have more Type 1 muscle fibers, you'll be more primed to perform sports that last longer, like road cycling. The size of the muscles will also affect energy use. This is why pro cyclists tend to weigh very little: the smaller you are, the less energy you'll need in order to do the work at hand, like get yourself up over that huge mountain pass.

- **Nutrition.** Fuel types and timing will affect how you perform and recover. This ties in closely with how well you've developed the energy systems and trained them with specific nutrient timing. Nutrition intake can also significantly affect hormonal balances in the body, as you'll learn later on.

When it comes to energy use, we can also break it down into three primary categories that determine how well you can turn energy produced into performance:

- **Skill and technique.** We group these together here, as the one will greatly affect the other. The more you practice a skill, the better you can refine your technique, and so they continually feed into one another.

- **Mental preparation and performance.** The better you prepare your mind for the event at hand, the better you'll perform. This is another area that many athletes fall short in, but the best of the best make it a point to train their mind, just as they train their body. Check out Lanny Bassham's *With Winning in Mind* for more on this skill.

- **Movement capacity.** This is where strength training comes into play, as the better you move, and the higher the quality of your movements, the more efficient and economical your body can be, requiring less energy to burn to perform. This is also why how you sit on the bike, how you pedal, and if you perform an interval sitting, standing, on the hoods, or in the drops matters. The better you balance and build your body via strength training, the better you're going to be able to perform on the bike.

When we talk about increasing power output, the vast majority of cyclists are very inefficient on the energy utilization side of this equation (with energy creation on the other side), which means there are a lot of performance gains to be made simply by focusing on movement. In this graphic from Joel Jamieson's *Ultimate MMA Conditioning*, it breaks down what your on-bike performances are built from.

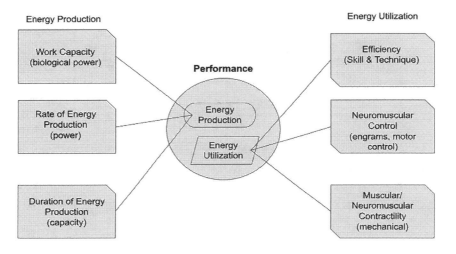

Image Source: Jamieson, Joel. Ultimate MMA Conditioning, *2009, p. 21.*

In the middle, we have performance. Your performances are determined by the energy you produce and your ability to use that energy efficiently and effectively.

On the left side, we have how your body produces energy. There are three main parts to producing energy:

1. **Biological power:** This is the total amount of work your body can do. Many refer to this as "fitness."
2. **Power:** This is how quickly you can produce energy for an effort.
3. **Capacity:** This is the length of time you can continue to produce energy. For many cyclists the focus is on training their FTP, or Functional Thresh-

old Power, which usually is referring to their aerobic energy system's ability to do work.

Put these three items together, and we now know how well your body produces energy. But the ability to produce energy does not determine your performances, as you need to be able to effectively and efficiently use the energy and turn it into movement. That's the right side of the graphic:

1. **Skill & technique:** This refers to how you ride your bike, how you pedal, your positioning on the bike, your ability to stay relaxed, breathe well, corner, descend, climb, sprint, eat, drink, etc.

2. **Motor control/engrams:** This refers to your ability to control the different parts of your body with as little energy use, and thus as much efficiency, as possible. This is built through a combination of on-bike skills and technique development, and through an intelligently designed strength training program that helps you move better.

3. **Mechanical work (contractility):** This is your ability to fire a muscle, or a group of muscles, in a way that moves your body. This is built through strength training and on-bike skills and technique.

By learning how to better move your body through the FUNdamental 5+1 movement patterns (addressed in Chapter 6), improving breathing patterns, and working towards better posture, you'll be able to increase your movement capacity and improve your skill and technique on the bike (as long as you actually practice them on the bike!). You'll not only see improvements in your strength and technique from your FUNdamental 5+1 movements, but you'll also make your brain more aware of where exactly in space your body parts are.

Now that we've covered power output and energy creation and use, next we'll learn how your body responds to the training sessions you do in order to get the results you're after.

THE 4 STAGES OF TRAINING RESPONSE

Understanding how your training sessions will create the changes that you want to see so that you can ride strong is very important. The better you understand your body, even at a very basic level, the smarter you're going to be when it comes to adjusting and changing your training program to keep you on track.

A basic understanding of how you plan and perform your training programs will lead to different changes in your movement patterns, your fitness, and in the end, your performance.

1. The Training Session: Specific Goals

During each and every training session, you need to have a specific goal and desired outcome in mind, relating to the changes you want to see from putting in the work in that area.

This is one of the reasons why many self-coached athletes tend to flounder and fail: They try to do everything in each training session, or they try to focus on too many changes in one training block. By training with a shotgun approach and trying to train too many things at once, they make it very unclear to the body exactly what changes they want to make. You want to be crystal clear with the body about how it should adapt to the training.

2. After the Training Session: Structural and Energy System Changes

As you endure specific training stress, your body will respond to the specific wastes and products made by the particular energy systems you are using, as well as the stresses placed on it from the muscles and tissues of the body.

This sounds complex, and it is, but just think of it like this: If you want to be able to climb mountains well, you need to stress the energy systems in the body, as well as the muscles, in ways that will help you adapt and get stronger to the forces and energy demands that climbing places on you. You cannot become a fast and strong climber riding only on the flats.

3. While You Recover: Adaptations

This one is really complex, and we're only now beginning to understand it, but put simply, when you stress the body in specific ways, it will turn on genes that will help you to respond as best as possible to the demands you're placing on the body.

While we put in all this time and effort into training, the missing key for many is the rest and recovery in between those training sessions, which is where the training effect, also called adaptations, actually take place. It's not just showing up and doing the work that matters; it's showing up, doing the work, and then taking the time to recover and allowing the adaptations to occur.

This is why sleep, nutrition, and stress management (life and training) are so important and must be focused on—that is, if you're serious about getting stronger, fitter, or faster.

4. While You Sleep: Tissue Adaptations

The last stage of training response involves your body adapting and building muscles and other tissues in order to be better at dealing with the specific stresses and forces that you are putting on it.

Many, or most, of the adaptations from training will occur while you are sleeping. Ever wonder why babies and teenagers spend so much time sleeping? Much of it has to do with their bodies changing, growing, and adapting!

While you sleep, the nervous system takes in all the information from the movements you challenged it with throughout the day, and it makes changes so that it can better perform those repetitive movements next time, with less effort. This means increased myelination around those nerves so that the signal can travel faster (like power lines from a power center) and the release of hormones to help the tissues and bones adapt.[1]

With all of these different factors of energy creation and use in the body, combined with the four stages of response to training, your body will become more efficient and economic and you will become faster, fitter, stronger, and more powerful as a cyclist.

But there is still one more thing we need to consider when it comes to getting the most out of our training. That is our posture and its ability to impact or change the effect exercise or training has on us.

THE IMPORTANCE OF POSTURE IN PERFORMANCE AND INJURY PREVENTION

Posture can tell us quite a lot about the abilities of an athlete (muscular imbalances, movement patterns they have adapted), as well as where they are on the fatigue spectrum.

Having the endurance for the muscles to perform the task at hand is the baseline for performance. This is especially true when it comes to riding the bike, for as soon as your posture starts to change, your technique will suffer, zapping you of your power, as well as alerting your competition to your wariness.

First and foremost, endurance athletes *must* have muscular endurance! And cycling is no exception. As a cyclist rides more and more, they begin to consciously or subconsciously pick up subtle cues about the riders around them. Shoulders rounded or elevated, hips wiggling a bit side to side, excessive leaning on the handlebars, and becoming fidgety on the bike are all signs that someone's tiring and the time to drop or attack is here or quickly arriving.

One of the first things that I look for when I meet a cyclist is their posture. How they carry their self tells me as much about their daily activities as their preferences for training. As I go through the movement screen with each athlete, it becomes more and more apparent to me how they ride their bike—where they are strongest and what kind of terrain fatigues them the quickest—and this is all before we even get on the bike!

The exercises to help address these postural issues are difficult, and many, if not most, athletes skip them due to frustration, because the exercises are technically challenging, or because they are not seeing any immediate results. The frustrating idea of instant gratification has infiltrated training. "Two weeks to lose five pounds" and "thirty days to a sexy six-pack" have become refrains of the fitness industry, and endurance athletes are no less guilty. "Twelve weeks to your fastest race" and "couch to 5K" have become parts of our little world. While you may be thinking that these are no "instant" results, they are. Some of these plans actually do work, but the fitness is short-lived, and a longer term (6–12 month) program is far better than the shortcut.

The approaches I have set forth in this book are not short-term or fast-return. While most everyone who uses my program will see at least a slight return on their performance in as little as 4–6 weeks, the true power of the program comes after sticking with it consistently for at least 16 weeks, if not a full calendar year. That's the minimum to really get your body stronger, fitter, and faster. Eight weeks for a solid base and to get much of the tightness and imbalances addressed. And then another eight weeks to make you physically stronger, with your strength gains seen and felt on the bike.

Can you really get stronger in 16 weeks? Absolutely.

Will it be easy? No.

You must be consistent, have focus during your workouts, and make sure that you are doing the essential things that are outside of the gym that make the big differences: nutrition, sleep, and recovery. Oh yeah, and don't forget about posture!

BREATHING, AT THE HEART OF IT ALL

Breathing may seem like something odd to include when it comes to strength training, or training at all. But while we may think, "Hey, I'm not dead, so I must be doing it right," there is actually far more to breathing—and learning how to improve our energy use and efficiency of movement—that we need to consider. In fact, over the course of time, the body works to decrease the amount of energy needed in order to complete a movement. This is what drives our development towards becoming more expert and advancing our skills and abilities on the bike.

To do this, we have to understand that movement not only comes from the central nervous system—the part of the nervous system that connects the brain and the muscles—but is also heavily influenced by the autonomic nervous system—the part of the nervous system that influences bodily functions such as heart rate, digestion, breathing, and recovery.

While we're not going to get lost down the rabbit hole here, as a lot of this is very technical and advanced, it's important for you to understand that movement affects recovery, and breathing is driven by movement and positions. Improved breathing will help improve movement, mobility, tissue qualities, and recovery.

It may seem silly when you first begin, but once you slow down, practice your breathing, and begin to feel and understand how you breathe at endurance and recovery-paced efforts as compared to hard efforts, such as lactate threshold, VO_2 max, and all-out sprints, you'll notice how different each is from the other. You'll also notice how when you're tired, it's even more different, and your ability to put the power down often decreases even more.

BREATHING AND RECOVERY

While we often think about the muscles getting tired and limiting our abilities, nervous system fatigue actually has a far bigger and far more reaching impact on limiting our performance, as it affects the whole body, not just the muscles used.

Breathing is incredibly powerful and can by itself shift the body from a "fight-or-flight" state into a "rest-and-recovery" state. You may think that in order for this to happen you have to meditate or focus on your breathing for long periods of time, but the body is incredibly dynamic and responsive. In fact, you can see these shifts happen in a matter of seconds, if you do it properly.

The ability to shift from the fight-or-flight mode into rest-and-digest is significantly impacted by the position of the body, especially the spine. This is one of the areas where cycling actually gives us a fairly large advantage over other sports, as our positioning on the bike, and especially the time trial bike, puts us in a position that helps us recover quickly.

If you think back to high school when your gym teacher had you running sprints, what's the first position you took when you were completely winded? Hunched over with your hands on your knees, trying to open up your upper back so you could "breathe." In fact, this same position helps you drive better breathing patterns to turn on your parasympathetic "rest-and-digest" nervous system.

BREATHING AND MOVEMENT

For many cyclists, neck, shoulder, and upper back pain, as well as hip and lower back pain and numbness and tingling in the hands and feet, are common occurrences. Either we ourselves have experienced it, or we know someone who has. And while a large contributing factor to developing pain in these areas comes from poor strength balance at the joints, breathing patterns also play big roles!

Shoulder and hip position especially are significantly affected by our breathing patterns. Here's how: When we inhale and exhale there are small, but significant, changes in the positions of different parts of the skeleton. When we inhale, our neck moves forward, the upper back extends up and back, while our lower back pushes forward, and our sacrum rotates down and forward. When we exhale the opposite happens: the neck extends (moves back), the upper back moves down and forward, and the sacrum moves up and back.

Even though the movements are relatively small, they can have a huge impact on the shoulders and hips. This is because we can get stuck in either an inhalation or exhalation position. Over time this can lead to the inability of the hips and shoulders to move through their full range of motion without pain or limitation.

While there is a lot more that we can dive into, let's stop here and summarize why breathing exercises and learning how to breathe properly is so important and must be included in your routine:

1. Breathing has an impact on the ability of the body to be efficient in its energy use and movement.

2. Being able to breathe properly helps us move the axial skeleton through its full range of motion, which impacts joint positions, especially at the hip and shoulders.

3. Improving how you breathe will allow you to perform and recover better between efforts, and between sessions.

You'll learn more about specific breathing exercises in Chapter 9, but for now just be aware that breath work should be included in each strength training session's warm-up.

---

1. Kathrin Bothe, Franziska Hirschauer, Hans-Peter Wiesinger, et al., "Gross Motor Adaptation Benefits from Sleep After Training," Wiley Online Library, December 23, 2019. https://doi.org/10.1111/jsr.12961.

CHAPTER 3 SUMMARY

- Along with sleep, nutrition & hydration, and interval training, the main determinants of performance on the bike include efficient energy use, power output, technical skills, and tactics & race strategy.

- Instead of buying speed with lighter equipment, you can influence your power output and speed far more by developing motor control, stress management, movement qualities, energy systems, skills, and techniques.

- Power output comes down to energy creation and energy use, and how efficiently your body can do both.

- Your training will show a response (changes in your movement patterns, your fitness, and your performance) in four stages: during the training session, after the session, while you recover, and while you sleep.

- Bad posture can be a limiter on and off the bike and can lead to injuries.

- Nervous system fatigue can be another limiter on performance. Breath work can improve energy use and efficiency of movement.

CHAPTER 4
SPECIAL CONSIDERATIONS FOR WOMEN

Much of this chapter comes from the resources of Dr. Stacy Sims. Most notably, the book ROAR[1] *was extremely helpful on the women-specific topics.*

While the majority of this chapter is devoted to the current best practices for women who are looking to gain fitness through strength training and cycling, and to understand the differences in training and recovery approaches between the sexes, the first two topics we'll cover here are vital to both sexes. I strongly encourage both male and female readers to read about Low Energy Availability (LEA) and Relative Energy Deficiency in Sport (RED-S) below, as these issues can have a big impact on everyone.

If you're a male coach who coaches both sexes, you need to be able to comfortably discuss subjects like menstruation and the pill in a professional, appropriate manner. If these subjects make you uncomfortable, find a way to get comfortable with them or get used to only working with one gender.

Do not ignore that you're uncomfortable! That discomfort is a part of the reason why women's sports sciences are still lagging behind men's, and we must change that culture. At the very least, educate yourself about the issues and how they are to be properly addressed and handled.

LOW ENERGY AVAILABILITY (LEA)

One of the biggest challenges in endurance sports is meeting our nutritional needs. And when we incorporate a strength training program, dialing in those nutrition demands is even more important.

Cycling is a sport where being lighter or leaner is seen as a huge performance aid (though this is *not* always true), and many cyclists have an incessant focus on eating less than they burn in their training in an attempt to drop weight to get faster or to improve their Watts per kilo.

While eating less may work for some athletes, there are many instances where riders—especially female riders—do not meet their minimum intakes that allow for proper recovery, rebuilding of the muscles and connective tissue, and maintaining appropriate hormonal balances.

While falling short on food intake here and there won't necessarily slow fitness and body composition progress, regularly falling short on nutritional needs can lead to a state of Low Energy Availability (LEA).

This is not just a female issue; it affects both men and women. However, because of the hormonal fluctuations that occur, women may suffer more detrimental effects, including but not limited to:

- excessive fatigue
- muscle loss
- frequent illness or injury
- stress fractures
- menstrual dysfunction
- inability to recover
- decrease in performance

HOW DOES LOW ENERGY AVAILABILITY HAPPEN?

With the health and fitness industry's obsession with numbers, calories in vs. calories out has become a popular practice. This involves basing the number of calories a day that you are consuming off of how many calories you are burning during your exercise session(s) that day. Monitoring the number of calories in (consumed) versus the number of calories out (expended) can help an athlete lose or maintain weight, so you can see why it has become so popular.

However, there are a number of problems with this approach.

First is the biggest problem. Most people aren't educated on how their body's energy needs go above and beyond the calories burned in their exercise sessions. To help explain this concept, I made an "Expert's Weight Loss Equation" video back in 2015, which you can watch by going to the HVTraining YouTube Channel.

The body has what are called "basal metabolic needs." In everyday terms, these are the calories needed to maintain basic body functions—like the energy the brain needs to run things (roughly 20% of your energy intake), breathing, circulation, nutrient processing, and other cell functions. Your basal metabolic rate, or BMR as it is called, is based off of the number of calories your body would need if you were to lie in bed all day, doing nothing.

But very few coaches or trainers will tell you about BMR and how you must meet these caloric minimums in order to maintain healthy bodily functions. It's not sexy or fun to talk about BMR, because it can take some middle-school level math to figure out. You can tell how popular BMR is from the total views on my video (around 500 views as of this writing), compared to my other videos, such as "Ride your bike faster: sitting properly for cycling" (~300,000 views) and "How to set up your cycling trainer for indoor biking" (~135,000 views). But BMR is something you *must* measure if you're serious about your health and fitness.

There is one more very important note about basal metabolic rate: The number you use to calculate your BMR will change based on how active your job and daily lifestyle are. If you sit at work all day, your number will be lower than someone who is standing and moving all day, such as a UPS driver or a surgeon who is in the OR for 4–6 hours a day. This is a small detail that many miss, which can have a huge impact, especially as training volume, intensity, or life stress goes up.

THE PRO'S BASAL CALORIC NEEDS EQUATION

Over the years there have been a number of quick and easy BMR calculators online that have become popular. However, while they may be quick and easy to use, many of them drastically miscalculate an individual's energy needs, due to not taking into account their level of activity throughout the day. Lifestyle factors like an active or inactive job, training sessions, and sleep are all important to consider.

Here is the pro's BMR equation, which is called the Basal Caloric Needs, according to the *ACSM's Resources for the Exercise Physiologists*[2]. This equation takes into account these important factors and will help you figure out your actual needs.

Step 1: Plug in your weight, height, and age into one of the equations below.

Women: 655 + (4.35 x weight in pounds) + (4.7 x height in inches) - (4.7 x age in years)

Men: 66 + (6.23 x weight in pounds) + (12.7 x height in inches) - (6.8 x age in years)

Step 2: Divide the number from above by 24 (24 hours in a day).

Step 3: Take the number from step 2 and multiply it by the number of hours of sleep you get per night (on average).

Circle this number (we'll call it "A").

Step 4: Take the number from step 3 and multiply it by one of the following, depending on your level of activity:

1.15 if you have a non-active lifestyle and non-active job: (A x 1.15)

1.2 if you have an active lifestyle and non-physical job (i.e., computer/desk job): (A x 1.2)

1.3 if you have a physical job: (A x 1.3)

Step 5: Take the number from step 4 and multiply it by the number of hours per day you are NOT sleeping.

Circle this number.

Step 6: Determine the average number of calories you burn per training session. If you have a power meter on your bike, this is really easy, as you can take the Kj total per ride. Another easy way to do this is to add up all the Calories burned in training over a week, and divide it by 7.

Circle this number.

Step 7: Add up the circled numbers from step 3, step 5, and step 6.

This is your Basal Caloric Needs per day.

Low Energy Availability happens when the individual is not eating enough to support their basal metabolic rate *plus* their training needs. This can happen one of two ways:

1. Purposefully not eating enough to support training + BMR with the idea of creating a daily caloric deficit
2. Maintaining daily caloric intake but not eating enough to support increased training demands (either higher intensities/more time at higher intensities, or increased training volume), which drive up energy needs

Signs and symptoms of LEA are pretty common in endurance athletes, but they are too often shrugged off as being normal or due to lack of sleep, stress, or "just not feeling so great." Signs and symptoms include:

- reduced training capacity
- repeated injury or illness
- delayed or prolonged recovery times
- change in mood state
- irritability and lack of focus
- failure to lose weight
- reduced or low bone density
- reduced libido
- cessation of or disruption in menstrual cycle
- excessive fatigue
- poor or interrupted sleep
- night sweats
- extreme hunger in the middle of the night

What makes LEA particularly challenging to diagnose and correct is our tendency to feel these symptoms and ignore them. Instead of dialing back our training or increasing our nutrition, we go harder, eat less, and get more stressed about our body not responding the way we expect or want, thus speeding up the downward spiral until we eventually reach an overtrained, injured, or burned-out zombie state.

I've seen this happen to more cyclists than I would care to admit, as well as quite a few coaches, including yours truly. Yes, I made the very same mistakes I am talking about right now. Thankfully, because of my daily logging—whether I was training that day or not—including how I felt overall and my general attitude towards life, I was able to quickly (after 3 months) recognize what was going on and correct it with the help of a sports dietitian.

CONSEQUENCES OF LEA

The health consequences of short-term, and especially long-term, LEA can be devastating and far-reaching. You must be careful about this!

If Low Energy Availability persists over a prolonged period of time, it can move into the classification of Relative Energy Deficiency in Sport (or RED-S, for short), which brings with it a whole host of other, far more critical health issues, as well as decreased performance.

RED-S

Relative Energy Deficiency in Sport used to be categorized as "The Female Athlete Triad" of:

1. Disordered eating
2. Loss of menstruation / menstrual disruption
3. Deterioration of bone health

What many coaches and researchers found, though, was that there was a large number of *male* athletes suffering from many of the symptoms that occur when an athlete has Low Energy Availability for a longer period of time. This led to the recategorization of "The Female Athlete Triad" to RED-S, as it allowed athletes of both sexes to be identified and properly treated.

Athletes who participate in sports where power (i.e., Watts per kilogram), body composition, or aesthetics give a significant competitive edge are at risk of developing RED-S. Examples of these sports include cycling, triathlon, running, gymnastics, ballet, dance, boxing, and wrestling, just to name a few.

Teenagers are particularly vulnerable to developing LEA and RED-S, due to their desire to please instructors or coaches, peer pressure, or wanting a body type or "image" they think they need to succeed in that sport.

HOW DOES LOW ENERGY AVAILABILITY PROGRESS INTO RED-S?

While Low Energy Availability can occur every now and again for short periods of time for many cyclists, such as over the course of a 3–4 day training camp weekend, these short time frames generally have relatively small negative effects on an athlete's progress and fitness.

However, if an athlete remains in a Low Energy Availability state for a prolonged period of time, their body will begin to make a number of adjustments to important systems, such as the metabolic (energy) system, endocrine (hormonal) system, and even changes to slow down new bone growth. At this point, an athlete has moved from LEA to RED-S, and this can lead to prolonged suppression of estrogen and progesterone production in women, and suppressed testosterone in men. These hormonal changes, while detrimental to performance gains even in the short term (1–2 days), can have a devastating effect on an athlete over a longer period of time.

Additionally, an athlete may experience:

- increased body fat, as the endocrine system signals the body to break down muscle mass and increase fat mass (muscle needs energy to maintain it, while fat is the storage of energy in the body)
- a decrease in power output during efforts due to metabolic systems slowing to conserve energy

When these changes occur, many athletes interpret them as signs that they are not training hard enough, or they are not limiting their calories enough. So they train harder and eat less, thus leading them even further down the road of LEA and into RED-S.

The length of time it takes an athlete to move from LEA into RED-S varies from athlete to athlete due to individual circumstances and differences. But athletes and coaches should be aware of the following signs and symptoms that extend far beyond the absence of menstruation, and even well before:

- recurring injury (muscle soreness, "niggles," other small injuries)
- recurring sickness (common cold, infections, etc.)
- unexpected tiredness
- disrupted sleep patterns (waking at night, lack of energy during day)
- change in mood/irritability
- decreased desire to engage in social situations
- problematic relationships with food (becoming picky or avoiding certain foods)
- staleness in training or lack of performance
- lack of progress in training or fitness

Not all signs and symptoms of RED-S happen only because of LEA. Other underlying health or medical issues may be the causes, and so a medical professional should be consulted to rule out nutritional deficiencies, hormonal imbalances, or other medical conditions.

RED-S and LEA are not female-specific issues, and we must all understand the root causes if we are to stay healthy, fit, and progressing. One thing you must ensure is that you are taking in enough protein to support your training and supply the necessary building blocks to repair and strengthen your muscles.

THE MENSTRUAL CYCLE AND TRAINING

Now that you have a firm understanding of LEA and RED-S, let's talk about the female menstrual cycle and how women can adjust their training to fit their cycle. This was one of the biggest lessons I learned as a male coach when I started digging into why my female athletes were not responding as well as my male athletes to their training programs.

While I was taught in high school and college that a female's menstrual cycle is 28 days, in reality it can range anywhere from 20 days all the way up to 42—and still be a normal, healthy cycle!

Because of the hormonal changes that occur during the menstrual cycle, training intensities will need to be adjusted in order to meet the athlete where she is and for what she is capable of handling. Nearly every female athlete I've worked with has noticed that for at least a few days each month, her legs feel heavy, she feels uncoordinated, and, as one athlete expressed, "I just don't have any pop."

These are essentially side effects of the hormonal changes that occur in the female body in the second half of her menstrual cycle, after ovulation, which is called the luteal phase.

HORMONAL CHANGES DICTATE TRAINING INTENSITY CHANGES

In the first half of the menstrual cycle, which is called the follicular phase, a woman's hormones are relatively stable, she is able to put out high intensities in training, she can recover fairly quickly between exercise sessions, and she is able to build lean muscle mass efficiently.

However, in the second half of the menstrual cycle (the luteal phase), there is a big influx of estrogen and progesterone that puts the body into a more catabolic (breaking down) state. These hormones cause a number of changes in the female body, including but not limited to:

- trouble maintaining body temperature
- loss of blood plasma volume
- decreased coordination

Understanding the basic principles of how a woman's hormonal state changes throughout her menstrual cycle and how she can appropriately adjust her training for these changes, can have a massively powerful impact on her abilities to train, race, and improve fitness.

In a research study published in 2017 by Lisbeth Wikström-Frisén et al.[3], it was found that women who trained based off their hormonal changes performed better and saw more gains when they trained in the follicular (low hormone) phase. These improvements included:

- stronger squat
- higher jump
- increased muscle mass
- higher torque production

Understanding how your body changes through your cycle can help you make the small (and big) changes to your training that will help you ride strong and feel great.

CHANGES IN TRAINING THROUGHOUT THE MENSTRUAL CYCLE

Tracking the menstrual cycle is something that is extremely simple to do, but it takes a little bit of work up front to figure out. Women can track their cycle with pen and paper, an app like the one I recommend here at HVTraining called FitrWoman—or if they want to be really specific, they can even purchase an ovulation predictor kit at a local drugstore.

Tracking the cycle is a really important part of matching training to personal physiology, as the follicular and luteal phases are not equal in length. In fact, the follicular phase can be shorter or longer and will depend on when the woman ovulates. Trying to estimate and guess ovulation and how to build training off of those guesses can lead to continued frustration as the athlete can still have days where she is a bit "off" and can't match the desired intensities or needed execution.

Remember, in the follicular phase, the athlete is able to push intensities, coordinate, balance, and mentally execute at her very best. In this phase, all systems tend to fire on all cylinders and she is able to recover from the sessions and build muscle mass effectively, so long as she is getting quality sleep and supplying the body with the nutrients it needs to do so.

However, from the day of ovulation she will move into a high-hormone phase. In this phase there are a number of changes that will occur and which must be taken into account when planning and executing training.

No two women have the same length of cycle, and in fact, due to life stress, nutritional changes, training loads, and even environmental factors, no two cycles for a single woman will necessarily be the same. Yes, they will generally fall within the averages, but as we read above in the LEA and RED-S sections, there are a number of factors that can negatively affect the menstrual cycle.

With that being said, if a female athlete has regular, consistent menstrual cycles that are highly predictable, it's a good indicator that the nutrition, training, and recovery strategies for this individual athlete are effective and that she is in a healthy state (hormonally). Sometimes a change in her cycle can be an early sign that something is off and needs to be assessed and corrected.

TRAINING BASED OFF OF RPE

In today's modern age of measuring everything with apps and carefully planning out the programming based off of previous wattage or testing every few weeks, many endurance athletes and general fitness folks have lost connection with their bodies and their ability to understand what their body is or is not capable of on a given day.

While this may not seem like a big problem, progress in fitness and performance is not linear. It doesn't show up on a scheduled time or on a specific day.

While we work hard to increase the chance that you'll be in your peak form at the time of a known competition, we cannot predict your fitness exactly. But we can set you up to be as close to top shape as possible.

Acclaimed strength coach Dan John, in his book *Intervention: Course Corrections for the Athlete and Trainer*, talks about the difference in fitness abilities as being like going to a park bench vs. a bus stop bench. When you show up to a park bench, you know you're going to see some birds. You don't know when, or what kind, but they'll be around. When you show up to a bus stop bench, you expect a bus to show up at a specific time and for it to be headed to a specific destination. Chances are very high that the bus will show up on time. . . . But sometimes it happens that the bus is early, late, or makes a wrong turn.

When it comes to training with female physiology, we see both of these kinds of benches. During the follicular phase, an athlete is working with more of a bus stop bench. With good nutrition, sleep habits, and program planning, she has a really great idea of what she can expect on a given day, for a given exercise. So she'll pick a weight, a set and rep scheme, and while she may need to make a slight adjustment based on how she is feeling that day, she can plan with pretty good accuracy.

However, during the luteal (high-hormone) phase, she will shift more towards a park bench scenario. She will want to lift some weights and get in some solid training, but she may not be exactly sure of what she can handle.

This is where training by RPE (rating of perceived exertion) comes in. Instead of planning to lift at a specific weight, the athlete can train based on how she feels. Not only that, but during the luteal phase, she should back off from the heavier weights and more technical movements, and instead focus more on the FUNda-mental 5+1 movement patterns, some coordination, and adjusting the workouts to meet what she can handle.

By training according to RPE at this time in the cycle, she can appropriately choose weights that feel heavy—because based off of her neuromuscular abilities at that time, they *are* heavy!

This may seem like a funny change to make, especially as it completely flips upside down the concept that an athlete should be incrementally stronger week to week. But by simply putting her head down and attempting to hit those prescribed weights, she can slow down progress instead of boosting it.

For female athletes, it's all about meeting them where they are, and letting their training align with what their body is currently capable of doing.

CHANGES TO TRAINING DAYS IN A WEEK

Rolling with the tide is an important consideration when it comes to modifying strength training (and on-bike training) in the luteal phase. Simply training a little less can actually be a huge step towards fast-forwarding progress and improving strength and fitness.

While there are a lot of details, when it comes to strength training, it boils down to this:

- Instead of 2–3 days of moderate to heavy strength training, more may be gained by moving to 1–2 days of lighter weights, with more balance and coordination focus.
- Introduce longer rest periods between sets.
- Aim for 2–3 days in between sessions.

While this may sound odd, if an athlete trains fewer days a week and at far lower intensities and weights, she can significantly improve her abilities due to the changes in her physiological status.

There is much more to this topic than we've discussed here. You can learn more by looking up Dr. Stacy Sims and her books on training for women.

Fall in love with your bike again, by planning and adjusting your training for your unique physiology and needs.

NUTRIENT TIMING

In the mid-2010s, a study[4] was published by a highly respected researcher, stating that "the 30 minute window after training to replenish glycogen has been found to be untrue." Health and fitness practitioners around the world rejoiced at this news, as it meant that they no longer needed to worry about getting a meal in immediately after their training sessions if they wanted to see progress.

Unfortunately for women, like the vast majority of sports research, this study was performed on college-aged men from 18–24. Upon further research[5,6] that looked specifically at women, it was found that this idea of not needing to replenish glycogen quickly is untrue for women in their luteal phase! In fact, women in the luteal phase need to eat at least 30 grams of mixed protein in a meal within 20–30 minutes of finishing their exercise session, in order to avoid the body going into a catabolic (breaking down) state. During the follicular phase, however, women were more similar to men and did not need to worry as much about how soon after their session they ate.

Be careful about what you read, and make sure to look at the actual research study, who it was performed on, and how they tested it. If you'd like to learn more about how to read a research article, take a listen to episode 30 of my *Strong Savvy Cyclist & Triathlete Podcast*.

PERIMENOPAUSE & MENOPAUSE CONSIDERATIONS

While we've spoken about the changes women need to make as they are going through their menstrual cycle in order to see better results from their strength and on-bike training, this really only covers around 35–40 years of an adult female's life cycle.

As a woman moves towards menopause (called perimenopause), the rules will change, and she will need to adjust her training in different ways, due to the fluctuations and changes that are happening.

As Dr. Stacy Sims talks about in her "Menopause for Athletes" course[7], menopause refers to a very specific and short time in a woman's life cycle when ovulation ceases. We often erroneously refer to menopause as the entire time before and after this short period, which can cause a lot of ambiguity and confusion about what's really going on. During perimenopause, or the 4–5 years (or longer) leading up to menopause itself, hormone fluctuations become larger and more extreme, and body changes begin to happen. But it's also during perimenopause, when the hormones are in constant flux, that you have an opportunity to set yourself up for greater success after menopause, so long as you take action right away. Steps you can take to help set you up for post-menopause success include:

- better nutrition
- better body composition
- better control of blood sugar
- improved bone mineral density

How you go about implementing the changes of perimenopause will be determined by whether you are in a cycle of high progesterone and low estrogen, or vice versa. Each will have a drastically different impact on your body's internal environment, and thus how you'll work to counteract those changes through strength training, nutrition, sleep, etc.

This is a much deeper topic than what can be covered in this book; however, you can look up Dr. Stacy Sims and her books or courses to learn more.

The take-home message for those of you in your 30s or 40s who are starting to see unpleasant changes in your training responses as you hit perimenopause is a very important one: *NOW is the time to take action and set yourself up for better body composition and health post-menopause. Don't wait!*

A HEALTHY WAY FORWARD

As you can see, when it comes to building a training program for women, there are quite a few things that must be taken into consideration and planned for appropriately. These considerations, once you understand them, are relatively easy to plan and adjust for, so long as the athlete pays attention to what her body is telling her, and where she is in her menstrual cycle.

One last big, important note: If a premenopausal woman is not menstruating regularly, she is not healthy. Menstruation is a healthy part of a woman's life cycle, and the absence or irregularity of the menstrual cycle is often a sign, be it sometimes an early sign, that something in her nutrition, recovery, or self-care is off and must be addressed.

If you or your athlete has been missing their period, or it has been irregular, seek out a qualified women's health medical practitioner to help determine the cause and get back to health.

If you'd like to read more on this, check out the book *No Period, Now What* by Dr. Nicola Rinaldi.

1. Dr. Stacy Sims, *ROAR: How to Match Your Food and Fitness to Your Unique Female Physiology for Optimum Performance, Great Health, and a Strong, Lean Body for Life.* (Rodale, 2016).

2. American College of Sports Medicine, *ACSM's Resources for the Exercise Physiologist,* 2nd ed. (LWW, 2017).

3. Lisbeth Wikström-Frisén, Carl J. Boraxbekk, and Karin Henriksson-Larsén, "Effects on Power, Strength and Lean Body Mass of Menstrual/Oral Contraceptive Cycle Based Resistance Training," *Journal of Sports Medicine and Physical Fitness* 57, 1-2 (2017): 43–52, doi: 10.23736/S0022-4707.16.05848-5.

4. Alan Albert Aragon and Brad Jon Schoenfeld, "Nutrient Timing Revisited: Is There a Post-Exercise Anabolic Window?" *Journal of the International Society of Sports Nutrition* 10, 5 (2013), doi: 10.1186/1550-2783-10-5.

5. Anna M. Gorczyca et al. "Changes in Macronutrient, Micronutrient, and Food Group Intakes Throughout the Menstrual Cycle in Healthy, Premenopausal Women," *European Journal of Nutrition* 55, 3 (2016): 1181–1188.

6. Julia M. Malowany et al. "Protein to Maximize Whole-Body Anabolism in Resistance-Trained Females after Exercise," *Medicine & Science in Sports & Exercise* 51, 4 (April 2019): 798–804.

7. Dr. Stacy Sims, "The Menopause for Athletes" course, drstacysims.com/courses.

CHAPTER 4 SUMMARY

Female cyclists have special considerations to take into account for their health and their training.

- Low Energy Availability (LEA) can happen when an athlete falls short on food intake, and it can have many detrimental effects, including excessive fatigue, muscle loss, frequent illness or injury, negative changes in hormonal levels, and more.

- The basal metabolic rate (BMR) determines the caloric minimums an athlete must meet to maintain healthy bodily functions.

- If an athlete is in an LEA state for a prolonged period of time, they can move into RED-S, which can lead to prolonged suppression of hormones and can have devastating effects.

- LEA and RED-S can happen to both male and female riders.

- Because of the hormonal changes that occur during a female's menstrual cycle, training intensities and programming will need to be adjusted to meet the athlete where she's at.

- Training adjustments may include training by RPE or changing the training days in a week.

CHAPTER 5
FOUNDATIONS OF A HEALTHY SPINE

This chapter has been proofed and approved by Dr. Stuart McGill[1], world leading back & spine expert, and author of over 250 published research papers.

Over the years, the main aches and pains of cyclists have changed, as we've learned more about how to make the machine more effective in how it rewards cyclists for the work they are doing and puts them into better positions to do that work. However, even with advancements in technology, much of which came about due to the ingenuity, imagination, and necessity of different riders throughout history, one big area of pain and discomfort continues to plague many riders to this very day: back pain. Specifically, lower back pain.

We've seen great improvements in bike technology thanks to riders like Eddie Merckx and Greg LeMond, and bike fitting has become better understood as it pertains to the human body thanks to Ben Serotta. But when it comes to our understanding of how the human element plays into the equation of pain and discomfort, especially when it comes to back pain, cyclists are far behind, and some would even say that we are in the dark completely!

Understanding the spine and how back pain occurs is incredibly important in helping you to stay healthy, and to get stronger and faster. I've kept this chapter light on technical terms to make it easier to read—but pay attention, as there are a few really important points here that will help you drastically improve!

BACK PAIN IN CYCLISTS

One of the common first pains we feel on the bike (after the backside from the saddle) is our lower back. As you'll soon understand, there can be a number of causes for a new cyclist's back pain. While I won't go deep into the details—I could write a whole book on this subject alone—what I will do is give you a solid understanding of how and why back pain occurs, and what you need to do in order to keep your spine healthy and strong.

Let me start with a personal story of a back injury that threatened my own future in the saddle. It happened on a random Thursday morning training ride in late April of 2010, on one of my favorite routes and at almost the farthest point away from home.

MY INJURY

Pedaling along in the mid-morning of a gorgeous spring day, just outside the city limits of Pittsburgh, PA, my left hip locked up, and I felt as if someone had taken a large knife that had been heated with a blowtorch and stabbed me with it right in the middle of the crease of the hip. The pain radiated up my lower back and through my entire left side. I was petrified, thinking that I had somehow either broken the neck of my femur or maybe dislocated my hip in my last tempo effort.

But if it was tempo, that wouldn't make any sense!

Slowly riding my way home at a pace the pain would allow me, thoughts were running wild in my head. What could I have possibly done? Could my riding career be over before it really began? And how could I coach cyclists without being able to ride?

As soon as I got home, I called on the sports medicine team that I used for my own athletes and set up an appointment for the next day with one of the physical therapists. It turned out that I had what's called Femoroacetabular Impingement (FAI). This injury resulted from the bone of the pelvis and the ball part of the femur growing in such a way that they physically collided when I pedaled due to my riding position. And that collision caused movements in my lower back.

My back pain was due in part to the FAI, but it was also due to poor midsection strength.

Let's pause the story here for a minute and get into the anatomy of the spine and hips, because these play a very important role in back pain for cyclists.

BASIC ANATOMY OF THE SPINE

The human spine is made up of 33 vertebrae. These bones help to support us and keep us upright, and they protect our spinal cord, which carries signals from the brain down to the different muscles and organs.

The spine has 5 distinct and very different areas. From top down they are:

- cervical spine (7 vertebrae)
- thoracic spine (12 vertebrae)
- lumbar spine (5 vertebrae)
- sacrum (5 vertebrae, fused together)
- coccyx (4 vertebrae, fused together)

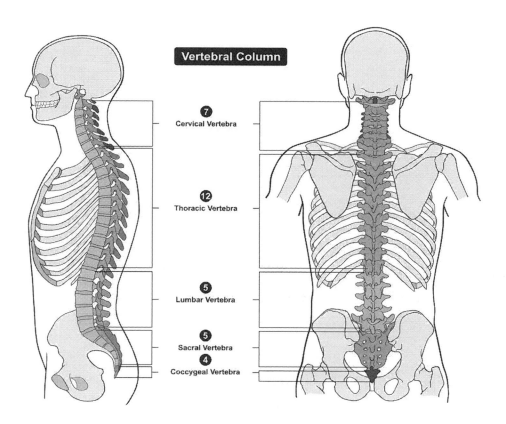

Image Source: Vertebral Column of Human Body Anatomy, Shutterstock.

Of the five regions of the spine, the lumbar spine is the biggest area of pain for cyclists.

Each of the sections of the spine are built to produce movement in specific ways, and to provide stability in others. When we perform movements that go against or above these different spinal sections' abilities, that is when we open ourselves up to a higher risk of injury of some type.

In order to help protect the spine, we must learn a few skills:

1. Good movement patterns that protect and bolster the spine's ability to deal with the forces at hand.
2. How to activate and fire muscles to produce not only the forces we need to perform a movement but also the stiffness to protect and stabilize the spine, and the rest of the body, in order to get the desired outcome.
3. How to breathe properly while performing these first two items.

MUSCLES DO MORE THAN PRODUCE FORCE

When most of us think about muscles, we think about them producing a force in order to overcome an obstacle. For example, if we think about the bicep moving, we think of it overcoming a force (such as a grocery bag of filled water bottles) in order to bring it up close to our chest in a "biceps curl" motion.

However, muscles in the body, and in particular in and around our midsection and spine, also work to produce appropriate stiffness in order to protect our spine and other joints, and to create movement.

Muscles need to stiffen in order to create movement? That doesn't make sense! It does, and here is how: If you're on your bike and you want to catch up to the riders in front of you quickly, you will push down on the pedals harder, to create more force (power) and thus more speed. But in order for the leg pushing down to create the force you want—forward movement of the bike—your glutes, midsection, and even upper body all need to stiffen so that the force is put *down* into the pedal, instead of your hips and upper body rotating up and away from the leg moving down.

If you'd like to learn more about this, take a listen to episodes 8 & 9 of *The Strong Savvy Cyclist & Triathlete Podcast* with Dr. Stuart McGill, and episode 23 with Lee Taft, where we cover this and other important performance and spine considerations.

STIFFEN YOUR SPINE TO PRODUCE POWER AND SPEED AT YOUR ARMS AND LEGS

I mentioned in Chapter 1 that one of our goals with the Vortex Method is to help you learn to create proximal stiffness to produce distal movement. It's not just the overall ability to maintain body position that we need from our muscles; it's also the ability to keep the joints that are moving, and our back, nice and stable while we pedal our bikes.

Getting your true core: all of the muscles between your neck, elbows, and knees, to produce proximal stiffness, so you only get movement from the hips and arms, are keys to a healthy, happy spine, and on-bike performance.

You see, the spine is much like a fishing rod. It's strong but flexible, with the different sections having various amounts of flexibility. This flexibility is one of the qualities that allows us as human beings to be able to do such a wide variety of activities like ride a bicycle, perform gymnastics on a balance beam, and bend and twist the various parts of our body into different positions in yoga.

But not all spines are built the same, and the different segments of the spine are built to be able to do different things!

DIFFERENCES IN SPINE SIZES

I have a friend who is just fantastic at yoga. He is about as bendy as they come, much to the chagrin of his wife. They're both around the same height, he weighs about 20 pounds more than she does, but no matter how much she practices her yoga poses and stretches, she just cannot perform the poses with the same position or stability that he can. It's a similar thing with one of his friends—the friend has the same build but is less bendy.

What's causing this? Do his wife and friend both just really stink at yoga? Is that even possible?

The difference comes down to their skeletons. And while there are plenty of differences that could apply to yoga, I'm going to focus in on their spines. Looking at the width of each of their spines, my bendy friend's spine is roughly the width of my index and middle fingers put together. His wife's spine is slightly wider than that, and his friend's spine is the size of my index, middle, and ring fingers put together.

The size difference in the width of the spines is one of the major factors that determines how flexible someone will be.

Other considerations include:

- natural muscle resting tone (do they feel like a dead fish when you shake hands, or do they have a firm grip?)
- ligament/connective tissue thickness (genetics and previous fitness and life activities)
- disc adaptations due to genetics and previous fitness and life activities
- ability to activate muscles around the spine that support it and produce stiffness
- previous injury to the back and its structures

These factors combined are responsible for determining how your body is able to deal with the specific forces that you are putting on it while cycling.

HOW YOU SIT ON THE BIKE MATTERS!

If you start to think about the back and how it is built, you begin to understand why bike fitting and how you sit on your bike matter. A LOT.

When we are riding, we have 5 points of contact with the bike (at most):

- hands (2)
- bottom of the pelvis (ischial tuberosity) (1)
- feet (2)

That's all we have to support ourselves while we whoosh down the road, track, or trail. But it's this support, and the position that we have to hold still for long periods of time, that can cause us to have back pain.

For many of us, when we get our first bike, we simply jump on and start pedaling, not giving a second thought to how we are sitting, or how we are supporting ourselves on the bike. While for short bits of time here and there this usually doesn't cause a problem, when we begin to get into regular training and riding numerous times a week, or for longer periods, we begin to see and feel the structures of the back break down.

Popular belief is that lower back injuries happen when you try to pick up a heavy weight that you're not ready for. While for many cyclists who put off strength training for much of the year and then head into the weight room, this may be true (discussed in episode 8 of the SSCT podcast with Dr. McGill), this is only one of the mechanisms that can cause a lower back injury.

We won't get into all of the mechanisms here, but instead we will focus on two that have a huge impact on back and spine health for cyclists:

1. **Repeated subfailure loading:** lifting light or medium weights repeatedly until the muscles/tissues fail due to fatigue
2. **Sustained stress over a long period:** staying in positions for long periods of time that stretch the tissues, decrease blood flow, and decrease muscle strength

Repeated subfailure loading can be seen in cyclocross and mountain bikers who are riding on very challenging terrain where they need to constantly lift and maneuver the front wheel. Sustained stress can be seen in road cyclists and time trialists. These two types of loading tend to be the most common, but they are not the only ways in which cyclists can hurt their backs. There are always a number of considerations that we have to take into account.

Having a bike fit performed by a professional and highly skilled bike fitter, who doesn't just throw you and your bike up on the stand and then move the bike to match measurements punched out by a computer, is absolutely paramount in keeping you and your spine healthy and strong.

WHAT SHOULD A GOOD BIKE FITTER DO?

A good bike fitter should spend some time talking with you, getting to understand what kind of riding you do, what your lifestyle off the bike looks like, what aches and pains (if any) you get on the bike, as well as what your goals and dreams are.

After the conversation, some bike fitters will ask you to go right to the assessment table or mat and will have you lie down. From here they will have you lift your legs, bend your knees, flex your hips, and do a few other movements by yourself. They may also ask you to relax while they take your leg/knee/hip/arm through different movements without you needing to do anything.

A good bike fitter will have you squatting, hinging, taking your hands overhead, and also performing a squat while you are on your hands and knees. All of these movements are recorded, either with video or by notes—and sometimes both.

After the conversation and the movement assessment, or even just the conversation, the bike fitter should have you do a light warm-up of some kind while they keep a watchful eye on you. This doesn't mean they are going to watch you the entire time, but they should spend at least 3–5 minutes watching what you're doing, walking around and looking at you from different angles, and even taking short videos.

From there the bike fitter will consult his or her notes and videos, and then will set you up on your bike or suggest which bike you should buy. It all depends on when and why you are seeing the bike fitter.

One of the big areas a good bike fitter will spend time on is your hips and lower back. As you may remember from my injury story, my back pain only began because of a hip injury.

THE ROLE OF HIP STRUCTURE

The muscles that cross over the hip joint and connect the leg to the pelvis and spine, such as the psoas and iliacus (together known as "the hip flexor muscles") and the quads, work to move the upper leg bone, called the femur, and produce power. However, if you do not have the muscular strength or the ability to produce the correct amount of stiffness at the spine, the power that you produce with the muscles at the hip will instead move up into the spine, causing the spine to move instead of putting the power down to the pedals.

This movement is pretty easy to see when riding behind another rider—when you look at the top of their jersey pockets, you can see the pockets moving (sometimes quite a bit!) from side to side, while the rider's shoulders and upper body do not move at all.

But this is not the only way in which the femur and pelvis can affect your lower back. When there is either not enough stiffness at the spine (proximal stiffness) to support the spine while the limbs move (distal motion), or if the bones are hitting each other, as I had with my injury, something called "micromovements" can happen at the joints and discs of your back. These motions push, pull, and twist the joint, which leads to the joint losing its ability to stabilize over time.

That is what happened to me. However, I didn't recognize the back pain as anything beyond the normal ache after a long climb or tiring ride until *after* my hip injury came out in full force. Had my hip injury not happened, as I continued to ride my bike and push my limits, my back injury could have progressed to the same point as a few of the riders I've worked with. Their pain had reached a place where they couldn't get power down to the pedals, despite feeling that their legs were capable of more.

Why does that happen? The loss of the ability to put power out due to the instability at the back is actually caused by the brain as it shuts down the leg muscles in an effort to protect the spine. While this is usually a late-stage sign of a back injury of some kind, unfortunately, there are a large number of cyclists (and triathletes) whom I've met or had as clients who have not sought treatment for their back pain until this point. The failure to recognize that back pain is not normal is largely due to the wide acceptance of back pain and discomfort in riders, which is sometimes even seen as a badge of honor in the world of cycling.

This is not a good practice. Instead, the ability to recognize "good pain" and "bad pain" is fundamental to enjoying riding our bikes and the sport for decades to come.

WHAT IS "NON-SPECIFIC BACK PAIN"?

Another problem that plagues cyclists, and back pain sufferers specifically, is when they go to a physical therapist or doctor to have their back pain assessed and are told that they have "unspecified back pain." The doctor may say, "You're a cyclist. … This back pain is in your head; it's just your body telling you you're working hard."

Unfortunately, even in today's modern age, an overwhelmingly large percentage of doctors and clinicians are not trained in the art and science of being able to do a thorough assessment in order to determine an exact mechanism and trigger of back pain. When a clinician or doctor uses the term "non-specific back pain," this often means that this particular medical professional does not have the skills necessary to determine what is going on.

Thankfully there is a resource out there to help you find a professional who *does* have the skills and tools necessary to determine the cause of your back pain, and to build you up with an intelligently built program. Dr. Stuart McGill's website, www. BackFitPro.com, is a fantastic resource to find qualified professionals who can help you. Dr. McGill has spent the better part of the last 30+ years teaching professionals from around the world how to determine back pain causes and triggers.

FOUNDATIONS FOR A HEALTHY AND PAIN-FREE BACK

While we've only just lightly touched on the topic of back and spine health (and there is much more to it), having at least an understanding of the causes of back pain, how it affects cyclists, and that there are a number of ways in which back injuries occur, you are now able to better understand the foundations of healthy, quality movement.

DAILY HABITS AND POSTURE

Learning how to move from your hips and not from your back is at the base of building a healthy and happy spine. This practice ranges from how you squat to pick something up and put it down to how you hinge from the hips while keeping your midsection appropriately braced and back in neutral. Lifting with a neutral spine is a necessity, as when you round your lower back, you are essentially "turning off" the muscles responsible for reducing shearing forces on the lower back. Put more simply, you're turning off muscles that help protect your back from moving in ways that can injure you.

As we move through the rest of this book, you'll begin to learn the foundations of good movement, understanding what makes up good vs. bad movement, as well as how to properly assess yourself or your athletes in order to help build them up with strength training, not break them down.

The oblique angle of the lumbar portions of the lower back and paraspinal muscles protect the spine against anterior shearing forces. However, these muscles only work when the spine is in neutral. The muscles are able to perform their job and pull against the forces. However, when the back is rounded, the muscles are not able to do their job of protecting the spine.

LEARNING TO MOVE WELL

Learning and executing appropriate core bracing strategies takes time, and it is not something that will happen overnight, or even in the course of a few weeks. We are changing how your body acts and responds to movements and needs throughout the day, and this means re-learning many strategies and movements that have become completely subconscious to you. Often, you're not even aware that you're not moving well!

If you're currently injury-free, I invite you over to the Human Vortex Training YouTube Channel, "HVTraining," to begin your strength training fundamental movements now as you work your way through the book and begin to learn how to build strength training programs. If you look at the "Playlist" section on the HVTraining YouTube channel homepage, you'll see a playlist titled "Foundations." These are a series of exercises that will help you build a solid core and movement foundations. The resources on the YouTube channel may be free, but if you listen to the cues, follow the directions, and are patient, you will see fantastic results.

---

1. Dr. Stuart McGill, *Low Back Disorders: Evidence-Based Prevention and Rehabilitation*, 3rd ed. (Human Kinetics, 2015).

CHAPTER 5 SUMMARY

- Understanding the spine and how back pain occurs is incredibly important in helping cyclists stay healthy and pain-free.

- When we perform movements that go against the spine's abilities, we open ourselves up to a higher risk of injury of some type.

- The muscles around the midsection and spine produce stiffness to protect the spine and to control and direct forces to create movement from the hips and shoulders, and at the limbs.

- A good bike fit and knowing how to sit on the bike will help you avoid back pain.

- If there is not enough stiffness at the spine micromovements can happen at the joints and discs of your back, leading to back pain or injury.

- Incorporating daily habits of good posture, spine sparing movement strategies, and learning to move well are the foundations for a healthy and pain-free back.

CHAPTER 6
THE FUNDAMENTAL 5+1 MOVEMENTS

Over the last 10–15 years, the fitness industry has been consumed with functional training, which usually involves some squats on a BOSU ball, balance training on an unstable surface, or training muscles through a specific and rather small range of motion. When I started to get into this functional training trend, I began to really question things. Why do we need to do so much on the ball? Why does a movement need to be done in as many of the three planes of movement as possible? Why do athletes need functional training?

Over the course of a few months of working with athletes and clients, it dawned on me—they don't, at least not always. This doesn't mean that we shouldn't utilize some of the functional training tools. We certainly use them, but only when an exercise is the best tool available for a specific athlete, at a specific time, to meet their specific needs.

However, there is another troubling part to this trend, especially as it pertains to weight training for cycling. Strength training programs that simply use exercises that mimic the same movements as on the bike can lead to overuse injuries and a decrease in your performance. These programs are marketed as cycling-specific workouts, and they do have exercises that are similar to cycling movements, but they do not incorporate the SAID (specific adaptation to imposed demand) principle.

The SAID principle states that in order to see desired sport improvements, you should place similar demands on your body in your training. This means that when done properly, movements that look nothing like their in-sport motions can improve the specific adaptations needed to benefit on-bike abilities and performance.

This is the primary reason why I believe that doing CrossFit for your strength training is one of the worst things you can do as a cyclist. CrossFit athletes are generally larger than cyclists and have the ability to work with heavy weights and odd objects for periods of time from 4–30 minutes. This is about as un-cycling-specific as one can get!

This is not a knock on CrossFit, rather, just a look at what a cyclist's actual needs are and how we can build them best. I worked in an international CrossFit box for half a decade, helping CrossFitters and athletes of all sports to really unlock their in-sport performances. Those who came to my classes regularly received appropriate substitutions of the WOD and MetCon work to meet them where they were in order to get them where they needed or wanted to be. However, to get what they really needed out of CrossFit, there were many changes to their programs that needed to be done. This was especially true for cyclists.

For instance, the squat, deadlift, and the clean (part of the Olympic Clean & Jerk), when done with proper loading, speed, and technique, can prove to be incredibly beneficial to cyclists in boosting their performance. But to do these movements at speed, under fatigue, and in a highly competitive environment like a MetCon, we now have a perfect recipe for an injury, as well as the loss of focus on what you actually need to get out of strength training. We'll cover desired adaptations to strength training in Chapter 12, but for now let's focus on movements.

WHAT IS OUR GOAL WITH STRENGTH TRAINING?

In order to become a better cyclist, you must ride your bike. If you focus on the important things like smooth and consistent effort, a smooth pedal stroke, and improving your climbing, cornering, braking, and sprinting skills, you will begin to see magic happen.

While these essentials are key to becoming a better cyclist, you also need to improve your abilities through strength training, which will increase the contractility of the muscles and how they produce stiffness at some parts of the body, allowing you to control motion produced at other points of the body, like your legs.

What you are looking to build through an intelligently designed strength training program is the body's ability to produce stiffness in your torso, to produce movement at your limbs.

PROXIMAL STIFFNESS TO PRODUCE DISTAL MOVEMENT

Put more simply, get enough bracing at your midsection to keep your ribs, spine, and hips steady so you can produce movement and power at your arms and legs.

Sadly, this bedrock principle is commonly scoffed at and pushed aside, as athletes and trainers look at the trendy and highly complex movements that they see professional athletes doing. From overhead squats to balance board single-leg deadlifts, the novel, more challenging movements that so many are looking to copy won't improve your performance or decrease your risk of injury. These cool and difficult exercises are the exact opposite of what you need to be doing. With these highly advanced movements, you'll twist and contort your body in an effort to copy the professional athletes, which totally defeats the purpose of doing the exercise in the first place.

As I mentioned earlier in the book, "joint position dictates muscle function." Recruiting muscles in the right order or to get them to produce stiffness and control throughout a movement is hard, often because they have been neglected for so long or just left to "do their jobs," which they cannot do if they have poor joint positioning.

Learning the FUNdamental 5+1 movements and how they form the very core of each and every movement you need to train will allow you to see faster, better results in the weight room and out on the road.

As you read this book, keep in mind that it doesn't just contain a bunch of regular exercises thrown together because they hit the major muscles involved in the sport of cycling. The Vortex Method is a highly structured approach, focused on form and technique and getting you into positions that will help you build a rock-solid core while improving your ability to breathe and to have better biomechanics out on the road, trail, or mountain. Ask any of the athletes with whom I've worked, and they'll tell you that I stress form, technique, and consistency.

The following chapters provide a good overview of a few exercises that every cyclist should be able to build up to executing. Exceptions include but are not limited to: 1) If you have had a previous injury to the targeted area, or 2) if you have been told by a doctor, physical therapist, or other medical professional that you should not be exercising the area.

If you are unsure of whether or not you are cleared to perform any part of the program laid out in this book, seek out a medical professional and ask them if the program is appropriate for you. As with any physical exercise program, you should consult your physician to ensure that you are physically capable of executing this program.

THE FUNDAMENTAL 5+1

There are six primary movements in the human body that we need to train in order to see strength gains and progression in abilities that boost and aid in sport and life performance. I call these the FUNdamental 5+1. The "+1" is for Rotary Stability, which is different from the other five movements. It requires you to know how to appropriately direct forces through the torso, as opposed to actually moving.

While many of us dread the thought of focusing on fundamentals or practicing the basics, it is in fact these very basic skills and tools that allow us to see *extra*-ordinary results in all aspects of life. From Warren Buffett in investments to Michael Jordan in basketball and Wayne Gretzky in hockey, many high-achieving people have consistently stressed mastery of the fundamentals. As it's been said, fundamentals are simple, but they are not easy to master.

When it comes to strength training, we really only need to focus on six major multi-joint movements, which I call the FUNdamental 5+1:

1. Push-Reach
2. Pull
3. Squat
4. Hinge
5. Press
6. Rotary Stability

Building your strength through proper movement patterns and great positions is just like building a skyscraper: the foundation takes time, effort, and careful planning, but when done properly you can build huge structures on top. Here we are working with an athlete to correct his arm position in his squats.

These six primary movements are key to an intelligently designed strength training program. Sure, bicep curls, tricep pushdowns, or squats on a stability ball will stroke your ego, but they are rarely a good use of your already limited time for strength training. There are far better and more efficient ways to get the results you're after! When we take a look at the actual movements and what the athlete's needs are, there are far more important and productive exercises.

1) PUSH-REACH

The push-reach movement is first on the list for cyclists and triathletes since they spend so much time in a reaching position on the bike. Due to the long periods of time in the riding position, the movement patterns for pushing tend to be broken and idiosyncratic—and just don't work well!

The most common response I get when a cyclist sees bench press or push-up variation on their training program is either a text or a quick phone call to me saying, "Hey, uh, I think you gave me the wrong program? I have a chest exercise here. . . ." But I assure you, this is intentional. Working to build a biomechanically proficient and stabilized push and reach pattern is absolutely integral to not only improving on-bike abilities, but also for posture and breathing!

Additionally, many cyclists complain of neck and shoulder pain, along with side stitches, so establishing a good push should be one of the focal points of a strength training program for cyclists. Due to the long hours in the riding position, the body will slowly adapt to the demands placed on it by tightening some muscles while lengthening others. In the case of cyclists, this often means a shortening of:

- pectoralis minor (small chest muscle)
- serratus anterior (under the scapula and pectoral muscles)
- scalenus (neck)
- intercostal muscles (between ribs)

These muscles play major roles in our breathing patterns, posture, and our ability to move the bike under us for cornering, climbing, and especially as we try to steer the bike down the road as we reach into our back pockets to grab some real food to eat. The inability to perform any of these skills on the bike is a huge impediment to performance and to riding comfortably.

When we push into a reach, we're extending the elbow while the shoulder blade moves forward and the rib cage moves backwards. Perhaps one of the biggest mistakes that many riders make is that instead of reaching forward, keeping their chest up and allowing the shoulder blades to move forward, they round their upper back in order to get their arms and hands further forward. Many riders are already performing a push movement in their strength training programs by doing a front plank, which, when performed properly, is a static reach. The challenge is that most riders are doing these incorrectly, allowing their shoulder blades to come back and together, or by rounding their upper back.

Learning how to push properly is absolutely key in allowing you to ride and perform better, but you need to take the right path to learn the correct movements . . . and jumping right to push-ups on the floor is not the way to go. In fact, most cyclists do push-ups so poorly they wind up with achy shoulders, necks, and elbows.

Start small, with an exercise such as a front plank to cue the proper position, and from there move to an incline rack push-up, where you can slowly begin to load the movement and work your way down to the floor from there.

Keep in mind that a pure push, like a basic bench press with heavy weight, is going to be a little different than a push-reach. When you're on a bench press doing heavier weights, you don't want to have your shoulder blades come as far forward on the rib cage as a push-reach. There are times and places in an athlete's program and progressions for both the push and a reach; however, due to the demands of our sport, we want to focus first on learning a push-reach, as it's far more relevant.

PUSH-REACH EXERCISES: Barbell Bench Press, Push-Up Variations, Front Plank

60 SECONDS TO FIX GCN'S PUSH-UPS

Back in February 2019 the Global Cycling Network (GCN) had a push-up challenge, and the contestants' push-ups were so bad that a huge amount of viewers commented that GCN needed to bring in a proper strength coach to show them how to do push-ups correctly.

That was my first opportunity to join the GCN crew, and we actually had a lot of fun fixing Hank's (also known as James Lowsley-Williams) push-ups. While I imagined that I would have at least 5 minutes to prep Hank and Dan Lloyd before we shot the segment, it turned out that I had just 1 minute to fix Hank up, on camera no less, and get him to pop out as many push-ups as possible (he did 25!). You can see how I cleaned up Hank's push-ups in less than 1 minute by checking out the video in the book's bonus section at www.HumanVortexTraining.com.

2) PULL

Also called "rowing," the pull is a movement that has huge potential to help cyclists, yet many make some relatively simple-to-correct mistakes that leave them injured and in pain instead of stronger.

For both pulling and pressing, keep the spine in a neutral position, elbows around 45 degrees to your upper body, and the shoulder blades relatively stable in a retracted (or "pulled back") position. You want to make sure that you are executing the pulling movement in a way that will keep your shoulders healthy and well.

Here's what you should look for:

- soft knees
- great posture with your whole abdominal hoop fired up
- a slight reach forward from your shoulders
- keep the upper back back
- begin the movement from the muscles of the mid-back by starting to bend the elbow as you also move the shoulder blade back at the same time (this is a hard skill to learn!)
- bring the shoulder blade(s) back towards your spine

Unfortunately, many well-meaning cyclists and trainers alike make one or more of the following common mistakes in how they teach or perform the pull, which leads to undesirable gains in strength, stability, and positioning of the shoulders:

- moving the elbow backwards while letting the shoulder round up or forward
- knees straight and stiff
- rounding the upper back instead of getting that reach
- using the spine/back to get the movement instead of the shoulder blades and mid-back
- letting the head move forward and back
- letting the chest/ribs move up and down through the movement

These may seem like relatively small mistakes, but when it comes to working with cyclists, and really anyone looking to improve performance or get rid of pain, these small mistakes lead to poor joint positions and training the muscles in the wrong way.

It's not uncommon for an athlete who learns or re-learns how to pull properly to come back a day or two later feeling muscles in their mid-back and under their armpit that they have never felt before. While we never use soreness to tell us if a training was good or not, we *do* use soreness to let us know if we are using and challenging muscles that haven't been used, or haven't been used properly before.

Just remember that less is more and that the vast majority of strength training sessions should be at an RPE of 5, 6, or 7. You should never feel like crawling out of the gym.

PULL EXERCISES: One-Arm Bench Rows, Seated Neutral Grip Rows, TRX Rows

A NOTE ON PULL VS. PUSH-REACH

When I was coming up as a powerlifter and young coach, there was a prevalent thinking that you should be doing a 2:1 ratio of pulling to pushing, as it "evened out" the upper body. However, through my experiences working with athletes over the 15+ years since, it's become very obvious that pushing and pulling are more similar to one another than different.

I cannot stress enough how this 2:1 ratio is misleading and that in order to get balance at the shoulders and upper body, you should be focusing instead on learning how to perform a proper reach in order to balance out the push and pull movements.

The shoulder blades are designed to move on our rib cage in a number of ways:

- forward (called protraction) and backward (called retraction)

- up (called elevation) and down (called depression)

- rotate up and out (upward rotation) and down and in (downward rotation)

Many (but not all) of the issues cyclists face with neck and upper back pain center around the fact that no one ever taught these vital movements or explained them and their important role in movement in the sport of cycling.

There are a growing number of bike fitter s who are becoming much more knowledgeable and aware of how movement and anatomy of the upper body affects performance on the bike, thanks in part to bike fitting certification and education programs like ReTul and SICI (Serotta International Cycling Institute). There are also new technologies (for example, LEOMO) that are helping athletes, coaches, and bike fitters to be able to better understand the human movement dynamics and how everything ties together.

The bottom line when it comes to pull: Shoulder blade movement and the ability to maintain good rib cage and spine position are going to determine if you're getting the desired results you're after or not.

3) SQUAT

The squat may seem like a pretty simple exercise, but it is in fact challenging to do properly by getting the movement from the right places at the right times. As cyclists we tend to think of single-leg movements like lunges as being more relevant to our sport. But, really, the lunge is a more advanced version of a squat!

The squat serves as the baseline of movement patterns and strength. Learning how to squat properly before getting into single-leg variations of the movement helps to essentially unlock more strength and power potential, and there is far more stability and strength that can be built from a two-legged squat than a lunge.

This doesn't mean that lunges aren't useful! We'll make use of lunges and step-ups later in the programming progression, after you've learned how to produce proximal stiffness to control distal motion. The squat is one of the best movements to help us master this skill for our sport.

Here is how to do the squat properly:

1. Upper body upright
2. Hips and knees bent (flexed)
3. Rib cage over the hips (stacked) with midsection braced
4. Knees over the toes (despite the myth that the knee shouldn't go over the toes)
5. Shin bone at a slight forward angle
6. The upper body and the shin bone pretty much parallel to one another (almost the same angle)
7. Connect to the ground through the bottom of your foot
8. Weight is in the middle of your foot—not on the toes or on the heels
9. Squat straight down

The upright upper body (torso) angle matching to the shin angle is a pretty tough thing for many cyclists, and it's not a perfect measuring stick for a squat (we'll talk about how the hip joint is designed here in a minute). But it does offer a lot of fantastic things you do not get in our sport if you do it right.

Many in the cycling world see the hinge as the ultimate exercise for cyclists, but I don't necessarily agree. The hinge certainly works muscles we don't use together much in our sport, but many of us are already in a static hinge on the bike. We need to strengthen the hinge through its full motion, but there is a lot we can improve by learning how to squat properly.

The squat and hinge are two big movements where we often see big differences between each person's anatomy. This is because when it comes to squatting and hinging we are dealing with a number of big joints, including the hips and the knees.

SQUAT EXERCISES: Goblet Squat, Barbell Front Squat, Landmine Low Grip Squat, KB Lunge, Side Lunge

UNDERSTANDING THE SQUAT AT A DEEPER LEVEL

While this book is written for those without a degree in anatomy or exercise physiology, when it comes to being able to increase your understanding of what a good squat vs. a bad squat looks like, we are going to have to get down into some deeper anatomy in order to help you better understand how truly individual these movements are, and more importantly, why.

If we're going to talk about cycling, strength, and improving your performance, we absolutely must talk about the anatomy of the hips, as they play a huge role in both bike fitting and strength training.

We like to think of our bodies as being 100% symmetrical. Our right matches our left, and our left matches our right . . . right?

Well, no. When it comes to our hips, there are a number of differences that we see from person to person, and even from hip to hip. One example would be the angle of the "neck" of your upper leg bone, the femur. The angle of the neck of the femur can range from 5 degrees all the way up to 20 degrees from hip to hip! Can you see how that might make it hard for you to have a normal squatting position?

While this angle of the femoral neck is one angle that can affect performance, there are a few more that we have to think about. Don't worry if it's a bit too technical for you—just take a look at the sketches here and notice the differences in these pelvic bones.

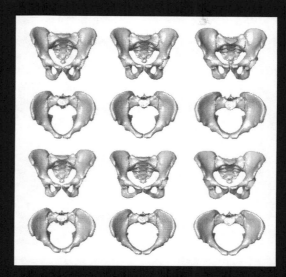

Anterior and superior views showing male (A) and female (B) pelvic mean shapes at age ~13 years old (left), ~25 years old (center), and ~80 years old. Image Source: "Developmental Evidence for Obstetric Adaptation of the Human Female Pelvis," Proceedings of the National Academy of Sciences of the United States of America, 2016.

I won't go into too much detail here, other than to point out the four other big considerations for the hips that we have to think about when it comes to squatting and deadlifting.

1. **Hip width:** Narrower hips usually do better with things like squatting and hinging, while wider hips tend to do better in taking the leg out to the side.

2. **Femoral neck angle:** If the angle of the connecting part of the upper leg bone has an angle closer to 90 degrees, you won't do very well at picking up or carrying heavy things.

3. **Positioning of the hip joint:** Forward or backward pointing of the hip joint is where an individual wants to get "super aero," but their hips literally won't let them. I've seen this quite a bit in bike fitting, and while I cannot see how the joint is positioned without an X-ray, I can feel it as we go through the hands-on assessment.

4. **Shallow vs. deep hip socket:** Imagine your hips are like one of two kinds of bowls. One bowl is really deep—perfect for some of grandma's homemade chicken soup with plenty of room for noodles, chunky vegetables, and lots of broth and croutons. The other bowl is very shallow. This one isn't very good for soup, but it is good for pasta, as the outside has a slight angle to it so your meatballs don't fall on the floor. As both Dean Somerset and Dr. McGill point out, hips can be the same: Some have deep hip sockets, which are great for marching and carrying heavy loads. These are called Celtic hips,

Continued...

as they are seen mostly from those of Irish descent. A shallower hip socket is great for deep squatting such as for Olympic lifting and gymnastics. These are called Dalmatian hips, and they are most often found in Eastern European countries.[1]

Understanding hip structure is really important so that you can discern good teaching and know your limits. There are a range of bone structures that will physically limit what someone is able to do and how they are able to do it. Just because one person is able to do something doesn't mean you can, or should.

Different hip shapes and structures can have a huge influence over what you can and cannot do in the weight room and on the bike. Understanding what your body is built for, as well as the reasons that you may not be able to do the same thing as your riding buddy, will help you better know your body and allow you to build your strength training program around what your body needs.

If this is all confusing or a little overwhelming, don't worry! For now, just keep in mind that all hips are not created equal, and this means that when it comes to the squat and hinge, you need to be aware that not everything may work for you.

4) HINGE

The hinge (specifically the deadlift) has quickly become a fan favorite of cyclists everywhere, as well as fitness enthusiasts everywhere, for a number of fairly good reasons:

- It's a move we don't do too much in our day-to-day life.
- It works many muscles we don't often work.
- It can significantly boost strength.
- Due to its full-body use, it can burn more calories than other moves.
- The ego loves to load up heavy weights and look strong.

I personally love the deadlift because it exposes weaknesses an individual may have. When I step up to the bar for a warm-up set of deadlifts for myself, I quickly know:

- how ready my nervous system is for the day's workouts
- what muscles are tight or not firing right due to fatigue or long hours on the bike
- if my breathing and bracing are where they need to be
- if I can produce force and strength from the correct places

It truly is a fantastic exercise, but it isn't necessarily the best move for all cyclists. It depends on what your personal needs are.

With the hinge, you get all the benefits of deadlifting, regardless of where you start the movement. Set yourself up for success, and not injury, by using blocks or other pieces of equipment to bring the bar up to your starting point.

But here's the thing about hinging: You don't need to do it from the floor to get the benefits. In fact, many of us cyclists have no need to do a hinge off the floor! This may sound a little extreme, but there is a lot of reasoning behind this:

1. As cyclists, we spend a lot of time with poor posture. When we ride, many of us round our backs so we can reach the handlebars. As we get tired, it gets worse and can lead to neck or shoulder pain.

2. Over the many hours we spend on the bike with our back rounded forward, the different tissues at our spine begin to slowly "creep." Over time this leads to these tissues not being able to do the job they were designed to do.

3. While all of that is happening, the muscles on our backside are begin-

ning to stretch as well. They begin to act like a Laffy Taffy that's been left in the car in the middle of July. . . . They're stretchy and loose and not able to do their jobs of supporting your back very well.

4. The bones themselves become weakened because they aren't being challenged to support heavy weight (although at the end of a long ride your upper body can feel really heavy!).

All of this can lead to injury, as Dr. McGill talks about in episodes 8 and 9 on the *The Strong Savvy Cyclist & Triathlete Podcast*. If we were to try to pick a weight up off the floor, because of the changes our body has gone through in order to help us ride longer, we can't protect our joints or move the weight in the way a normal body is designed to!

But this doesn't mean we should avoid hinging. Actually, quite the opposite! It means that building up hinging strength is really important to helping us keep our backs and hips strong and healthy. Working on the hinge from positions where you can move as the body and muscles are meant to is the place to start.

Good hinge technique: Hips are high and back, shins are vertical, back is straight, chin is tucked, and shoulder blades are back and down.

How do we do this? We begin from the top, with the weight in our hands and standing tall, and we work our way carefully and controlled through the range of motion while keeping great technique.

We'll cover this later in the testing and programming chapters, but if you're already doing some strength training and are doing some hinges (usually some kind of deadlift), I'd strongly encourage you to take a video of yourself doing the hinge from the side. (You can prop your cell phone up against a weight and switch the camera around to selfie mode to take the video.) See if you're able to keep your back straight, and lift the weight by using your *hips*, not your back. It's a small, but very important, detail that can really supercharge your training results and help keep you from getting injured.

HINGE EXERCISES: Hex Bar Deadlift, KB Deadlift, Landmine Deadlift, Kettlebell Swings

5) PRESS

The press is an overhead, ideally near-vertical, movement that most cyclists cannot do. In fact, for many cyclists, they do not see a problem with losing the ability to reach up overhead purely from their shoulder, as they don't think it makes them a faster rider or more athletic.

Unfortunately, as mentioned for the push-reach movement, having good, healthy movement from your shoulder is actually really important to riding your bike powerfully and comfortably—and to breathing well!

Just because you're able to do a movement doesn't mean that you're getting the

Overhead pressing is often lost on or extremely difficult for many cyclists. This can have far-reaching negative effects on performance.

movement from the right places. For many cyclists, this is very true when it comes to overhead movements. When asked to take their arm and reach up overhead, the arm comes forward, and as they reach the end of where their shoulder can move, they crank on their lower backs and throw their head backwards in an attempt to get their arm overhead. With a proud look on their face they proclaim, "See! I told you I can do it!" and then lower their arm back down. Counting down from 5, I wait as they ask, "What are you counting for?"—at which point they try to grab their lower back and tell me, "See, I told you my back hurts, and now it's really hurting!"

As Mister Rogers sang, "Everything grows together because you're all one piece."

Most riders don't think about losing the ability to lift their arm overhead with good movement patterns until it's too late, or they are far down the path of dysfunction. I've had a few riders who have developed "frozen shoulder" as young as the ripe old age of 35, due to neglecting their shoulder health and strength. It can be incredibly scary to realize that you cannot move your arm throughout your normal day, let alone that you cannot ride your bike. But it's actually really easy, and a little fun, to keep your shoulder healthy and working well.

Pressing overhead is a neglected movement for cyclists, but if we want to have fun on the bike for many years to come, it's an important move to train.

The press movement is one that we may not train traditionally because as cyclists we don't necessarily need overhead strength in the same amounts we need for other movements. Instead, we'll train the press to maintain a good balance of strength at the shoulder, as well as to make sure that the supporting muscles are strong and firing at the right time so we can keep our shoulders healthy.

The exercises to keep your shoulders healthy aren't necessarily what you think they are, and often you'll only use one arm at a time. This is a great way to work on your overhead pressing motion and your rotary stability, which every athlete can use as much of as they can get!

PRESS EXERCISES: Overhead Press, Landmine Press, Half Kneeling Landmine Press

6) ROTARY STABILITY

Rotary stability is the "+1" of the FUNdamental 5+1 movements, but not because it isn't just as important as the others. Literally at the core of it all, rotary stability is your ability to keep your hips and your rib cage from moving in opposite directions from each other.

Sounds simple? It's not!

If the core is all of your muscles between your neck, elbows, and knees, and you need to learn how to stabilize your ribs and hips together, it will take a lot of work and focus!

In my Strength Training for Cycling certification course, we spend quite a bit of time learning how to perform an on-bike/on-the-trainer movement analysis. Often this section is met with questions like: "Why are we doing on-bike testing for a strength training certification?" When we are riding our bikes, we are trying to steer the bike down the road while pushing down on the pedals. If we don't learn how to connect our rib cage and our hips together, these two parts of our body will move opposite of one another, instead of working together.

You can easily see this when riding behind someone. You'll see their shoulders rock to one side while their hips twist the other way. Not only is this movement pattern sapping power out of their pedaling, but it's also slowly wearing down the tissues of the discs in their back and other supporting ligaments. This is a recipe for lower back pain at some point in the future.

This can easily be avoided by learning how to produce rotary stability, but it takes patience and attention to detail. In order to train rotary stability you have to first start by building a rock solid foundation around your spine, learning how to activate the different glute muscles while you are bracing all the muscles of your midsection in the right amount, to keep your spine nice and neutral.

Over the many years of working with cyclists and other athletes, I've developed a highly potent hip series that helps in learning these skills. You'll learn them in the warm-up section of the book, but if you'd like to start now, look ahead to the "Hip Warm-up Series" in Chapter 15 and start practicing them 2–3 days a week.

Planks and side planks, when done properly, can be a part of rotary stability and core training, but until you actually train the muscles in a full 360 degrees, hitting all of the muscles in ways that teach them to keep your spine strong like a steel beam while allowing movement to happen at the hips and shoulders, you're not getting what you really need.

Because of how important the skill of rotary stability is, you'll notice that we begin and end many of our sessions learning or practicing this skill. The key for rotary stability is to build strength-endurance and great habits, but this takes time and careful practice. No rushing through these exercises! It's all about *how* you do them and being in the correct positions.

ROTARY STABILITY EXERCISES: Side Plank on Knees Hinge Pattern, Side Planks, Bird Dog

CHAPTER 6 SUMMARY

- Functional training and exercises that mimic on-bike movements won't necessarily improve your performance and could cause you injuries. They are useful only at specific times and for specific needs.

- The FUNdamental 5+1 movements take a structured approach, focused on form and technique and building you to have better posture, positions, and biomechanics on the bike.

- The six multi-joint movements you'll focus on are: push-reach, pull, squat, hinge, press, and rotary stability.

- Due to the long hours in the riding position, the push-reach movement needs to be trained properly, and it is good for posture and breathing.

- Small mistakes with the pull movement, if uncorrected, can lead to poor joint positions and training the muscles in the wrong way.

- Understanding hip structure is important to performing a good squat and will help you know your limits.

- The hinge can expose an athlete's weaknesses in their movement patterns, muscles, and breathing—but can also help keep the back and hips strong and healthy.

- Overhead pressing is often neglected by cyclists, but it can help maintain a good balance of strength at the shoulder and prevent shoulder injury.

- Rotary stability will keep your hips and rib cage from moving in opposite directions from each other, allowing you to produce more power.

SECTION 2: THE VORTEX METHOD

CHAPTER 7
COMPONENTS OF AN INTELLIGENT STRENGTH TRAINING PROGRAM

Building a strength training program requires more than just throwing together a bunch of exercises and choosing set and repetition ranges—but, unfortunately, very few folks understand or know that the process needs a little more thinking and planning. For the time you put into your strength training, you should have the best information that exists to get you the best possible results.

There is nothing wrong with starting with a basic workout; we all start somewhere. In fact, I still have my old Steno notebooks where I wrote down and planned the strength training programs for myself and my clients, and I too started with simple sets and repetitions. But as I worked with more and more clients and athletes, and got deeper into my own training, it dawned on me that there is way more that we can (and should) be getting out of strength training.

Many trainers may not be aware of, or know how to fully take advantage of, the six components of an intelligent strength training program. The next several chapters will go into detail on each component, with specifics on how and when to do each. The six components of the Vortex Method are:

1. Soft Tissue Work
2. Breath Work
3. Dynamic Warm-up
4. Explosiveness/Power/Jumping (involving low reps and high power)
5. Strength & Correctives
6. Postural Challenges/Rotary Stability

Note that the last three components make up the main strength training program, but all six are very important. Soft tissue work uses foam rolling or trigger point therapy to help decrease stiffness and stimulate the muscles so you are in a more relaxed and ready state (Chapter 8). Breath work puts you in a better state of hormonal balance and readiness, which allows you to be primed to perform in the workout (Chapter 9). The dynamic warm-up is the last part of the strength training warm-up, and this is where you address major muscular and movement issues and prepare for that day's movements (Chapter 10). The main strength program uses a variety of exercises, jumps, and challenges, and detailed instructions and photos are found in Chapter 15 or on the Human Vortex Training website in the "Book Bonus Content" section.

We want to ensure that every strength program is built with each component carefully planned in advance. This will not only make you stronger, but it will also help you to move better, recover faster, and be able to return to a hormonal homeostasis much quicker—something that will have massive positive effects across your life and sports performance.

In order for you to get the most out of each strength training session, especially as an endurance athlete, it's incredibly important that you properly prepare the body and mind for the workout you have ahead of you. This means that each and every session is going to start with the same thing, as you build a familiar routine to rev up the body for the work you're about to do and cool down the mind from everything else that's going on in your life outside of that particular workout session.

Building yourself a repeatable and familiar warm-up routine is something that is so easy to do that it's also incredibly easy not to do, which is why most people don't.

THE IMPORTANCE OF A ROUTINE

As human beings, we are incredibly sensitive to routine. This starts out early in life when we are infants and continues until the day we die. We find comfort in routines and predictable paths for our days and activities. For better or for worse, routines often define our lives, what expectations we have for ourselves and others have for us, as well as what our results will be.

In his book *The Power of Habit*, author Charles Duhigg shares the psychology, physiology, and chemistry of why habits don't "just happen." He says habits are a deep-seated response to something that is going on in our lives. The challenge for us is that we have to move from having unconscious habits, where we just float along passively in life, to conscious habits, where we choose what we do and how we do it.

The pre–strength training routine should be purposeful, and over the course of time (usually 2–4 months) it will allow you to compound your progress and eventually see fantastic results.

The goal isn't just improvement in your warm-up exercises. You want to get into a habit where you teach your mind and body how to tune out all the distractions and dial in for the task you are about to take on. You'll find that getting into a routine for every strength training session will also help you better dial in before rides and other events in your life—like, say, that big presentation you have at work.

Building a strength training warm-up routine allows you to train yourself to let the rest of the day and its distractions melt away. You can begin to focus on how your body is feeling and moving, as well as on the main focus of that day's training session.

A WARM-UP IS NOT A WASTE OF TIME

Warming up is an absolute necessity for strength training, and training in general, but many individuals skip any kind of warm-up outside of maybe 3–5 minutes on the exercise bike, and then they jump right into the workout. This rushed approach can significantly increase your risk of injury, as well as decrease the training results you see. A proper warm-up serves you in a number of ways that prepare the body and mind to best perform each and every session on a number of levels.

1. **Increased core body temperature:** This allows the muscles, nervous system, lungs, and energy systems to be better prepared to move and perform.

Which leads to . . .

2. **A shift towards a more homeostatic, or chemically balanced, state:** This means the body is going to be even more ready to put out better performances.

Which leads to . . .

3. **Changes in blood pressure:** This is the body's fight-or-flight system warming up and getting ready for the fight ahead.

4. **Changes in hormonal status:** This is where the body begins to change its inner chemistry by changing the hormones (the strongest drugs known to mankind) that are released into the body, as it prepares you for the upcoming stressors. The stress of the environment will have a big impact on what changes will occur. This is incredibly important to know and understand if you are a highly competitive athlete who will be competing in big races. Knowing what the pre-race warm-up environment will look like can change how you set up and practice your strength training warm-up to better match and prepare you for those demands.

Which leads to . . .

5. **Increased mental alertness:** This allows you to be more aware of how your body is moving and feeling, and for you to be more responsive to stimulus, whether it's a dog chasing you on the bike (hopefully not!) or walking up to a bar to lift it with intent and strength (more on intent later).

But before you get into the movement warm-up, you need to connect with your body, bringing it and your mind into a more balanced and relaxed state. You can accomplish this by doing a small amount of soft tissue work with the foam roller, lacrosse ball, or other trigger point tool, followed by 1–2 basic breathing exercises. This simple routine will allow you to anchor each and every strength training session, and you will be able to really connect with your body on a number of levels.

Following the soft tissue and breath work, you'll then start your dynamic warm-up. The dynamic warm-up can range anywhere from 3–7 different exercises that help address major issues you have, as well as prepare your body for great movement patterns and improved technique.

Only after you've completed these three steps (soft tissue work, breath work, dynamic warm-up) should you get into the main workout. This may seem like a lot, but when you plan it right, these three steps should take you no longer than 15–18 minutes total.

Here is a look at how these six components might look in a single training session:

SAMPLE DAY'S SESSION	EXERCISE OR MOVEMENT	TIME
Warm-up		
Soft Tissue Work	Foam Rolling	3–6 min.
Breath Work	Crocodile Breathing	3 min.
Dynamic Warm-Up	Side-Lying Windmill Sofa Stretch Side-Lying Straight Leg Lift Hip Lifts McGill Crunches	10 min.
Main Strength Program		
Explosive/Power/Jumps	Hands on Hips Vertical	45 min.
Strength & Correctives	Barbell Squats	
	Landmine Deadlifts	
	Half-Kneeling Landmine Press	
	Seated Neutral Grip Rows	
Postural Challenges/Rotary Stability	Suitcase Carries	

In this next section of the book we're going to take a deeper look at each part of a strength training program, to help you understand why we do it and how you should be planning and performing each part.

CHAPTER 7 SUMMARY

- The Vortex Method has six components to its strength training program: soft tissue work, breath work, dynamic warm-up, explosiveness/power/ jumping, strength & correctives, and postural challenges/rotary stability.

- Soft tissue work, breath work, and the dynamic warm-up all make up the strength training warm-up and are important for preparing the body and mind for the workout, and are where we address major movement or muscle imbalance issues.

- Building in a regular routine for every strength training session will lead to good habits and better results.

CHAPTER 8
SOFT TISSUE WORK

Soft tissue work, or trigger point therapy as many call it, is not new to cyclists. Back in the early 2000s foam rollers were just beginning to appear in physical therapy clinics and more advanced strength training gyms across the U.S., but not too many people really knew what to do with them.

Thanks in part to CrossFit, as well as the Internet, foam rolling, The Stick, and lacrosse balls began to make their way into cycling and strength training. Since then, foam rolling and trigger points have taken off and have become a staple of every gym, spinning class, and pre-race parking lot around the world.

Foam rolling can be a fantastically useful tool, but only when used correctly and in the right amounts. Both of these points tend to get lost on many riders, as they simply foam roll the areas they feel are tight, without giving much thought as to why they may be tight and if foam rolling is indeed the right thing for that area. On top of that, and I was guilty of this myself many years ago, they use the foam roller for 20–30 minutes at a time, with much of this time on 2–3 specific muscles!

Before we get into how to properly utilize foam rolling or trigger point therapy, let's first talk about why it's important and why you should be doing it—in the correct amounts and on the right areas.

FOAM ROLLING: A VALUABLE TOOL . . . IN THE RIGHT AMOUNTS

Why does foam rolling work? Truth be told, we still don't *really* understand why foam rolling and tissue release works—but we know that it does.

When done properly, foam rolling can:

- decrease stiffness
- decrease pain (due to muscles pulling unevenly at a joint)

- improve mobility
- help you tune into your body's tight areas
- allow you to learn some anatomy and get a better understanding of your body

While foam rolling can help in the proper amounts, too much can actually hurt you and slow down your progress. I found this out myself back when I had a hip injury. Ironically, it was one of those injuries where I did nothing wrong in my training. I just wasn't aware of how to train for my body structure. I have hip sockets that are deeper than normal, more forward-oriented, and this led to my problems. In the long run the injury was a blessing in disguise. It pushed me to learn more about hip and back pain in cyclists and triathletes, which has helped me become a leader in the field of strength training for athletes.

Foam rolling at physical therapy sessions helped me move much better and with far less pain. While at home, I spent 30–45 minutes on the same muscle groups, which helped me feel amazing for the next 2–3 hours. But after that, my pain returned many times stronger than it was before!

Why did this happen? Because muscles have three jobs in the body when it comes to movement, and they are in the following order of importance:

1. To protect a joint from injury.
2. To stabilize a joint while a nearby joint moves. Think about lifting your arm straight ahead. Your bicep has to stabilize your elbow so your hand and forearm don't flop around.
3. To move a joint.

When a muscle tightens, we cannot just foam roll it or stretch it. We have to first take a look at how the body is moving, think about what activities and movements we've done in the last 2–3 days that may be affecting our body, and only then can we figure out if we should be stretching, foam rolling, or activating/lightly using the tight muscle.

By spending such a long time using the foam roller to release the muscles that had tightened, I was forcing my muscles to violate rule #1. In response to this, my body doubled down and made those muscles tighten up even more!

So how do we make sure that we're getting just the right amount of foam rolling? Aim for just 3–6 minutes total, 3–5 days a week, as a part of your strength training and on-bike training warm-up routine. The key with foam rolling and soft tissue work is to not go all out and roll until all the tension is gone. Rather, it's about consistency and hitting high value target areas on a regular basis.

For cyclists, the high value target areas are what I sometimes call The Super 6:

1. **Front of the shins** (tibialis anterior)
2. **Quads**
3. **Gluteus medius** (the glute muscle just above your belt line on your rear) with a tennis or lacrosse ball
4. **Chest**
5. **Lats**
6. **Thoracic extension** (being able to arch backwards slightly with your upper back)

These Super 6 are great starting points for most riders new to soft tissue work, as these muscles tend to be very tight and out of balance. Keep in mind that the order that you work these areas matters a lot, and while it's often personal preference if you start from the bottom up, or from the top down, you want to keep moving from one end of the body to the next. This will help you to get more out of foam rolling, as you systematically work the muscles.

But remember the time limitation for this! You don't want to spend any more than a total of 3–6 minutes on the foam roller. The easiest way to do this is to set a timer for 20–30 seconds for each spot on each side. No more. If you've been spending 10–15 minutes working on the foam roller, boy are you going to be in for a surprise!

If done correctly, the foam roller will go from being a meditation-style activity to one where you are moving relatively quickly from spot to spot, working the foam roller back and forth. And by the end of your 3–6 minutes, you'll have broken into a light to moderate sweat.

Now we have not only gotten the target areas to relax and open up a bit, but we have your core body temperature up, the nervous system has been woken up, and you've had to start using your midsection bracing to help you complete your foam rolling.

Trigger point and foam rolling work can be very helpful when used properly. Pictured here are members of the White City Racing Team performing Trigger Point with a lacrosse ball after day 1 of training camp in 2017.

SHOULD YOU FOAM ROLL EVERYTHING FROM HEAD TO TOE?

This is a good question, and while there are some times where foam rolling every-thing may be the right thing to do, these times will be few and far between—that is, if you're following an intelligently designed strength training program!

As I spoke about in Chapter 3, two major parts of creating and using energy effi-ciently to increase power output are the quality of your movements and coordina-tion. These two factors are major focuses of the Vortex Method, and over time you should see improvements in these areas. The joints will have a better balance of strength, and the muscles that were tight and desperately needed foam rolling a few months ago should decrease their need, hopefully all together!

If you feel that you have to foam roll all the muscles in your body, or you find you still need the same amount of foam rolling after 4–6 weeks of rolling these areas 6–8 weeks into your strength training program, you really need to go back and reassess if your program is effective.

If your program is highly effective, you should be able to get yourself into better posture, get full 360-degree breaths and get air into the correct places, be able to move better, and should see or feel that you need less and less foam rolling.

As you can see, foam rolling is much more than a simple warm-up or recovery tool. If you know what to do and understand how to "read" what it's telling you, it can be a highly valuable tool for assessing if your programming is effective, and if you or your athlete is responding well to it.

For some, what we've just covered about soft tissue work will be enough. If you're not someone who is interested in going a little deeper into how to get the most out of your foam rolling, go ahead and skip ahead to the next chapter. If you're looking to get a bit more from foam rolling, read on!

GETTING THE MOST OUT OF YOUR SOFT TISSUE WORK

To maximize your training gains and performance, we need to go a little deeper with soft tissue work. This section will be especially useful for competitive riders.

There are two major areas to think about when it comes to soft tissue work and why it's so important for us.

1. Load Management

Load management has to do with how much load (total weight and stress) you're placing on the body and muscular system in a training session. Your load tolerance will depend on your strength training age (as mentioned in Chapter 2), injury history, and tissue qualities. Load tolerances will also vary from sport to sport based on the demands placed on the tissues. Just because you have been training seriously and riding your bike regularly for the last five years does not mean that your tissues or structures of the body are prepared to deal with the same loading tolerances as someone who has been strength training year-round for five years.

In order to increase the abilities of specific tissues and structures of the body to be able to deal with and adapt to certain training stresses, you need to systematically improve the body's ability to deal with the forces you place on it.

If you want to be able to squat or deadlift well and to lift heavy things for these movements without hurting yourself, you're going to need to slowly and incrementally challenge the muscles and structures *consistently* over time, in order to build up their abilities to deal with these forces.

This is one of the many reasons why year-round strength training for cyclists is so important, and breaking this approach is why so many cyclists hurt their backs, knees, and shoulders when they hit the weights in the fall/winter, after not having picked up a (relatively) heavy weight for the last 6–9 months. To avoid the risk of injury due to large jumps in training load, we need to think about how we are loading the body just like we think about our on-bike training.

If you are riding with power, and especially if you use TrainingPeaks or Golden Cheetah, you'll be familiar with CTL (Chronic Training Load) and ATL (Acute Training Load). When you're dealing with soft tissue qualities, the responses to training will take longer than those from your metabolic, or energy system, training. Unlike the changes in ATL and CTL that you can see within 24–72 hours after a ride, changes to tissue quality takes much longer, with time periods much longer than a week.

So if you want to maximize your tissue qualities and tissue adaptations, you must take this into consideration. This means keeping with small increases (<5%) in total load for a movement per training session or training week. This is *especially* true for those who are returning to strength training/resistance training after a break lasting longer than 2–3 weeks.

2. Ideal Muscle Resting Length

The muscles of the body each have what's called an ideal resting length, where the muscle is neither too tight nor too loose to work at its highest level of performance. When a muscle is at its ideal resting length, the ability of the muscle to hold just the right amount of tension will mean that the muscle is primed and ready to be fast and powerful!

While some riders make the mistake of thinking that the muscles should adjust in their length in order to make them as "aero" or "cycling specific" as possible, what happens when we have poor muscle resting length is the body is worn down much faster than when the muscles are at their ideal resting length. Your ability to recover is also going to drop significantly, which will decrease your ability to train frequently and to refine or learn skills and techniques necessary to succeed at higher levels.

PUTTING IT ALL TOGETHER

Soft tissue work is important as it helps keep the different parts of the muscles working well, and moving well, while also helping pull your attention to areas that tend to be tight or stiff. By properly managing the amount of load you're placing on the body in each session, and using the foam roller to help better understand your personal tight areas, you can really dial in your dynamic warm-up and corrective exercises to help you work on these weaknesses.

FOAM ROLLING FOR WARM-UP VS. RECOVERY

An important note to make about the soft tissue work as part of the warm-up for each strength training session is that this kind of foam rolling is and must be different in nature than the foam rolling you do for recovery purposes.

Many people think of the foam roller as strictly a recovery tool, but it can be used as a preparatory tool, helping to increase blood flow, helping the body to connect with different muscles and areas, and helping you get mentally focused for the task at hand. It's very important that you have a sound understanding of the differences between foam rolling for recovery vs. warm-up, so here is a cheat sheet:

	WARM-UP	RECOVERY
Time per location	20–30 sec.	45–60 sec.
Primary locations	5	5+
Goal	-Work what is tight, what feels good -Increase blood flow to prepare for activity -Increase mind-muscle connection -Increase muscle resting length -Trigger Sympathetic Nervous System (SNS)	-Work to restore muscle back to ideal resting length -Improve deep muscle blood flow to remove waste and aid recovery -Improve body awareness -Trigger Parasympathetic Nervous System (PSNS)

Understanding the differences between these two approaches to foam rolling will help you make sure that you are getting what you need out of your foam rolling at the correct time.

CHAPTER 8 SUMMARY

- Soft tissue work involves foam rolling or trigger point therapy and is very useful when used correctly and in the right amounts.

- Foam rolling, when paired with corrective exercises and an intelligently designed strength training program, can help decrease stiffness, decrease pain, improve mobility, help you tune into your body's tight areas, and help you understand your body better.

- Too much foam rolling can actually hurt you. Aim for just 3–6 minutes total and include as part of your strength training warm-up.

- Focus your foam rolling on the Super 6 high value target areas: front/side of shins, quads, gluteus medius, chest, lats, and thoracic extension.

- Getting just the right amount of load to allow you to see improvements, along with ideal resting muscle length, are keystones in improving performance.

- Foam rolling as a warm-up has a different purpose and application than foam rolling for recovery.

CHAPTER 9
BREATH WORK

Poor breathing patterns can have massively negative impacts on performance, recovery, and adaptations that occur due to training. Earlier, we talked about the general practice of breathing and why it's important for us to improve our postures and positions. In this chapter, we're going to talk about why and how we add breathing exercises into our strength training routine, and why we do it right after soft tissue work.

Breathing serves as the foundation for many vital functions of the body, and when done correctly, helps us to better recover and adapt from the stresses we go through on a daily basis. Breathing properly also affects the positioning of different joints in the body, the ability for us to stabilize our upper body, and also the resting length and use of different muscles in the body.

THE DIAPHRAGM AND BREATHING MUSCLES

Part of how proper breathing helps us to perform better is in the positioning of the diaphragm. In order for the diaphragm to work best, it needs a full range of motion and to be lined up with the pelvic floor muscles so that it can do its job correctly and effectively. If we don't have good posture and breathing patterns on the bike, the diaphragm is not positioned well and the whole mechanism suffers, as you can see illustrated here by Dean Somerset.

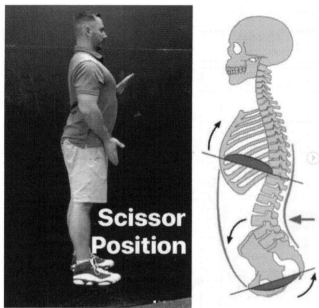

Photo: Dean Somerset, used with permission

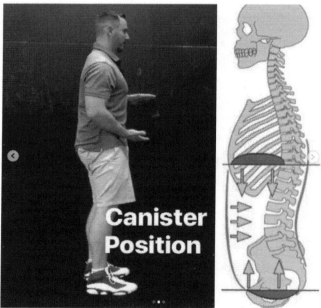

Photo: Dean Somerset, used with permission

Keeping great posture allows the curve in your lower back to remain neutral, which also puts the joints into their ideal positions, allowing the muscles of the midsection and torso to perform their jobs better.

Because we're often not taught how to breathe properly and many of us don't naturally have great postural strength, we can keep riding our bike and going along the
path of least resistance without ever addressing our breath and posture issues.

But this is a huge problem! As you continue to train without addressing your
posture and your breathing patterns, the secondary respiratory muscles become
overused and tighten up. Simply put, these muscles kick in and work when your
main breathing muscles (like the diaphragm) cannot do their jobs properly.

Secondary respiratory muscles include:

- pectoralis minor (the upper, outer part of your chest)

- serratus anterior (the muscles just under your chest)

- trapezius (the muscle on the back of your neck)

Recognize most of these muscles? The reason why you may recognize them is
because they are the very same muscles that some riders complain about being
tight, painful, or limiting when they are out on the bike! Because of how we are
positioned as we ride, many of these muscles are pushed to their limits relatively
quickly as we begin to rack up more time on the bike.

THE IMPORTANCE OF A QUALITY BIKE FIT

Many of the problems you have with breathing muscles getting tight and painful can be delayed, or even prevented, by having a good bike fitter work with you. You want your bike to fit
you and your body's needs, not the other way around.

If you've been through three or four bikes in the last two years, and you just can't seem to
find one that feels comfortable, look for a bike fitter who has the SICI Sizercycle, or the GURU
Sizercycle. It's a really cool machine that allows the bike fitter to figure out what your needs
are so he or she can then recommend certain brands or even specific models and sizes to help
get you comfortable out on the road!

THE WARM-UP ORDER IS IMPORTANT

Doing soft tissue release before the 1–2 breathing exercises in your warm-up allows the breathing exercises to be able to have a much better effect. The muscles that you've just spent time releasing will now be closer to their ideal resting length, which means you will be able to move air more easily and to get air into the right areas.

Once you have the muscles at better resting lengths, you can get much better breaths. This will allow your breath to:

- have the diaphragm and pelvic floor move together
- create great intra-abdominal pressure
- help the parasympathetic nervous system turn on
- help with healing and tissue repair

For these things to happen, you need the diaphragm to move well as you breathe in and out. The diaphragm movement in good breathing patterns also helps to "self-massage" the psoas and to keep the joints, especially those of the ribs, moving well. Because of this connection between the diaphragm and the hip flexors, learning how to breathe can help relax the hip flexors, decrease lower back, neck, and SI joint pain, as well as activate the core, including the all-important pelvic floor.

I cannot stress enough how important the order is: soft tissue release, *then* breathing exercises!

Additionally, performing breath work early in the workout will help you:

- separate your workout from whatever else is going on in your day
- bring you into an improved state of homeostasis and balance on a mental and physiological level, allowing you to perform better
- use breathing to open up

All of this in your warm-up, simply by learning how to breathe properly. Now *that's* a win-win!

BUILDING BETTER BREATHING IN YOUR WARM-UP

Building breath work into a strength training program is relatively simple, but as with anything, in order to have its intended impact, it needs to be done regularly with attention to detail. Learning to breathe properly is an important task that can pay off in faster recovery and even in allowing you to produce more power on the bike.

In order to get the most out of the breathing exercises, you ideally want to be in a quiet place where you can focus on slow, steady breaths, getting air into the upper back and sides, and getting long, full, deep breaths. You don't need to spend a lot of time on the breathing exercises. I'll usually prescribe 1–2 sets of 4–6 breaths. That's it.

There are three basic positions you can use to build your improved breathing patterns in your warm-up:

1. On all fours (called quadruped position)
2. Lying on your back (called supine position)
3. Lying on your stomach (called prone position)

Note that these are not the only positions; they are just the best places to start. As you move through all three of these positions, you'll begin to see and feel changes in:

- Posture
- Your ability to hold powerful positions
- FUNdamental 5+1 movement strength and stability
- Your ability to put power down, and to recover quickly

BREATHING EXERCISES

There are a couple of breathing exercises that are simple but not easy. The following exercises are what I use with new Human Vortex Training (HVT) athletes, as they learn how to breathe properly and begin to reset their bodies. When done properly, these will teach you how to expand your rib cage and your belly to get a full 360-degree breath.

Crocodile Breathing

I call this Crocodile Breathing because when you do it correctly, your flanks move in and out, just like the big ol' crocs on the banks of the Nile.

For this exercise, you'll need to lie on your stomach in order to help you expand your flanks (sides) and to take full, even breaths. This is what is called "back body expansion," also known as breathing into your back.

Many riders find that when they learn how to perform the Crocodile Breathing exercise correctly they feel their lower back, neck, and shoulders all release. Quite a few riders have found "extra power" in their legs on longer and more challenging rides because of this exercise. Learning how to breathe the right way and how to save those secondary breathing muscles until you need them will make you a more energy-efficient rider!

You can do this exercise by lying on the floor or on a yoga mat, depending on what you prefer.

1. Lie down on your stomach with your toes pointed behind you, ankles resting on the ground.

2. Place your hands flat, one on top of the other, underneath your forehead, making sure to keep your neck neutral. Your eyes should be looking straight down at the ground.

3. Relax your shoulders and let your elbows come out to the sides, away from your ears.

4. Keep your shoulder blades relaxed, but back and down.

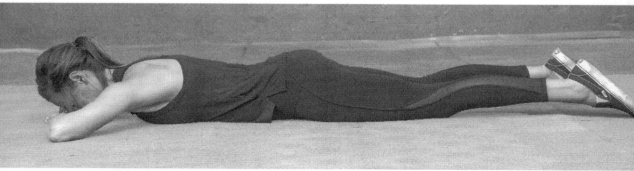

Crocodile Breathing BEGIN

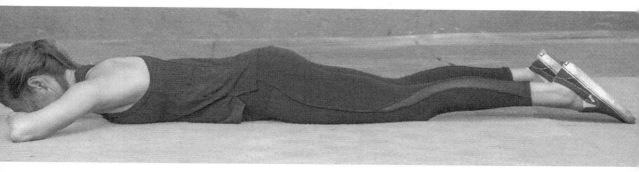

Crocodile Breathing END

5. Take a long, slow inhale through your nose for 3–5 seconds, while thinking about *relaxing* your hips and bringing that air into the area between your shoulder blades, into your lower back, and your sides.

6. Hold your breath for 2 seconds, feeling the middle of your back and lower back open up, and your neck and shoulder relax.

7. Breathe out through your mouth for 5 seconds.

This may look like a simple exercise, but it's very challenging to do correctly. Take your time in learning how to do it properly with consistent practice 2–4 days a week, and you'll be massively rewarded. As you master this exercise, you will want to get a solid 3–4 weeks of great breathing for each and every repetition of 2 sets of 5 breaths, before you move on to Sphynx Breathing.

Sphynx Breathing

Sphynx Breathing can be a really great breathing exercise, but as cyclists who tend to have lower back discomfort and loss of movement at the upper back and shoulders, we must begin this exercise with an air of caution. We *never* want to cause or create pain, especially in our backs, with any of our exercises.

For that reason the Sphynx Breathing exercise has three distinct levels. If you are a healthy rider with no back pain or history of back pain, you can start at level 3. If you are unsure, or have had a history of any kind of back pain, first check with your doctor to make sure it's okay to perform this or any exercise from this book, and then begin at level 1.

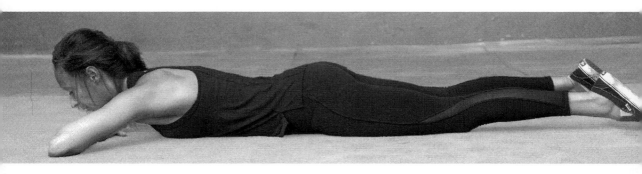

SPHYNX LEVEL 1: SINGLE FIST

1. The first level of Sphynx Breathing is going to look pretty similar to Crocodile Breathing, except that instead of having your forehead on your flat hands, take your non-dominant hand, make it into a fist, and rest your chin on the fist with your eyes looking forward.

2. Rest your dominant hand on the floor just in front of the fist, and be sure to keep your shoulder blades relaxed and your back towards your spine.

3. Breathe in the same fashion as Crocodile Breathing.

4. When you can perform 2 sets of 5 repetitions relaxed and pain free, move to level 2.

SPHYNX LEVEL 2: TWO FISTS, STACKED

1. Take your non-dominant hand and make a fist. Place this fist, pinky on the ground, under your chin.

2. Take your dominant hand and make a fist. Place this fist, pinky towards the floor, on top of your non-dominant hand.

3. Place your chin on top of your stacked fists, and breathe in the same way as with the Crocodile Breathing, except now think about keeping your shoulder blades back and down, but relaxed.

4. While breathing in through your nose, think about the shoulder blades as floating on the rib cage, relaxed and able to move forward and back as your ribs inflate up and out with air.

5. Breathe in, trying to fill the sides of your ribs, as well as the area right in between your shoulder blades, with air.

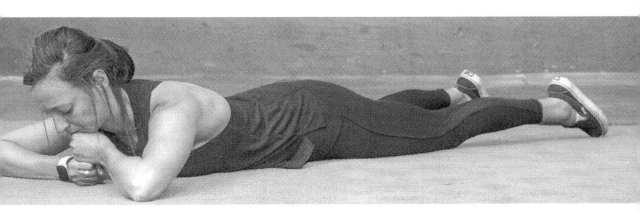

6. When you can perform 2 sets of 5 repetitions relaxed and pain free, move to level 3.

SPHYNX LEVEL 3: ELBOWS

Unlike the first two Sphynx Breathing levels, you will now put your forearms on the ground, elbows at 90 degrees, and allow your shoulder blades to move freely, while you think about filling your rib cage with air in all directions. This is a very tough position for many cyclists to master, as it closely copies the riding position, but now you want to allow the shoulder blades to relax back and down, while having them move freely in a rhythm that matches your breathing.

It's not uncommon to feel a stretch in your stomach, hip flexors, or even quadriceps in this position, due to overly tight muscles. None of these should cause pain, but if there is any kind of sharp stabbing, pulling, or tingling, stop the exercise immediately and carefully return to the Crocodile Breathing position before trying to get up.

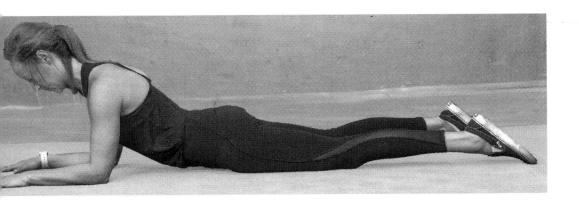

Here's why Sphynx Breathing is a great breathing exercise:

1. Due to the positions cyclists need to be in for long periods of time, many of our back muscles have become stretched out, especially in the upper back.

2. As mentioned in the FUNdamental 5+1 chapter, many riders have poor push-reach movement patterns, and the Sphynx Breathing progression lets us begin to work on it in a static manner.

3. In order to get great breathing patterns we need feedback. By starting on your stomach and working your upper body up off the floor in a slow progression, you will learn more quickly how the different parts of your body are moving with each breath.

4. This level 3 position for Sphynx Breathing is very close to your riding position, which gives you a faster learning curve to breathing better on the bike. However, do not skip ahead to level 3! Take your time and move through the progressions as outlined above.

Even if you feel that you're more advanced, try this exercise for at least two weeks before you move on. It's never a bad idea to shore up your fundamentals!

FINAL THOUGHTS ON BREATH WORK

As you can see, there is quite a lot to learn when it comes to breathing. The key to improving breath work is to start at a level that you can control and quickly learn how to progress. It is not about going as hard as you can and pushing the limits each and every time. This approach is also not the way to see strength gains and progress. You want to do things consistently over time, with attention to positioning, postures, and how and where you are getting the movements.

Breathing exercises allow you to: 1) access and use many different muscles that are often neglected and left untrained, and 2) train your mind-body connection, as these exercises force you to slow down, tune out everything else around you, and really connect.

I'll close this chapter on breathing by mentioning one of the underlying but very important reasons to start each and every session with 3–6 minutes of soft tissue work and 1–2 sets of breath work. These two kinds of work provide a buffer between everything else that is going on in your life and the time you are using to train to improve yourself physically and mentally. Perhaps the foam rolling can be breezed through on some days, but the breath work cannot.

I cannot stress enough how important the order of the workouts (soft tissue work, breath work, dynamic warm-up, etc.) are for you, and this is just one of the many reasons why we have written our strength training programs like we have here at Human Vortex Training. Follow the recipe, and you'll have amazing results. Attention to detail and focus on great execution matter.

CHAPTER 9 SUMMARY

- Proper breathing patterns have a huge impact on performance, recovery, and adaptations to training, as well as your ability to recover between efforts on the bike.

- Breath work should be incorporated into your warm-up, just after soft tissue work when your muscles are closer to their ideal resting lengths.

- Breath work can help relax the hip flexors, decrease lower back, neck, and SI joint pain by getting muscles to relax & joints to move better, as well as activate the muscles of the midsection

- Breathing exercises don't take a lot of time. You just need 1–2 sets of 4–6 breaths.

- The Crocodile Breathing exercise will help your lower back, neck, and shoulders release, and may give you extra power in your legs on longer, more challenging rides.

- The Sphynx Breathing exercise has three distinct levels, depending on your history with back pain and discomfort.

CHAPTER 10
DYNAMIC WARM-UP

The first 6–8 minutes of a session—yes, that is how long it should take to get both foam rolling and breathing done—have stimulated the muscles to move into a more relaxed and ready state. The combination of the foam rolling and the breath work will have not only gotten the nervous system and muscles ready for the session ahead, but when done properly, they will have also helped turn on your parasympathetic nervous system, which is your "rest & digest" mode.

You may be wondering why this is a good thing if you're about to get into a strength session. It all comes down to the order of operations and how you want to prepare the body for peak performances.

FAST IS LOOSE, AND LOOSE IS FAST

Have you ever watched a sporting event with a great athlete in a high-pressure situation? That's a make-it-or-break-it time, and the stakes are high. One mistake or slip up is a certain loss.

What do you notice about the all-time greats? They're cooler than an ice cube in the Arctic. Many of them may have a game face on during high-stakes moments, but watching them move you'd think they're just playing a game of Thursday night pick-up with their friends.

Great athletes have practiced over and over again how to not allow stress to cause them to get nervous or tighten up. In fact, most have spent many hours mentally putting themselves in that very tense situation during their practice sessions. And in those imaginary situations they make it feel real, while they train their bodies and minds to stay relaxed and cool under pressure.

Soft tissue work and breath work are similar. You're not trying to amp up like a high school linebacker before the homecoming game. Instead, I want to teach you how to connect your body and mind, to move from stress (over work, your training plan, the big ride coming up, etc.) into a more balanced state.

It's from this balanced, relaxed—yet alert—state that you will perform your best. From strength training and bike racing to family events and big work projects, learning how to stay calm, cool, and relaxed while alert and dialed into your body and your surroundings will allow you to perform your best.

This is one of the many reasons why the ordering of the six components is so important:

1. Soft tissue work
2. Breath work
3. Dynamic warm-up
4. Explosiveness/Jumps
5. Strength & Correctives
6. Postural Challenge/Rotary Stability

THE DYNAMIC WARM-UP

The dynamic warm-up—the last part of the strength training warm-up—will get the muscles moving, help work on problem areas consistently, and get the body at 100% alertness and readiness for main sets. While each of the six components of a well-designed strength program is important, the dynamic warm-up is an area that is often either overlooked completely or given too much attention.

The keys to a sound, effective, and well-built dynamic warm-up are:

1. Be progressive; move from general to specific.
2. Improve and challenge proprioception (where the body is in space).
3. Include 1–3 corrective exercises that will help address major movement issues.
4. Keep moving to raise core temperature and alertness.

Along with these four keys, also try to include some kind of (appropriately) challenging balance or coordination moves. The dynamic warm-up is a great place to put these kinds of bodyweight movement challenges, as they are fun, mentally engaging, and help teach better coordination.

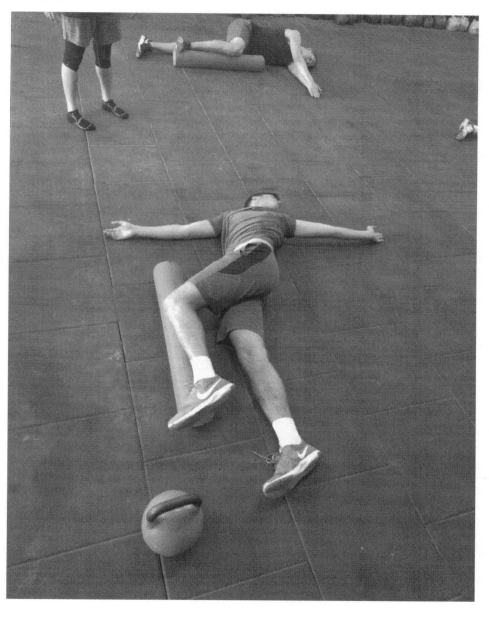

Dynamic warm-ups are critical to your success. They are where you address major muscular and movement issues, as well as prepare you for that day's movements.

Some like to argue that low-level plyometrics or ground-interaction drills like track runners do in their warm-ups should be considered "musts" in the dynamic warm-up for cyclists. I would say that while these movements certainly can offer riders benefits, be very careful about how early in the development program to include them. This is especially true for anyone over the age of 18 who is racking up considerable (8+ hours) ride time in a week, as their tissues may need a bit of work to be able to deal with the forces these exercises produce.

But here's the great thing about plyometrics and ground-interaction drills: They can be slowed down to teach better posture, technique, and control! This allows us to program the low-impact and movement-improving versions of these exercises into the dynamic warm-up . . . when appropriate.

Only so many things can be accomplished in a single training session. And when it comes to the dynamic warm-up, you're really looking to create a warm-up that repeats two of the exercises prescribed on all strength training days. These two exercises, often called "corrective exercises," will be those that get after your 1–2 biggest movement challenges. There is a wide variety of acceptable movements that can be used, but the right one will depend on the athlete, their needs, and where in their strength training regimen they are, as well as where in their riding season they are.

Let's look at how a well-designed dynamic warm-up would look.

LINEAR AND LATERAL

The first two movements are very general and "big-movement" focused. While these two movements are not in a specific order, during the high-volume ride time of year I like to get to the straight-ahead, linear stuff first. The body is getting a lot of this movement, and it's an easy way to see what possible hot spots there are.

MOVEMENT #1: LINEAR

These include light jogging, bodyweight walking lunges (forwards or backwards) with 90-degree knee angles, marches, or an exercise I call "Statue of Liberty," just to name a few. If you'd like to see what each of these looks like, just head over to the bonus section of the website under "Exercise Library," and sign in with the password THEVORTEXTRIBE to get access to the free resources.

The idea behind these movements is to start with something familiar to the body, yet slightly different. Again, movements 1 and 2 can easily be switched around without worrying about changing the programming too much. Go with what feels best to you or your athlete. Just don't keep changing them every session. Stick with your order for two weeks. If after two weeks it's not getting the job done, or you're not sure, switch 1 and 2, and try it the other way for two weeks. Then go with whichever order felt best.

MOVEMENT #2: LATERAL

We already get a ton of straight-ahead, linear movement in cycling, so if we want to truly prepare for increased performance, we must teach and refine the body's ability to move sideways. What's both great and tough about lateral movements is that many riders won't have great coordination or balance as they begin. But remember, it's not speed you're after here. It's learning and refining movements, which helps light up your nervous system and gets you ready for the day's strength session.

When you do lateral movements, start at slow speeds, teaching footwork, coordination, and good body positioning. Don't worry about the speed of the movement. If you take the time to learn how to move with great body positioning, the body will adapt over time, and you'll be moving quicker and will be more agile.

Some of my favorite lateral movements include "ballerinas," side lunges, cariocas (usually for more well-coordinated individuals), and for more up-tempo work, the Figure 8 drill. You'll find these movements also shown in the "Exercise Library" in the bonus section on the HVT website.

Ballerinas	Low-level plyometric style exercise focused on coordination and lateral movement
Side Lunge	Medium to high challenge—requires strength and stability
Cariocas	Dynamic movement involving high level of coordination to turn hips while stepping over or behind the other leg
Figure 8 Drill	Reaction and speed drill; can be done at any pace, requires planting, change of direction, and moderate levels of power

For movements 1 and 2, you don't need to do too much here; 2–3 short, focused rounds are usually more than enough. Usually these are done over a distance, such as "down the hallway and back 3x" (the hallway in this instance is a short, 20-foot walkway), or "2 x 10 feet each way" (for lateral movements).

Again, keep in mind that these movements are here to get you ready for the strength session ahead, not to be a warm-up like a ride. You do not need more than 2–3 minutes total for both of these.

TORSO STIFFNESS PREPARATION

MOVEMENTS #3 AND #4

These tend to be 1 or 3 movements that will target the biggest weaknesses or areas where you just don't have good muscular control or coordination. For many cyclists, these two exercises are usually going to target either the upper back or the hips.

Many people think that we are targeting "the core" here, and they're technically right. Yes, we *do* hit on the core here, but we do it in a way that is teaching the rider how to *create proximal stiffness to produce distal motion*. This is one of the biggest things to remember, as once you begin to be able to do this, you are well on your way to unleashing the full neuromuscular abilities you have within you!

Okay, so this proximal-distal thing . . . what is it again, and how do upper back and hip exercises help? Learning how to brace your midsection—all the way around—in the right amounts, to allow you to keep your rib cage and hips locked together, is necessary to being powerful and to greatly decreasing your risk of injury.

This sounds easy, but most find it incredibly hard to get the right muscles to fire together, let alone at the right time. If someone is a true beginner, this may mean that their dynamic warm-up movements 3 and 4 need to be very basic to help them learn this bracing.

Examples of beginner torso stiffness movements are:

EXERCISE	GOAL
Bird Dog Progression, Level 1 (arm raise)	Proper core bracing to only see movement from arm/shoulder blade
Shielded Breath, Seated	Learn how to brace and create intra-abdominal pressure
Side-Lying Straight Leg Lifts	Learn to fire glute medius muscle while bracing midsection appropriately
Clamshells	Learn to turn off tensor fasciae latae muscle while firing glute medius muscle and bracing midsection appropriately
Half Clamshells	Learn to turn off tensor fasciae latae muscle while firing glute medius muscle and bracing midsection appropriately to resist twisting motion
Blackburns	Ribs down, abs braced (appropriately); learn to fire mid-back muscles only, and get movement from shoulder blade only
Incline Bench Y's	Ribs down, abs braced (appropriately); learn to fire mid-back muscles only, and get movement from shoulder blade only
Prone Glute Activation	Learn to separate glutes from hamstrings while appropriately bracing the midsection

Examples of intermediate movements 3 and 4 would include:

- Bird Dogs, Level 2 (leg only) or 3 (leg & opposite arm) with dowel on spine
- Hip Lifts
- Frog Hip Lifts
- Incline Bench Y's with 2-second pause or squeeze at top
- Inchworms

As athletes, we tend to want to skip ahead and do the technical or hard stuff, but remember that building durable and lasting strength takes time. You need to build postures, good movement patterns, and learn how to produce stiffness and control where you need to, in order to get the most power and speed out of your body somewhere else.

Fight that temptation to skip ahead to intermediate exercises. There is nothing wrong with performing "beginner" exercises for 2–3 months in a row while you learn how to connect with your body to get the movement you want and need.

More often than not, because you'll be getting these two target exercises 2–4 days a week, do 1 set of 3–15 repetitions, depending on what you can handle technique-wise. Especially after high-ride volume or high-ride intensity days, it's not uncommon to need to do fewer repetitions due to neuromuscular fatigue. Listen to your body and remember that *quality* is what you're after here, not just slogging through to "git 'er done."

PLYOMETRIC MOVEMENTS

MOVEMENTS #5 AND (IF NEEDED) #6

Exercises 5 and 6 in the dynamic warm-up will be where you can add some very low-level plyometrics, such as jumping rope, light bounding, skipping, or some kind of lightly weighted focal movement (non-plyometric), like a basic goblet squat for technique, or even a very short set of light single-leg kettlebell deadlifts.

Perform 1–2 sets of 8–12 touches or repetitions with great technique and form.

For a more upper-body non-plyometric focused workout, you can do exercises like:

- Wall Scapular Slides
- Wall Spinal Stabilization
- Back on Corner Shoulder "No Money"
- Foam Roller Y's to W's

Or simply, just do an easier version of a push-up, pull-down, or row.

This is where you need to understand your body, its needs, and working to correct imbalances.

PUTTING IT ALL TOGETHER

These six movements collectively make up the dynamic warm-up, which should take you about 10–15 minutes total. Going from general to specific, here is how they stack up in a session:

THE MOVEMENTS OF THE DYNAMIC WARM-UP			
Movements		Examples	Instructions
1	Linear	Jogging, Lunges, Marches	2–3 rounds
2	Lateral	Ballerinas, Side Lunges, Cariocas	2–3 rounds
3	Mid-section	Bird Dogs, Clamshells, Blackburns, Hip Lifts, Incline Bench Y's	1 set of 3–15 reps
4			
5	Plyometric	Jump Rope, Bounding, Skipping, Goblet Squat, Wall Scapular Slides	1–2 sets of 8–12 touches or reps
6 (if needed)			

CONCLUSION OF THE DYNAMIC WARM-UP

The dynamic warm-up is a highly misunderstood and drastically underutilized portion of a strength training program that many trainers skip completely—or they just fumble their way through some very general movements. Understanding the role of the dynamic warm-up and the huge impact it can have on you as a rider will better equip you to build a powerful strength training program.

As you go to build your dynamic warm-up, keep in mind that the most powerful dynamic warm-ups are those that:

- Focus 100% on the task at hand—no talking to others!
- Transition from one exercise to the next quickly and efficiently
- Have the order of the movements correct
- Progress from general to more training-session specific
- Address the biggest 1–2 movement issues
- Are quick, but not hurried. Take your time! We want GREAT technique, great body positions, and the correct muscles working.
- Are quality-focused, with 1–2 sets maximum
- Put you in a light sweat by the time you're done

Following the system provided here in this chapter will help you to build a highly valuable dynamic warm-up that addresses movement issues and works on imbalances—so you can begin your main program for the day primed and ready to crush it.

CHAPTER 10 SUMMARY

- The last part of the strength training warm-up—the dynamic warm-up—will get the muscles moving and the body alert and ready for the main sets.

- The dynamic warm-up is where you consistently address your strength imbalances through corrective exercises.

- The keys to an effective dynamic warm-up are to move from general to specific, to improve and challenge proprioception, to include corrective exercises, and to raise core temperature and alertness.

- Your dynamic warm-up should include 5–6 movements that address lateral, linear, mid-section, and plyometric needs.

CHAPTER 11
RESISTANCE TRAINING

When putting together an intelligent strength training program, deciding on the exercise order is important. This may come as a surprise, but just changing the order of the exercises themselves can change what results you get 6, 10, or 12 weeks later—or even longer.

Think of exercise order like making brownies: You can have all the right ingredients, but if you don't put them together in the correct order, the brownies can come out tasting and looking awful. Well, when it comes to exercise prescription and planning, it is even more important to put the ingredients in the right order. You can always throw out a bad batch of brownies and start again. But you only get one body, and it really sucks to miss out on a goal event or a few weeks of the best riding of the year because of an injury that should have been prevented with a few tweaks to your program.

Remember, our #1 goal of adding strength training to your regimen is to keep you healthy, moving well, and performing at your best.

THE VORTEX METHOD OF STRENGTH TRAINING

When it comes to writing strength training programs, there is a lot to be said for keeping it simple. You'll find that there isn't anything super complex about the Vortex Method. In fact, it's relatively straightforward and easy to understand. Like most successful athletic programs, there is a large degree of simplicity in the approach, and complexity is only added when and where it will have a large positive effect.

But while this method may be simple, it isn't easy.

THE BEDROCK FOUNDATION

The deeper and better we make the foundation of a highly effective strength training program, the better the outcome will be. The foundation is heavily reinforced by the soft tissue work, breath work, and dynamic warm-up that we've previously talked about. I cannot stress enough the importance of the previous sections in setting you up for success; they must get the attention and care they deserve.

Only after we have those three pieces in place can we get into the main program. For the main program, make sure to:

1. Order exercises in a way to improve strength systematically and address weaknesses and imbalances.

2. Pair exercises together to aid in improved positioning, breathing, and movements.

EXERCISE ORDER

While some may say that exercise selection is most important, and it certainly plays a big role in a strength training program, the ordering of the exercises has a bigger impact on the outcome of the program.

Exercise selection really comes down to meeting the individual where they are and choosing from the FUNdamental 5+1 movements. We'll talk a little about exercise selection in this chapter, but you'll find the exercises and progressions I've used for the last 10+ years in the exercise library on the Human Vortex Training website.

When it comes to exercise ordering, there are only a few rules. When in doubt, go with the simplest solution. Simplicity rules when it comes to programming, and while it may not be sexy, it works. That is where many coaches and athletes go wrong. They want to do more complex or technically difficult exercises because they think that's where they should be. Keep it simple, stick with the fundamental order we lay out here, ensure that you're "dosing" the exercises appropriately, and through consistency, you'll see big gains.

Following these five simple rules for strength training programming can lead you to fantastic results:

1. **Power & explosive exercises first:** Many well-intentioned coaches and athletes put their power or explosive work at the end of their strength training sessions, at a time when they're mentally, physically, and neurologically tired. Their thinking is, "I need power when I'm tired in the ride/race, not when I'm fresh, so I'll do this in my training as well." But by doing their power exercises in a fatigued state, they are actually losing many of the benefits they are after.

   Performing power exercises at the end of your strength training, or after a bike ride, is like firing a cannon from a canoe—you're not going to get the outcome you'd like.

   What you want is to perform power exercises like jumps, bounds, skips, throws, and Olympic lifts immediately after you finish your dynamic warm-up. Performing these exercises when you are fresh allows you to be able to get the movements from the correct places and to be able to fire your muscles with maximum power.

2. **Address the major FUNdamental 5 first:** For many of you, your first thought is to do either a squat or a hinge. . . . But that isn't always the correct choice. You'll need to see what movements are needed first. For many cyclists, this will mean push-reach or press movements.

3. **Pair the major FUNdamental 5 movements with a complementary or corrective exercise:** This will depend on your movement needs and what part of the training year you are in. The Vortex Method takes the work out of this for you by pairing movements up. We're not only making the most out of your time strength training, but we are also helping your body to learn how to move better and more efficiently.

4. **You do *not* need to do all of the FUNdamental 5+1 in a single workout:** This is a mistake many self-coached riders make when it comes to strength training, and it often leads to burnout and poor results. As you've already learned above, the dynamic warm-up allows you to get a little of each of the FUNdamental 5+1 and to consistently work on your weaknesses.

5. **End with a global challenge to rotary stability:** Rotary stability may be the "+1," but working it at the end of the training session allows you to work on one of the areas that can significantly boost your on-bike power: your ability to keep great postures and positions on the bike when you're fatigued.

These challenges should be low intensity and built around the idea of getting the whole body to work together to resist the separation of your ribs from your hips. These exercises usually will not be done with heavy weight or resistance, due to the fatigue you've built up through the session and the need to get muscles to work together.

Some exercises that you should avoid when writing your program include isolation exercises, like bicep curls, tricep push-downs, and other single-joint movements. These kinds of movements will sometimes find their way into a program for a few select riders, but that is only because they have a true need for a specific exercise at that time, and it is the best tool. However, for 99.9% of riders, those exercises are a complete and utter waste of time and energy that you don't have to waste.

IT'S NOT JUST THE ORDER, BUT IT'S HOW YOU DO IT

The appropriate ordering of the exercises cannot be stressed enough. As you learn how to best order the exercises in your training program, you'll begin to not only feel better, but you'll also move better.

Much like a computer program, our bodies are incredibly sensitive to the inputs we give it. By building your strength training program in the following order, you are programming your body to work better, be more efficient, and be able to express that out on the road where it counts:

Power → major movement to work on → corrective/complementary exercise → rotary stability

If you stop reading the book right here, jump to the online exercise library, and build your strength program around these five rules, you'll already see a 30–50% increase in your results compared to what many coaches and personal trainers are practicing right now.

That's a big increase!

But that's not all. . . . We still have three areas that are not often talked about or practiced that will help you increase the results you get many times over.

The best part? They're easy to understand and even easier to put into practice.

WHY YOU SHOULD NOT DO A 1RM

While many programs suggest performing a 1 repetition maximum to determine the correct weights to use, as cyclists, this advice can do more harm than good. As our sport of cycling requires no stress of the body under loads or much external resistance, the body is not prepared to handle heavy loads, especially one repetition maximum.

Instead, you can train by Rate of Perceived Exertion, a simple scale of 1–10, with 1 being very light, and 10 being maximal. Or you can train 2–4 weeks from perceived exertion, and then perform a 10 repetition maximum effort, and then use an online calculator to determine your e1RM (estimated one repetition maximum) to determine the correct loads.

RPE	FEELS LIKE	NEED A SPOT?
10	Absolute Max Effort	Definitely need a spot
9	I could do 1 more rep with good technique	Another rep with a good spotter, but it's really heavy
8	I could do 2 more reps with good technique	Another rep on my own, but not more
7	I could do 3 more reps with great technique	Another 3 reps on my own, don't need a spotter
6	I could do 4 more reps with great technique	No spotter needed; I'm working, but not that hard
5	I could do 5 more reps with great technique	I'm working a little, but no spotter needed
4	I could do 8 more reps with great technique	Just warming up
3	I could do another 10 reps with great technique	Nope
1–2	Air	80–100 reps, no problem

EXPLOSIVE MOVEMENTS

Tempo movements can help unlock a lot of strength, but to unlock the type of strength needed for sport, we require a different type: explosive strength. Explosive strength does not have a set tempo, except that you will take your time to get into a great starting position, keeping just enough tension in your body to hold this position, and then *explode* with great technique to create maximum velocity!

Explosive strength is in the same family of strength as speed strength, as these both require a more dynamic approach in order to train properly, and the velocity or speed of the movement has a huge impact on the outcome. Examples of explosive movements are kettlebell swings, cleans, snatches, and jumps.

By performing these movements with a moderate to heavy weight, you are not going to improve your explosiveness! For many cyclists, this is one of the most misunderstood and poorly executed part of a strength training program, because when we think about developing power and explosiveness, we either think heavy weights or lots and lots of jumping until we're tired.

But in fact, there is much more to explosive strength. We need to consider a few things before deciding how to execute these parts of our program: Are we training the metabolic system (energy system) to be placed under stress for longer periods of time? Or are we trying to get the nervous system and muscles to become more powerful in how they move the body?

1. **Is our goal to increase the nervous system and muscles to be able to create maximal force?**

   For this kind of training, we absolutely must perform our power exercises with lighter weights and faster speeds. And even in partial ranges of motion.

   When it comes to building the body's ability to coordinate its systems to produce maximum power and force, we need to work on building the neuromuscular connections and refine the different parts and systems of the body for max power output. This kind of training is what we want to begin with. However, this kind of training can be hard for cyclists to wrap their heads around, as it means using lighter weights (around 20–30% of estimated 1 rep max), and resting for 4–5 minutes in between rounds.

   That's a long time in between sets, and you won't really "feel tired" from these efforts. But you're not supposed to feel out of breath and exhausted from these! We're slowly charging up your nervous system like a defibrillator and asking it to deliver a maximum charge for 2–7 sets of 1–4 repetitions.

   As you progress from beginner to intermediate, the weights used (% of estimated 1 rep max) won't change too much, but they will slide up to 30–50% of estimated 1 rep max. These movements will include Hang Cleans, Hang High Pulls, Drop Cleans, as well as jumps and true plyometrics. For the jumps and plyometrics, we do not use added weight until much later, and even then it is very little. However we *do* program the jumps, partial jumps, and plyometrics starting from 2–4 sets of 2–5 repetitions.

Take your time in between repetitions to set up for the starting position you want, and focus your mind and body to give 100% power to that one repetition, as if it is your only repetition for the day. The keys here are maximum recovery for the nervous system between sets and stopping sets when the power decreases.

2. **Do we want to build the energy system's ability to maintain less than true maximum power output for longer periods of time?**

Perhaps this is what many cyclists have in mind when they think of power training. This approach is often taken to extremes, where riders will do box jumps or other plyometrics at the end of their workouts. They have the mindset of "I have to be sore and tired for it to count or work!" But that couldn't be further from the truth.

In fact, if you want to actually build your power and power-endurance, you must take into account tissue and movement quality, and understand those two things will greatly impact your body's ability to put out power for longer periods of time.

This ties into our need to work on better postures and breathing. If you go back to the chapter on breathing and posture, you'll remember that our ability to take deep, slow breaths and move air efficiently has a huge impact on our performance and our ability to return to homeostasis, i.e., recover faster between sets and between workouts.

Getting the correct amount of rest time in between sets and using the correct weights (loading) will determine what results you're going to get from your strength training.

STRENGTH TRAINING

For the strength training section of your workouts, a common structure is 2 or 3 pairs of exercises, where you move quickly from finishing the first exercise right into the second exercise, and then rest for a prescribed period of time.

The rest period between sets is important, as it will determine the kind of adaptations and changes you'll get from your strength training. Rest periods of 90 seconds or less will push your training results to be more metabolic in nature.

Rest periods of 2–4 minutes will push your training more towards hypertrophy and maximum strength. And lastly, rest periods of 3–7 minutes will push your training towards neurological changes. However, for these exercises they must be explosive, with correct loads.

PROGRAMMING ORDER

The order of the exercises is very important, as you want to make sure that you are building your biggest areas for improvement when you are still fresh. And there will often be a hinge, squat, overhead press, or a horizontal pull—major multi-joint movements that will help you build strength, stability, and power. Which one you choose will depend on what your biggest weakness is, as well as where you are in your training year, and whether or not your focus is on technique.

If you are working on a more technical, heavy movement, you'll want to do it early in the strength training session when your nervous system is fresh, and you'll want to pair it with a complementary corrective or strength movement.

PAIR EXERCISE EXAMPLES

An example of paired Strength + Corrective exercises = Front Squats + Half Kneeling Banded Lat Stretch

Pairing these two exercises together allows better, cleaner movements by challenging you to maintain posture and produce movement in the front squats, and then immediately use your breath, hamstrings, and glutes to be able to open up your lats. The whole time you're activating and tying together these muscles to better work together as the latissimus dorsi muscles gain length.

An example of paired Strength + Complementary exercises = Hex Bar Deadlift + Pull-ups/ Lat Pull-down

These two exercises work well together as they allow you to hit the lower portion of the posterior chain in the first exercise, while getting a variety of loads moved (light all the way up to heavy). You then immediately follow this by putting the stabilizing and supporting muscles—in this case the latissimus dorsi and arms—through a full range of motion.

While many cyclists avoid the overhead press, gaining stability and cleanliness in this movement pattern can help you significantly improve your performance and power output. Be smart about how you program these in, and be sure to start with basic strength exercises through the range of motion that you can properly do, and provide a good, solid base (ribs and pelvis locked together) before you think about moving forward into power and explosive press moves.

Pressing for power/explosiveness is not a prerequisite for top cycling performance; however, creating stability in this fashion can give you more options to develop your speed and power on the bike, especially jumping out of the saddle on a climb.

Remember, it's not the weights that matter. It's the ability to create stiffness in the spine, rib cage, and hips—to produce movement and power at the arms and legs.

TEMPO

While Tempo may sound complicated, it's actually really simple:

Tempo = The speed at which you perform each part of the exercise

Understanding how tempo affects results and how to put it into a program is part of the "secret sauce" of the leading professionals in the world of strength training.

I'm going to keep it super simple and give you the four most common tempos that cyclists should be using in their strength training to get cycling-specific results. But first, let's talk about the four numbers and what they mean.

UNDERSTANDING TEMPO

Tempo is written with 4 numbers, but we'll demonstrate it with letters, like this:

A-B-C-D

The first letter (A) is really important, as it will make sure that you do the exercise correctly and start from the correct position. A is the number of *seconds* you should take to *lengthen the major working muscle* for the given exercise.

This is important because the lengthening (or eccentric) part of the movement must be the first. It sets you up for success for the rest of the set.

Examples of the lengthening part of the exercise:

- Lowering the weight to your chest for a bench press
- Lowering yourself towards the ground from the bar for a pull-up/chin-up
- Lowering the bar towards the ground in a deadlift
- Letting the weight move away from you for a seated row
- Letting the bar move up for a seated pull-down

The second letter (B) tells you how many *seconds* to *pause and hold tension and position* once you've reached the end of the eccentric part of the movement.

The key here is to keep your muscles tight and engaged, and only go through the range of motion through which you have good strength, control, and stability for.

Examples of the pause and hold part of the exercise:

- Brushing a box with your butt for a box squat
- Holding the bar with the shoulder blades and spine stabilized for a bent-over row
- Holding the bar lightly touching your chest with tension for a bench press
- Holding the top part of a pull-up while keeping your abs engaged and shoulder blades drawn down and together

Holding the position and great muscle tension is the whole point here—and will help you move towards mastery of that movement and position over time.

The third letter (C) is the number of *seconds* you should take to *shorten the major working muscle* for the given exercise.

Examples of the shortening part of the exercise:

- Raising the weight to your chest for a bench press
- Pulling yourself towards the bar for a pull-up/chin-up

- Lifting the bar off the ground in a deadlift
- Pulling the weight towards you for a seated row
- Pulling the bar down towards your chest for a seated pull-down

The fourth and last letter (D) shows how many *seconds* to *pause and hold tension and position* once you've reached the end of the concentric part of the movement.

The key here is to keep your muscles tight and engaged, and to only go through the range of motion through which you have good strength, control, and stability for. Some call this the end of a repetition, or returning to the starting point.

Examples of this pause and hold part of the exercise:

- Standing tall with the bar on your back for a box squat
- Holding the bar at arm's length with the shoulder blades and spine stabilized in a bent-over row
- Holding the bar at the starting point with good tension and position for a bench press
- Returning to the beginning position of a pull-up while keeping your abs engaged and shoulder blades in good position

Holding position and great muscle tension is the whole point here—and will help you move towards mastery of that movement and position over time. You don't want to relax.

HOW TO USE TEMPO FOR BETTER RESULTS

As I mentioned earlier in the book, there are different kinds of strength, and in order to get the type of strength you need to succeed as a cyclist, you need to train for that specific kind of strength by applying appropriate tempos. Let's talk about the four most common tempos you need to include in your program to see cycling-specific results.

1. **3-1-3-1 tempo:** Learning movement control, core control, and preparing the body for heavier, more explosive training

The 3-1-3-1 training tempo is a fantastic way for you to begin your strength training program for a number of reasons. It will:

- Expose breakdowns and weak points in the FUNdamental 5 movements
- Help you learn how to produce core control while moving
- Build tissue strength and resiliency with more time under tension
- Use more of your muscles' motor units as you fatigue
- Use lighter weights to see great results

The 3-1-3-1 tempo is a great place to start your strength training cycles in the fall or winter, as it will help get you on track quickly, giving you lots of great feedback while you build up the tissues' and nervous system's abilities to be ready to handle your upcoming training. The 3-1-3-1 tempo has also proved itself to be an all-star for mid-season strength for those who travel a lot, or who have high demands on their time.

2. **2-1-1-1 tempo:** For speed and power development

The 2-1-1-1 tempo is great for power and explosiveness, as it teaches you to control the weight through the eccentric portion of the movement, master the "loaded" position, and then explode up to the end position. Technically, the movement will take less than 1 second, but you want explosion and production of power.

For beginner and intermediate riders, the last number may be a 1, but the most important thing is to make sure you get your setup right before you go again.

The 2-1-1-1 tempo is used in the early to late base period, as well as through the riding and racing seasons, as it allows you to train power and explosiveness.

3. **2-5-1-1 tempo:** For starting strength or power

The 2-5-1-1 tempo is used to help build starting strength, but only when you don't have the equipment necessary to start the weight off in the right position to meet your abilities and needs. The loading (% of e1RM used) for the 2-5-1-1 tempo is really important; using weights that are too heavy can lead to injury.

Examples of exercises that we would use the 2-5-1-1 tempo for:

- Hang power clean
- Hands on hips jumps from bottom

By stopping for 5 seconds you are taking away the ability of the muscle to use stored energy to produce the power you are looking for.

4. **Self-Paced tempo:** For general strength base / movement learning

That's right, go at your own speed! However, you need to make sure that you are not zipping through an exercise and losing your ability to control the movement and produce stiffness. For most, this self-paced tempo usually winds up being around 2-0-1-0, but it does vary from person to person, although usually not by too much.

Usually, we'll use self-pacing for exercises like box jumps, bounds, and skipping. However, because many athletes and riders rush their setup in between repetitions, sometimes we'll give them a "reset tempo," usually 3–4 seconds. This just reminds you that you should not rush through the set, but make sure that you are learning and mastering the correct starting position.

When understood and programmed in correctly, tempo-based movement will allow you to focus on the specific kind of strength you are building and to get the neuromuscular and tissue qualities that you need in order to improve your performance out on the road. Simply adding the tempo to your lifting can be a big booster, but you can't just drop in tempo and expect to see results. You need to make sure that you're resting enough between your sets, so that you are putting the right kind of stress on your body's systems.

CHAPTER 11 SUMMARY

- The deeper and better we make the foundation of a strength training program, the better the outcome will be.

- Exercise order matters. Do the power and explosive exercises first, and end with rotary stability work.

- A common structure for strength training is to pair 2 or 3 exercises, a strength exercise paired with corrective exercises.

- Tempo, or the speed at which you perform each part of the exercise, will make sure you do the exercise correctly to get the type of strength that you need or want from the exercise.

SECTION 3:
TRAIN

CHAPTER 12
REST PERIODS: NEUROMUSCULAR OR METABOLIC APPROACH?

In or around 2013 strength training saw a surge in "HIIT," also known as High Intensity Interval Training. This kind of interval training with short rest periods can be useful, but many cyclists find it can actually hold them back from the results they are looking to get from their strength training.

Here's why: During every activity that we do with our body, we use a variety of different energy systems and we challenge our body to produce energy to meet its demands. Many cyclists who train with a workout program or a coach will quickly recognize this, as their training programs are built to challenge different energy systems in a structured fashion in order to get to the desired result. However, while training the energy systems may use, or even require, shorter rest periods, when it comes to training the neuromuscular system, you need more time between sets to get the desired results.

While we're not going to do a deep dive into the energy systems here, it is important that you understand how big of an impact taking the proper rest periods in between your working sets is. Improperly planned and executed rest periods can completely derail your strength training results. This has to do with shorter rest periods taking the work and stress away from the nervous system and muscles, and instead turning them to the energy systems, as well as the local muscles' ability to produce and use energy.

METABOLIC OR NEUROMUSCULAR

Strength training, and the results you get from it, occur on a spectrum. Like any spectrum, you are either going to the right or going to the left. There are no compromises, and the end results will be pretty different.

On one side of the strength training spectrum, you have metabolic adaptations. This is where you are building up the trained muscles and movements to be more effective and efficient with their work capacity. Think of it like a factory that you want to become more efficient and to produce more sprockets with the same amount of workers.

Metabolic changes will be what you get from strength training when you lift with relatively short rest periods (30–90 seconds) in between sets. This is the big focus of High Intensity Interval Training.

This kind of strength training can be fantastic for those who are sitting most of the day and are not getting much physical activity. It can also be a good approach for short, specific training blocks that focus on a weaker area or movements that may be holding back a cyclist from their performance as they approach a peak race or a race with very special demands. An example of such a race is The Tour of Tucker County (West Virginia), which features some of the most challenging climbing terrain in the U.S.

However, for the majority of cyclists, training for a metabolic response may not be the right method, as they're already placing a lot of metabolic stress on the muscles from their riding.

On the other side of the strength training spectrum is neuromuscular adaptations, and this is what most cyclists need to train. Neuromuscular changes will be the result of strength training when you lift with rest periods that match the specific results that you are training for in your lifting.

Examples of appropriate rest periods are:

- 3–5 minutes (hypertrophy, maximum strength)
- 4–6 minutes (speed-strength, explosive strength)

WHY DOES IT MATTER?

Our body performs work primarily in one of two ways, physiological or mechanical. When we strength train, we can affect the outcome of the training stress by either: 1) placing more stress on the energy systems (physiological) by taking shorter rests, which doesn't allow the systems to completely recover, or 2) placing more stress on the mechanical system by allowing the energy systems to recover more completely and giving more time for the nervous system to recharge in between efforts. The concept is far more complex and there are many important details, but this explanation should at least give you an idea of how it works.

As cyclists, we get a *ton* of metabolic work done on our bikes, as we should! The main focus of our sport is to produce the highest average power for the duration of our event, and to have the nutrition and energy-saving strategies nailed down, so that we can use tactics and bike handling skills to get over the finish line before anyone else in the field.

But when it comes to strength training, the biggest rewards don't come from putting more metabolic stress on the body. They come from nervous system adaptations and the resulting ability of muscles to be recruited at a higher level of effectiveness and efficiency in order to produce the needed movements, using a lower level of movement threshold and in a more efficient manner.

Improving strength in this manner is done by allowing the neuromuscular and metabolic systems enough time in between sets to recover, and by getting the nervous system to *max output* for the movement being trained.

Performing strength training in this fashion—with proper rest periods in between sets in order to get a more neuromuscular response, combined with continual learning and refining of on-bike riding skills like bike handling, pedaling, cornering, and braking—is where a truly intelligent strength training program shines!

But as I hinted at above, it's not just the rest periods that will have a huge impact on the results you'll get from your strength training program; it's also selecting the correct weight.

WEIGHT SELECTION: LOADING FOR SPECIFIC RESULTS

For many, when they think of strength training, they think of putting a heavy weight on the bar . . . or the machine they're about to use with a predetermined number of repetitions. The end of each set will be marked with technique breaking down, a burning sensation in the working muscles, or some fatigue.

But performing your strength training in this way actually neglects one of the most important variables that you need as an athlete, not as a general fitness fanatic. Namely, you need to manipulate your weight to meet your desired muscular and energy system needs to see sport-oriented adaptations.

Loading goes even deeper than this, as it also determines the velocities (speed or tempo of lift) that you train at. Understanding this is incredibly important, as training speed-strength or explosive strength with the wrong loads will lead you down the wrong path of results, and possibly even injury.

An important note before we get into the proper loading percentages based off of your *estimated* one repetition maximum (e1RM): No matter what your desired outcome is, and how much you do or do not load on the bar, it is your *intent* when moving the weight that has an absolutely tremendous impact on your strength development.

If you're looking for the best results from your strength training, every time you pick up a weight, take a second to think, focus, and commit your whole being to putting all you have into it, and moving it with the correct technique and tempo/speed required to get your desired result.

It doesn't matter if it's a 2.5 pound weight that you're adding for a shoulder exercise or if it's a 250 pound deadlift. Each and every time you go to touch a weight, focus your whole being on mastering the weight and allowing your body to work 100% focused in on your desired result.

Intent matters. A LOT.

Now back to proper loading. This table shows how to load for specific outcomes for intermediate and advanced strength training athletes:

	% E1RM	REST BETWEEN SETS
Strength	80–100%	3–5 min.
Power	70–100%	3–6 min.
Speed-Strength	50–60%	0.5–2 min.
Explosive Strength	20–30%	4–6 min.
Hypertrophy	60–85%	2–5 min.

If you missed it, I want to point out an important small detail in the above table. These percentages are for *intermediate and advanced* strength training athletes. If you're a beginner at strength training, you'll use a slightly different model because your strength will rapidly change and improve.

The below table for beginners (first 6–18 months of strength training) is much more subjective since efforts are based off of feel, but it works extremely well.

	PERCEIVED EFFORT (RPE SCALE 1–10)	REST BETWEEN SETS
Strength	7–8	3–5 min.
Power	8–9	3–6 min.
Speed-Strength	3	0.5–2 min.
Explosive Strength	2–3	4–6 min.
Hypertrophy	6–7	2–5 min.

This table shows a very important difference from beginners to intermediate or advanced athletes in how they properly load their exercises. A beginner's load will change quickly relative to estimated 1 repetition maximum, because the nervous system will adapt relatively quickly, making it difficult to load properly.

There is just one last piece to a well-designed strength training program for cyclists: when to program your strength training sessions in relation to your on-bike training. I will discuss this important concept in the next chapter.

CHAPTER 12 SUMMARY

- The two different primary adaptations—neuromuscular and metabolic—
  require different amounts of rest periods in between workout sets.

- Metabolic changes require short rest periods (30–90 seconds) in between
  sets, and neuromuscular changes require longer rest periods (3–6 minutes).

- With weight selection, you need to choose weights to meet your desired
  muscular and energy system needs to see sport-oriented adaptations.

CHAPTER 13
THE 5 STAGES OF THE STRENGTH TRAINING YEAR

Strength training for cycling performance is very different from strength training for general strength. As such, it will require us to look at strength training as a tool to help us build our abilities in a pretty different light.

I have to mention the elephant in the room. Cyclists, as a whole, are incredibly weak and do need general strength before they can begin to build strength for very specific sports results. I don't say this to offend anyone, but as a strength coach I know this to be true, and it's one of the reasons why simply starting strength training with a general plan can be incredibly beneficial . . . so long as you're learning proper technique for each movement.

And that is where the training year, for strength training, begins. There are five stages to the strength training year.

1. **Anatomical Adaptation** (helps you attain better movements at the joints and refines appropriate movement patterns*)

2. **Hypertrophy** (builds cross-sectional strength and stability)

3. **Maximum Strength** (develops strength in movement patterns)

4. **Conversion to Sport** (develops speed, power, and if appropriate, agility)

5. **Maintenance** (develops strength-endurance for movement patterns and maintains abilities)

---

*The higher the level of the athlete, the more difficult this gets, because they have moved certain ways in order to get where they are.

These building blocks require focus and attention to detail. There are examples of all five phases of strength training programming in the sample training plans at the back of the book.

STAGE 1: ANATOMICAL ADAPTATION

The first stage of strength training for cycling, triathlon, or any sport involves going through the FUNdamental 5+1 movements with little to no weight, allowing you to learn how the body feels and moves. The first stage has to do with technique, learning better movement patterns, and improving motor control and tissue qualities.

This stage of training is often very difficult to get adults to spend enough time on, as they have a need to *feel something* from their workout. They think, "I'm an adult! I can handle it!" and they want to challenge themselves in the gym. Like a hard hill repeat interval, they think they need to feel the effort.

Unfortunately, this thought process is a bit broken and leads many endurance athletes who hit the gym looking for strength training to boost their biking or running power into a world of pain, which takes away from their enjoyment of the gym, and over (usually a short) time, to stop doing strength training at all. And then I hear:

> *"I'm too sore to ride."*

> *"I can still feel my glutes from last Monday's squats."*

In the anatomical adaptation stage, you are actually looking for difficulty levels of 5, 6, and 7 (and occasionally an 8) for each set and for your overall strength training session. This concept is very foreign to many triathletes and cyclists who are used to pushing hard and "knowing a good workout when they feel it."

This stage lasts 3–6 weeks, and the point is for the body to begin to adapt to the new kinds of demands we are going to place on it, to allow us to learn (or begin to learn) the techniques we will need to safely and successfully use strength training to boost our power and performance, as well as to help us get into the new routine.

Stage 1: ANATOMICAL ADAPTATION

Length: 3–6 weeks

Focus: Tissue and structural adaptations to strength training, learning technique for movements with low loads

Target session perceived exertions (1–10): 5 & 6

STAGE 2: HYPERTROPHY

Hypertrophy has gotten a bad rap in the endurance sports world, but in truth, you need it if you want to increase your cycling power or drop your running and swimming times. Don't worry, unless you're training on the bike or for your swim/bike/run less than around 6 hours total a week, your risk of putting on tons of muscle is going to be slim to none. Your body will prioritize that which it's being asked to do most. (And if we're being honest here, if you consider yourself a cyclist or triathlete and are training *less* than 6 hours a week total in your sport, we need to have a whole different kind of conversation.)

Dean Somerset and I spoke a little about this when he joined me on episode 10 of *The Strong Savvy Cyclist & Triathlete Podcast* in 2019. Dean also wrote a blog post, "Resistance Training for Endurance Athletes," about this topic all the way back in 2010, which quoted some research from 1999 that shows endurance athletes can reap great benefits without bulking up. That's over 20 years ago, yet the myths still lives!

The muscular hypertrophy stage will generally last 6–12 weeks, depending on your strength training age (*not* your cycling training or triathlon training age!), your strength and performance goals, your physical needs, as well as where you are in your training year. During this phase it's a good time to be doing the *opposite* on the bike, run, or swim—meaning that if you're pushing for hypertrophy in the gym, you might want to do endurance, tempo, or even short sweet spots in your sport.

The adjustment is pretty simple once you understand the five stages of strength development as covered here and make the appropriate changes to your strength training program.

Stage 2: HYPERTROPHY

Length: 6–12 weeks

Focus: Growth in muscle size, strength, and thickness, along with connective tissue strength

Target session perceived exertions (1–10): 6, 7, and occasionally 8

STAGE 3: MAX STRENGTH

Only after you've gone through the previous 9–18 weeks' worth of preparation will you turn to max strength. This stage involves: learning the techniques of each movement, learning how to appropriately position yourself and breathe through the movement, and allowing for the mind-muscle connection to be developed in order to produce the stiffness needed to do these weights and movements properly. But above all else, you *must* get the tissue adaptations before using heavy weights.

Taking the time to set the table properly will allow you to reap massive benefits from this stage and will significantly decrease your risk of injury.

When doing the programming for max strength, it's important to note that you are *not* doing maximum efforts or weights for each and every movement! Rather, you'll select 2–3 movements that you know need improvement in order to allow you to see great results, and then you'll match those exercises with movements in the hypertrophy or strength-endurance ranges in order to improve your ability to perform stronger for longer.

Stage 3: MAX STRENGTH

Length: 6–12 weeks*

Focus: Increase max strength, increase mind-muscle connection (neural drive), practice new skills of creating stiffness in the torso and spine to move from the legs and arms

Target session perceived exertions (1–10): 6, 7, and occasionally 8

*The sample plans have just 6 weeks of Max Strength. For more advanced athletes, the Max Strength phase can be done twice, for a full 12 weeks.

STAGE 4: CONVERSION TO SPORT-SPECIFIC STRENGTH

The conversion to sport-specific strength is far easier than it sounds, yet so many riders and coaches completely neglect it. This phase of the strength training year is where the magic happens. This is when you use on-bike intervals and efforts to help you make the most out of your strength training.

In this stage, your strength training will dial back to 1–2 times a week in the gym, usually for shorter, highly targeted workouts. The sessions will be timed in ways that will help you carry over the gains from strength training onto the bike. You'll also be performing movement sessions at home 1–2 times a week to help you keep balance and strength as your ride time goes up. These movement sessions are usually 10–20 minutes long and don't require much effort.

While it takes a little more planning to match the on-bike program with the strength training programming so they work in chorus to help you ride stronger and faster, the results are well worth it. You'll learn a few of the best intervals and efforts to add to your on-bike programming in Chapter 16, but note that it's not about "big gears," but rather getting the right intervals and cadences to help you tap into your newly found strength and coordination. That last part—skills—tends to catch a lot of people by surprise, but it makes all the difference.

Learning and practicing skills such as braking, cornering, bumping, and sprinting all help you learn how to take your newly developed strength and proprioceptive abilities (knowing where your body is in space) and put them smack into your biking abilities.

Stage 4: CONVERSION TO SPORT-SPECIFIC STRENGTH

Length: 5–12 weeks

Focus: Take strength and new abilities shown in sport through specific interval work, skills practices, and careful planning of strength and in-sport sessions

Target session perceived exertions (1–10): 5, 6, and 7

STAGE 5: MAINTENANCE

The most commonly skipped stage of strength training for true performance cyclists is maintenance. This phase will vary rider to rider, based on your time available, access to equipment, and energy management.

For the majority of us, maintenance during our high-ride time of the year will consist of 2–4 days a week of a 10–15 minute strength session right after we get off the bike. This helps us to keep the muscles that help maintain our balance and posture firing well, as long as we can still get the nervous system fired in beneficial ways. If you train this way, you will *not* need heavy weights, but rather moderate to moderate-heavy weights.

The other option, for those who have time and energy available, is to do 2 days a week of those very same 10–15 minute routines post-ride at home, and then hit the gym 1 day a week for moderate-heavy to heavy weights, but with a very di-aled-in strength routine 1 time a week. This heavy lift at the gym should be based off of RPE, *not* your historical weights from the last 6 months to a year! This will allow you to get enough neuromuscular stress without frying yourself on rides.

Choose 1 day a week to hit the gym for this 30–45 minute strength session, which includes 4–6 minutes of soft tissue work, 10–15 minutes of dynamic warm-up, and then 2–3 pairs of exercise to keep you moving.

Stage 5: MAINTENANCE

Length: 5–12 weeks

Focus: Keep and slowly progress strength and abilities gained to this point

Target session perceived exertions (1–10): 6, 7, and 8

PUTTING IT ALL TOGETHER

The sample training plans at the back of the book use these five stages for a full year of strength training.

TRAINING PLAN OVERVIEW FOR THE YEAR	
STAGE	**LENGTH**
Anatomical Adaptation	4 weeks
Hypertrophy 1	6 weeks
Hypertrophy 2	6 weeks
Max Strength	6 weeks
Max Strength 2 (advanced)	6 weeks
Conversion to Sport-Specific 1	5–6 weeks
Conversion to Sport-Specific 2	5–6 weeks
Maintenance 1	5–6 weeks
Maintenance 2	5–6 weeks

If you want to truly see health and performance gains from your strength work, it's vital to move through at least the first four of these phases throughout the year.

While maintenance may not appeal to you, and in fact may not be needed if you're not logging tons of miles or time in the saddle at any one point in the year, approaching your strength training with these stages as a template of how to structure your training year will allow you to build lasting strength, which will improve posture, breathing patterns, and even overall functions for your muscles and joints.

Keep in mind that when I say "function" I am talking about "joint positions dictating muscle functions" and the work to keep your body as balanced as possible so that you can ride long and strong for many, many years to come.

CHAPTER 13 SUMMARY

- There are five stages to the strength training year: Anatomical Adaptation, Hypertrophy, Maximum Strength, Conversion to Sport, and Maintenance.

- The Anatomical Adaptation stage involves going through the FUNdamental 5+1 movements with little to no weight, allowing you to learn how the body feels and moves.

- The Hypertrophy stage focuses on growth in muscle strength, thickness, along with connective tissue strength and some muscle size, although this is usually blunted by your riding.

- During the Max Strength stage, you won't be doing maximum efforts or weights for each and every movement—just 2–3 select movements.

- The Conversion to Sport phase is when you focus on using on-bike intervals and efforts to help you make the most out of your strength training by converting strength gains to on-bike performances.

- The Maintenance stage is often skipped by cyclists but is very important to keep and slowly progress strength and abilities gained to this point.

CHAPTER 14
PROGRAMMING: WHAT'S THE BIG IDEA?

When and how do you plan your strength training days and your bike training days? The answer is, and always will be, "It depends!" This is because there are a lot of different variables that have to be taken into account when planning a program. Let's take a look at the major factors and how you should plan your training based off of them.

Cycling is so often used by athletes in other sports to help either recover from tough training sessions with low impact or to help build a better general endurance base. This tradition stretches back many decades and has even included athletes like Arnold Schwarzenegger in the 70s.

For those who focus on cycling as their main sport, much of modern day training is based off of high-intensity interval work and making sure that we're getting enough time to recover and adapt between our training sessions. You *are* getting adequate recovery between sessions, right?

To help you plan your training, I'm going to give you the major building blocks and teach you how to understand when and how to change them in order to get the recovery, adaptation, and results you both need and deserve. Remember, training without recovery and adaptation is just building yourself to an injury. Without recovery and adaptation, training will prove futile!

TRAINING WITH RPE

As with all great works of art, we first need to have a base layer. In our case, the base is understanding how to grade a workout's intensity.

For many of us, the first thing that comes to mind when we hear the words "high intensity" are VO_2max workouts or 1-minute, all-out intervals where each interval leaves our lungs and legs screaming for oxygen and relief, our bodies feeling sapped completely of energy, and our vision cross-eyed. Yes, this would qualify as high intensity for riding intervals, but when it comes to strength training, we rate intensity quite a bit differently.

Intensity for strength training is based off of:

1. The **speed** of the movement

2. The **load** of the movement

3. And, lastly, the level of recruitment of the **nervous system** for the movement

Notice that each of the strength training intensity parameters is *per movement*, not per workout. This is incredibly important!

While many strength athletes (especially Olympic lifters) measure intensity by percentage of 1RM, for those who have a focus in cycling, we have to measure our intensity a bit differently, as our main focus is not on moving a heavy weight but on increasing our ability to get stronger and more powerful out on the bike. For this, and a few other reasons, we'll use perceived exertion (RPE) to measure the intensity of each set, each exercise, and each training session.

Most cyclists (and endurance athletes in general) don't get nearly the recovery and adaptation time they need, which leaves them in a chronically sub-optimal training state. Using RPE to measure your effort and intensity in the gym will allow you to "meet yourself where you are"—on that day, at that time, in those circumstances—a skill that athletes at the highest levels develop, grow, and practice over years in their sport. Additionally, RPE tends to be accurate within 90–100% of actual effort for most people[1,2], especially as they move towards heavier weights. In fact, one study[1] found that those in the RPE group had a slight advantage when it came to lifting 1RM in testing at the end of the study!

RPE has gotten lost a bit since the advent of power meters and heart rate monitors, but oddly enough, as we learn more about the connection between the brain, perception, and pushing the limits of human performance, as Alex Hutchinson discusses in his 2019 book *Endure*, the more dialed in we are, if we just listen to our bodies.

RPE AND THE INDIVIDUAL

Yes, using RPE is playing the averages, but remember, we are talking in broad strokes/ big-picture terms, because you, your training stress, your level of on-bike and strength train- ing, life stress, sleep quality, nutrition, and a number of other factors are incredibly unique. In a perfect world, I'd work with an athlete 1-on-1, where we would determine their intensity for each workout, exercise, and set. But even then, if they've been strength training for less than two years, we're going to use RPE (perceived exertion on a 1–10 scale).

WHAT ABOUT ADVANCED STRENGTH ATHLETES?

You may be thinking, "Using RPE is great for beginners, but what about cyclists who have been strength training year-round for 2+ years?"

For those of you who are a bit more advanced, and yes, even those of you who want to get more technological and scientific, I have a few words of wisdom: First and foremost, learn to listen to your body, not a number on a screen. The rewards are far reaching and will pay you in spades later down the line.

Not good enough for you? Okay, if you want to use a little technology to help you out, you can use tools like the "CNS Tap Test" app to help you measure your ner- vous system's readiness for the day. It's super simple, but it takes 2–4 weeks of using it on a daily basis (both right and left hands) at the same time of day—or at least at the same point in your warm-up—to help you figure out how "ready" your nervous system is.

If you get a lower score than your usual average, you're probably a bit under-re- covered or stressed. Dial down the weights a little, but keep the RPE the same as usual. The weights don't matter as much as the stress on the system does!

If you'd like to get a little more technological, you can use tools like a PUSH band, which gives you velocity measurements of the bar/dumbbell/kettlebell. This will help you see if you're putting out the forces you need to in order to get the results you need. However, don't just go out and purchase a PUSH band because it's mentioned here. Take time to learn how your body is moving, what the different RPEs feel like, and what your body is telling you day to day. For many, the addition of these tools comes far later down the road.

TOOLS VS. EQUIPMENT

It's important to understand the difference between tools and equipment, as equipment is 100% necessary, whereas tools help you dive deeper into things. For example, your bike is a piece of equipment. A power meter or heart rate monitor is a tool, allowing you to dig deeper into what you are actually doing on the bike.

When it comes to strength training, kettlebells, dumbbells, barbells, and bands are all equipment. Tools would include any kind of technology or device that you would use to help you better understand your abilities. So for many HVT athletes, their cell phone (and its ability to take videos of them lifting) is a tool.

WHAT RPES DO YOU WANT?

For 95% or more of strength training sessions, you want to walk out of the gym feeling like the day's workout as a whole was a 5, 6, or 7. You don't want to feel your legs or arms trembling or wonder if you'll be walking or falling up or down the stairs. You want to walk out of the gym feeling as though you've done some work but still have some left in the tank.

And you want to do that *consistently* 2–4 days a week, 365 days a year, for as many years as possible. Strength training is not like cycling, where there are quite a few intervals and even training sessions that are body-crushing 8, 9, and 10 (even those should be carefully added and monitored in your on-bike program).

Within each workout, RPE and intensity will vary widely from training block to training block. But as a general rule, keep in mind the following intensity (RPE) levels for each of the following types of training goals for different exercises.

TYPE OF STRENGTH TRAINED	RPE PER REPETITION
Explosive Strength	9–10 (explosiveness, NOT weight)*
Speed-Strength	9–10 (speed, NOT weight)**
Max Strength	8–10 (10 is RARE!)
Strength	5–7

*Explosive Strength = Weight is 20–30% e1RM but intensity is 9–10
**Speed-Strength = Load is 30–50% e1RM but speed is 9–10

These distinctions are absolutely key in ensuring that you're getting what you need out of each set and exercise. If you're working by RPE and feel that you're at a 10 as far as explosiveness, but in general you aren't "feeling it," lower the weight. The same goes for the speed squats.

Speed squats are generally done with a very light weight, usually 20-30% of your estimated one repetition maximum, and are done at the fastest speed you can do while keeping perfect technique. Moving at those fast speeds causes the exercise to *feel* like an RPE of 9-10, even though the weights are light.

This may seem somewhat contradictory, having a light weight feel hard, but this is where we get into the nuances a little bit. RPE is about *perceived* exertion, not a straight percentage of a measured maximum weight you can do for a lift. Training by RPE allows you to better dial in to what your body is capable of doing on that day, at that time, and in those conditions—something that is really important for athletes, especially when we are dealing with the nervous system.

With RPE, you can obtain your desired results while taking into account your daily condition. Feeling tired? Instead of loading the weight up to what you did last week, or what some spreadsheet says you have to do, put the weight on that *feels* appropriate for the desired RPE.

A great practice to get into is using your phone or a GoPro to record yourself from 90-degree angles (front, sides, or back) for exercises. The visual feedback will tell you how you are moving and help you learn and check technique. This plays into RPE-based training, as you'll be able to see if the RPE feels off because your technique is better or worse that day, also tipping you off to possible weaknesses and areas to improve on.

ARRANGING THE TRAINING WEEK

Now that we've discussed how to appropriately measure intensity for strength training, we can talk about how to arrange your training week to help you recover and be fresh for rides and races.

This is a big challenge for many beginners in strength training, as the soreness they encounter in the first few weeks can limit their on-bike riding. If you understand what we talk about next, you'll be able to take advantage of something powerlifters, Olympic lifters, and athletes of other sports have been doing for decades to help them gain higher levels of strength and performance.

THE 3 TYPES OF RIDING WORKOUTS

If you're not following some kind of structure for your riding, you may get stuck in your fitness and especially in your strength training. Many recreational riders who don't follow a plan don't think about how the riding they're doing affects their bodies (and minds), and thus are constantly playing a bit of Russian roulette with their abilities to recover and adapt.

Don't take this to mean that every rider should be on a highly structured training plan year-round. That would be disastrous to our sport on a number of levels. Rather, you should be mindful of the rides you are doing and the impact that they will have on your body and your ability to recover and adapt before your next riding or strength training session.

This process is actually really simple, as training sessions on the bike (conditioning) and with resistance training can be put into one of three categories:

RECOVERY	Very easy, breaking a light sweat, also called a "movement session"
STIMULATION	Just hard enough to feel a little tired immediately after, but great in the next 2 hours
DEVELOPMENT	Still feel it that night, and occasionally a little the next morning

When you look at your training sessions in this fashion it becomes much easier to understand the toll each training session takes on your body and mind—and what it will take to not only recover, but also adapt.

Remember to think about all 4 pillars of athletic success when it comes to the adaptation process:

1. Neuromuscular
2. Hormonal
3. Cardiorespiratory
4. Metabolic

The workouts from development day are going to affect the hormonal system, which means the recovery process is going to be different than if you are doing a stimulation training session.

TIME BETWEEN BIKE & STRENGTH TRAINING SESSIONS

Understanding how to categorize each of your training sessions allows you to get a firm handle on how much stress you've placed on the body and mind. Now comes the more challenging part: How much time in between sessions of the same kind of session?

When you understand the time needed between sessions of a similar load, it's relatively easy to build your training week—so long as you are smart about how you balance your training schedule.

TRAINING LOAD	TIME BETWEEN WORKOUTS OF SIMILAR LOAD	STRENGTH WORKOUT EXAMPLE	ON-BIKE WORK-OUT EXAMPLE	RIDE INTENSITY FACTOR & TSS*
Very Large (Development)	72 hr.	Max Strength session	Peak race, very competitive group ride, 40km TT	>0.85 IF 250+ TSS
Large (Development)	24–48 hr.	Explosive Strength focus, speed focus	Tuesday Night Worlds, 20km TT	0.85–1.15 IF 200–225 TSS
Medium (Stimulation)	12–24 hr.	Normal Strength session	75–90 min. Lactate Threshold workout	0.65–0.80 IF 150–200 TSS
Small (Recovery)	10–12 hr.	Movement session with 30% of your normal working weights for 2 x 15 each	Cafe ride, re-covery ride, 2 hr. pure endurance ride	<0.50 IF <125 TSS

*IMPORTANT: Power numbers for training zones must be recent +/- 8–12 weeks, either via Power Profile or Field Test

STRENGTH TRAINING PROGRAMMING: GETTING IT RIGHT

Everyone thinks that programming is so easy. You just take a few exercises for areas you want to target, put them together in a generally structured fashion, and BOOM! You have a strength program.

Many of the strength training programs for cyclists out there are so general that they fall short of the quality information athletes really need. Sadly, because *something* is better than nothing, and because there are some results accomplished from these programs, no one really questions them or asks if they can do better.

Programming for endurance sports, and specifically for cycling, can get incredibly complex and can be very challenging. The key is to make sure that you are providing the correct training stimulus at the right time while not making it too complex. If you can do that, you can build a highly potent training program. The movements should be challenging enough—meeting you where you are and offering the best option for your needs at that time. But you do *not* want to train everything all at once.

CONSISTENCY IS THE WINNING FORMULA

The biggest rule for all Strength & Conditioning Coaches is simple: Keep the money on the field. This means that our number one goal is to keep you injury-free, out there doing your sport or profession, and able to perform and train consistently from week to week, month to month, and year to year. To that end, it is crucial in this program that you not go to failure for any exercise, but rather, to *technical* failure. What I mean by that is you should stop the exercise or set at the point where you have lost the ability to execute the movement 100% technically correct.

Unfortunately, so many athletes (and the general public) go until repetition failure—they do as many repetitions as they can, which leads to "cheating," be it arching the back, bending the back, swinging the weight up, etc. Aside from opening you up to risk of injury, this does little to nothing for your overall fitness. And this is one of the many reasons why we *don't* perform a 1 repetition maximum

Exhaustion, soreness, and fatigue immediately after a session or the next day are not our goals. We want mostly 5, 6, and 7 for our perceived exertions.

for any of our major movements like the squat, deadlift, or bench press. Cyclists just don't develop the tissue qualities, and definitely not the movement qualities, necessary to deal with those kinds of forces while out on the bike.

As we get into programming and the actual exercises themselves, it is imperative that you pay attention to the technique and form with which you are executing the exercises. Poor focus leads to poor technique and poor technique leads to incorrect movement patterns. Progression in strength programming and your abilities does not come simply by just putting in the work or getting in your repetitions.

Progress in your strength and riding abilities comes from paying attention to technique and form, breathing and posture, and recovery and *adaptation* between sessions. Why the stress on adaptations? Because without them you're just tiring yourself out and not seeing any actual improvement. This is a trap many endurance athletes find themselves in, as they mistakenly believe that they're only progressing if they're tired after a session. You need to adapt to a given training stress, which requires quality sleep, sound nutrition, stress management, and enough recovery time in between training stresses to allow the desired changes to take place.

I have athletes whom I have been coaching for more than three years, and Bird-Dogs *still* make them sweat buckets and throw colorful language at me when they finish each set. These exercises are hard to execute correctly, and that is a big part of their potency.

PROGRAMMING STRENGTH TRAINING + RIDING SESSIONS

A bike training week for most cyclists often looks something like this:

MONDAY	Off or Recovery Ride
TUESDAY	Training Ride
WEDNESDAY	Off or Wednesday Night Worlds Race
THURSDAY	Training Ride
FRIDAY	Off or Short Sharpening Ride
SATURDAY	Race or Long Group Ride
SUNDAY	Race or Long Group Ride

Over my 10+ years of coaching cyclists, this template holds true about 70% of the time, and so we'll use it as our basic template for putting together the training week.

In order for us to plan out strength training, we need to follow the general rules of how soon after each type of training session we can return to training. Recovery and adaptation are the key drivers we base our planning around.

So let's take a look at a rider's training week on the bike. Here is a sample week from a cyclist we'll call Laurie. Laurie is in the middle of her Build period, which for most northern hemisphere riders will happen October–March.

DAY	RIDE	TRAINING RIDE TYPE
Monday	Off or Recovery Ride	Recovery
Tuesday	Training Ride	Development
Wednesday	Off	
Thursday	Training Ride	Stimulation
Friday	Off or Short Sharpening Ride	Off or Recovery
Saturday	Long Group Ride or Race	Stimulation or Development
Sunday	Long Group Ride	Stimulation

Women-specific training considerations are discussed in Chapter 4, a chapter dedicated to the subject since there is a lot to talk about. But for the sake of our sample here, we will say that she is in the first half of her menstrual cycle, called the luteal phase, which is a time when she is hormonally comparable to her male counterpart.

Laurie has a pretty busy-looking schedule, but overall she has a great balance to her training:

- at least 1 day completely off from training a week
- 1 development day
- 3–4 stimulation days

While she *could* do 2 development days in a week, due to her job (and life stress), she has found that keeping the really hard workouts to Tuesdays works really well for her.

Another way to look at Laurie's training week is as a bar graph. Notice the development training ride on Tuesday has the most intensity, following *after* her low-intensity recovery day on Monday. Her three stimulation rides later in the week are at a moderately high intensity.

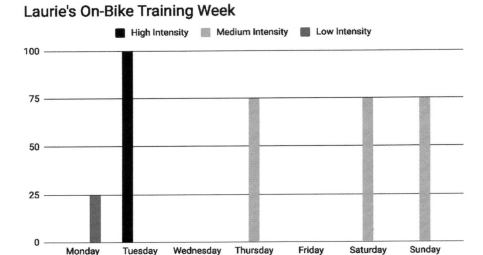

Laurie's On-Bike Training Week

It may look like a pretty packed training week, but it's possible we can actually get Laurie three strength training days in this week. The bar graph below shows how Laurie can add her three different strength sessions based on her riding sessions that week.

Monday = movement session

Tuesday = a solid development session, usually moderate loads, to get some good work done

Friday = a solid, short stimulation day to fire up the muscles and nervous system for the weekend or riding and racing

Wednesday is Laurie's recovery or "off" day from both riding and strength training in the week.

Depending on where in the season you are, the Friday workout will vary. During your Base and early Build periods on the bike (October—March for northern hemisphere road cyclists), Friday will usually be a Max Strength day. This is not necessarily ideal when it comes to powerlifting and for those who are looking to add more weight to the bar. But for our purposes, lifting heavy things on Friday in a short, focused session can have great results and really complement what you are doing on the bike.

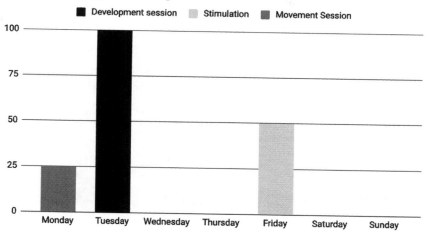

Laurie's Strength Training Week

■ Development session   ▨ Stimulation   ▨ Movement Session

Of course, adjust as needed. If you're planning back-to-back weekend rides that are going to push you to the limits on the bike, you will want to back down and make Friday a shorter stimulation workout, aiming for two working sets.

This may seem a little odd, but performing the strength training in this fashion actually makes for better results, by allowing the individual to perform one session in the morning and the other in the evening. Preferably, you would want to perform the bike in the morning during the summer high-volume riding season and the strength in the morning during the winter, but it doesn't matter so long as it is consistent.

Lifting on one side of the day and doing strength on the other allows you to increase the training stress, while affording a full day of rest each week. While this may seem counterintuitive, doing your strength training in this fashion allows your on-bike work to remain as the focus, while the strength training complements your riding. These two different kinds of training will complement each other based on the hormonal response to each stimulus.

While there needs to be more research done on this specific topic, you do want to have at least 6 hours in between the bike and the strength training so you don't retard adaptations from either strength or on-bike work.

Most important for the strength routine is consistency regarding the time of day when the session is performed. You can, and should, adapt the resistance used and training density to match where you are in the season and your perceived exertion.

There really is no one-size-fits-all way to organize a training week, as it is so incredibly individualized and really does come down to your ability to recover and adapt between sessions and your time available. If you're disappointed to hear this, don't worry. I'm going to give you some examples from the most common categories that riders tend to fall in. You'll be able to see how you can adjust your strength training period to meet these different situations.

RIDER #1: THE WORKING PROFESSIONAL

The working professional rider is also called the "time-crunched cyclist" (thanks to Chris Carmichael's book of the same name), and this group has a growing number of riders. These folks are serious about their cycling while professional at something else. Though busy and limited on time, they want the biggest return on their time training.

Usually working a job that requires 45–60 hours a week, these riders will benefit far more from workouts that are short, sweet, to the point, and which are easy to get done on a consistent basis. Some, but not all, of these riders have families or other social obligations that are important to them, and thus the time they carve out for the bike is precious and something they look forward to.

For the riders in this category who have no pre-existing pain, injuries, or issues on the bike, strength training will consist of 3–4 short, pointed strength training sessions a week, all tied to their bike training sessions.

The strength training sessions should be done either immediately before or immediately after their on-bike training, depending on the time they have. This will mean that during the Base period, they may decrease their total ride time by 10 minutes in order to get a 10–15 minute strength training session in.

The first objection that always comes up with this recommended decrease in riding is that it will mean less training, and thus less fitness. However, when strength training is done properly, the decrease in riding will help. When your riding sessions are shorter, you're able to push a little harder, or focus on recovering faster in between efforts, thus making you a more metabolically effective rider. It's the *quality* of the high-intensity sessions that will determine your long-term athletic progression, not the quantity. Joe Friel's book *Fast After 50* demonstrates this well, and while the target audience for that book is masters athletes, the principles do generally carry over to younger athletes as well.

However, there is a caveat. If you are training for long road rides or races or endurance MTB races where the actual event is over two hours long, you may only have two hours available of on-bike time a handful of times between now and your race. (For example, you may have eight rides in total that will be over two hours long over the three months leading up to your event.) In this case, *do not* chop off the 10–15 minutes for those specific training sessions. You'll need each and every one of those rides to help you dial in your specific adaptations and abilities to deal with those event demands.

That is why I'm not just teaching you strength training for cycling, but instead, *intelligent* strength training for cycling!

Now let's take a look at what the busy, working professional rider's weekly schedule looks like during Base and Peak periods, and how they could include strength training into their weekly training schedule:

Time Crunched Base

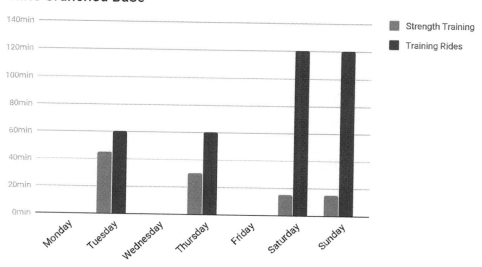

Due to the small amount of available time for the time-crunched rider, both strength and riding sessions are on the same days, with only one day (in this chart being Tuesday) needing a dedicated strength session and a dedicated on-bike session.

For a total of 100 minutes of work on Tuesday, the rider is able to get enough of a stimulus to allow them to perform a shorter strength session two days later (Thursday) alongside the bike, and two very short and focused workouts after the rides on the weekends (10–15 minutes).

While not ideal, it works well.

Time Crunched Peak

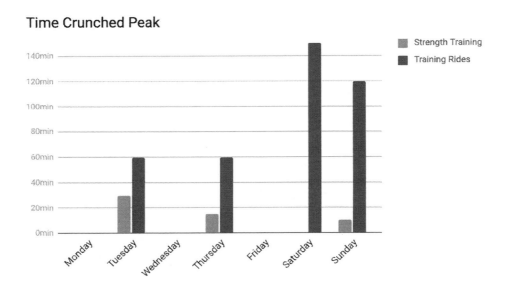

During the Peak time, the time-crunched rider will do similar training as they did in the Base period, but with shorter, more focused strength sessions, all separate from the bike. This will mean 2–4 dynamic warm-up exercises and 2 sets of 4–5 exercises that are planned out in a way that they can get the rest periods they need to get the results they want.

It would look something like this:

Dynamic Warm-up
1. Statue of Liberty
2. Side Lying Windmills
3. Side Planks
4. McGill Crunch

Main Set
A1. Double Kettlebell Hover Deadlift
A2. Bird Dogs
B1. 1-Arm Kettlebell Rows
B2. Inchworms

In this fashion, the rider is able to rest appropriately between rounds of a given exercise, while performing the complementary exercise, and then rest for 1–2 minutes after. In total, the program should take about 20 minutes to complete.

RIDER #2: THE SOCIAL CYCLIST

Much like the time-crunched rider, the social cyclist is usually working a job that requires 35–45 hours a week of their time. However, where these riders differ from their time-crunched cousins is in the important fact that their social life, and sometimes even family life, are built around the sport of cycling. They tend to have social lives that are heavily based on riding and training, and their friends, spouses, families, and significant others tend to be heavily involved in riding as well.

Due to the blending of other areas of their lives into their riding, these riders tend to have a bit more time per week to train, on average between 8–10 hours a week. While it might sound like for these riders it is easier to get strength training in due to the greater time availability, it's about a 50-50 split between those who find it easier to get in strength training and those who find it difficult to get it in due to how woven into their lives being on the bike is.

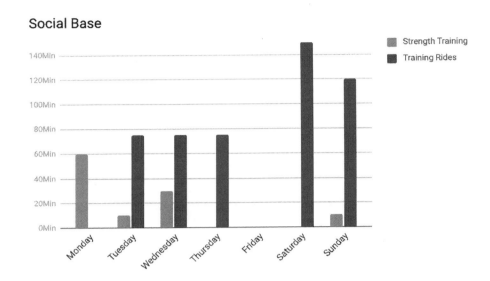

Social Base

For these riders, it can actually be a little bit tougher to get them to do off-bike train-ing. But they should aim for at least 1, if not 2, dedicated strength training sessions a week, along with 1–2 sessions a week immediately before or after their rides.

These charts show how the strength training and on-bike training can stack up during a week of the Base and Peak periods:

For the social rider's Base period, there is a fully dedicated day (Monday) to strength training right after the weekend of high-ride volume. This day will usu-ally be a Stimulation day, where they will work at lower loads and intensities but focus in on their major weaknesses and needs.

Tuesday, in this case, is a short movement session done immediately after the bike, focusing on movements that counteract the long hours in the saddle. Wednesday is the heavier, shorter, and much more focused strength session, at the opposite end of the day than the riding (either morning or evening).

Sunday's strength session is once again like Tuesday, in that it's immediately after the bike and focused on weaknesses in the rider and helping counteract the time on the bike.

Social Peak

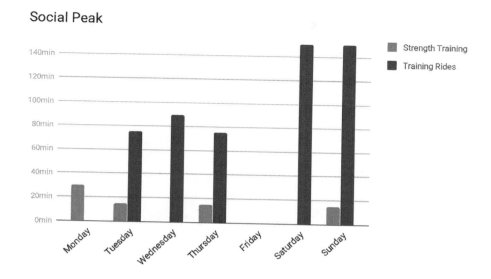

During the Peak time of year for the social rider, Monday's session is turned into a development day, but they are careful with the loads, instead focusing on great technique for all sets and repetitions.

Tuesday's and Thursday's sessions are post-ride, aiming at common areas of weakness or needs of the rider.

Sunday's strength is after the ride, focused on the 2–3 areas the rider needs more strength in, and this day will help prepare the rider for the following Monday's development day.

RIDER #3: THE PROFESSIONAL'S PROFESSIONAL

Also known as the "biking is life!" riders, these are the riders who are always on their bikes—rain, shine, snow, or sleet! They often log 14–18 hours of riding a week. Some will include their single-speed or commuter bike time to and from work in this total ride time, while others don't.

While these riders are often the hardest to sell on the benefits of taking some time off the bike to do strength training, they are almost always the staunchest allies of strength training for cyclists once they learn how easy it is to put it into their schedule, and how big the changes they feel and see out on the bike are!

As a coach, I don't have a *favorite* type of rider to work with, but I will say that the "professional's professionals" are some of the most fun to work with, as they are almost always thinking about how work from strength training ties into their riding, and vice versa. This comes from their deep passion for and love of the velo lifestyle, which is one of the reasons they are some of the hardest to convince to give it a shot, but once they do . . . look out! They tell *everyone* they talk to about how much more they are enjoying riding and how much they are getting out of it from this "thing called a kettlebell and a few giant rubber bands."

For these riders, the strength training program is almost always going to be highly personalized—to meet them where they are and to allow them to see and feel how easy and rewarding strength training can be.

Success takes consistency and understanding that there are some rules that can help you make it more likely to happen.

Because of their year-round, high-riding volume, these riders will fluctuate from having an "easy riding day" (oftentimes 1.5–2 hours!) with a dedicated 45–60 minute strength training session, to 2–4 times a week of 12–20 minute pre- or post-ride strength, all the way up to a fully dedicated 3–4 days a week of 60–75 minute strength training. But don't be fooled—on the biggest strength days, they commute to and from the weight room by bike!

After reading about these three common types of riders and how a strength training program can be adjusted for each, I hope you can now see why so many cyclists have avoided strength training—but didn't need to!

THE UNSPOKEN RULES TO SUCCESS IN TRAINING

Every single one of the athletes whom I have coached who has had massive success—whether in cycling, triathlon, running, basketball, or CrossFit—has possessed, or sought out, the unspoken rules to success.

Now, once you read the five rules below, you'll probably think to yourself, "That's it? Those are the unspoken keys to success?" Yet very few individuals possess all of them or practice them regularly. The good news is that they can be learned, and when practiced, they can become a regular, transformative part of your training.

RULE #1: CONSISTENCY

You MUST show up and do the work. Consistently.

Not a single athlete whom I have coached to great success has sought a magic pill to help them succeed. They show up ready to work every day. They don't let the minor aches and pains get them off track. They figure out how to train with or around the aches and pains safely, and they *listen* to what their body is telling them.

I can write (and have written) some of the best, most cutting-edge training programs out there, but because the athletes didn't consistently do the workouts as written—often because they wanted to do what their friends were doing, or "just ride"—the program went to waste, and they were disappointed in their results.

The bottom line is that you *must show up and train consistently* if you want to see the results you've been after.

RULE #2: FOCUS

You must learn how to focus and not get distracted.

In today's day and age, it's incredibly hard to focus. We are bombarded all day long by ringing cell phones, text messages, emails, etc. We have been slowly trained to be distracted by 3-minute or less YouTube videos, 15-second advertising clips, and a host of media and technology vying for our time.

Teach yourself to have laser-like focus. Before you start a workout, turn the cell phone off, or put it on airplane mode. Put your earphones in. All that should be on your mind is the exercise you're doing. No YouTube videos (unless for a short check on the exercise technique), no texting or messaging. You're here to work out, not converse.

RULE #3: ACCEPT REALITY

You can't be your best 365 days a year. Or even 30 days a year.

While it's important to be strong and to push, you have to both understand and accept the fact that you will *not* be able to put out your biggest numbers, or to lift your heaviest weights, over 95% of the year. Thankfully, in cycling this concept has gotten easier to explain to folks, as we now hear about racers having a "peak" or "prime" time of year, where for 7–14 days they are at their strongest.

Know this. Accept this. Expect this. That is why we re-test the energy systems' threshold abilities multiple times a year. That is why this program tells you to never miss a repetition. You must learn how to listen to your body and understand when to push and when to back off.

RULE #4: IT'S MORE REWARDING WITH A FRIEND

Having a training partner can be greatly overlooked, especially in cycling. Many beginners see cycling as an individual sport, unfortunately, but that's far from the truth. Having a regular training partner can not only help you get through tough training sessions, but it is also a great way to share lessons you've each learned and to help push each other. Perhaps one of the "secrets" to my coaching success is encouraging up-and-coming riders to ride with the more experienced, higher-level athletes whom I coach.

Work to find a riding and lifting partner with whom you can share the journey. They'll not only help you get going on the tough days, but they'll also help push you to better and higher efforts and successes.

RULE #5: DREAM BIG, ACT SMALL

This is perhaps the biggest thing most athletes who are starting out miss, specifically those who start in a sport after the age of 16: They don't dare to dream big.

Your aspirations should be big. Don't just dream of making it to the NBA; dream about being a *star* in the NBA.

Of course, you can't plan three steps ahead. If you have just begun riding a bike in the last three months, aiming to be a Cat 1 by the end of the year is too big a step. Start by setting realistic and attainable goals. Can you make the timeline ambitious? Sure . . . but set one!

Don't measure your future by your past. A new day begins again tomorrow morning. You're a new person in the morning. You're not the same person you were yesterday. You've learned new things and have a different view of the world now. Make the most out of every day!

Aim to get 1% better than the day before, *every single day*!

A WORD ON BODY COMPOSITION

So let's talk for a moment here about the elephant in the room. Triathletes, runners, and even cross-country skiers have bought into strength training to improve performance in sport. So why are *cyclists* so stubborn about strength training?

One of the biggest excuses that I hear coaches and athletes make for why they won't strength train is that they'll put on unnecessary weight. Here's my issue with that: Weight does not tell us anything but gravitational pull!

While professional cyclists will often complete the Grand Tours with an unhealthy percentage of body fat (they'll even admit it), far too many average cyclists have become completely obsessed with Watts per kg and their overall weight. If you're at all in the cycling community, you will easily be able to think of, off the top of your head, at least 10 friends who stay within 5–8 pounds of their peak riding or racing weight year-round.

That's just not healthy.

While it is systematically stressful to stay at your ideal "racing weight" year-round, not allowing yourself enough fluctuation *up* from that race weight can compromise your immune system, as well as hurt the body's ability to hold on to fat-soluble vitamins, which are so vital to performance and recovery. Oh, and let's not forget that the ability of the body to repair soft tissue damage is also bolstered by appropriate weight gain, which can be made up of fat, or muscle, depending on your needs. Additionally, it allows your body to maintain hormone levels.

Why am I talking about all this? Because so many cyclists like to blame weight gain on strength training, or they fear weight gain and cite it as the reason they won't include strength training. I'm here to tell you that most cyclists don't have a healthy handle on their weight throughout the year. Less is not always better.

Now, let me share a secret with you that I learned when I was competitively powerlifting and when I decided to toe the waters of natural (drug-free) bodybuilding: It's *hard* to put on muscle mass! It takes a concerted effort, a *lot* of calories, and a lot of hard, persistent work. Unless your genetics have programmed you to balloon up like Popeye after having a can of spinach, you will not gain pounds upon pounds of unwanted weight by strength training.

Going to the weight room will not only allow you to achieve better neuromuscular connection to your body (a cornerstone for all athletic performance), but it will also allow you to understand the principle that joint angle and position completely dictate muscle function.

Finding your ideal race weight is about performance and about having an ideal body composition and body fat percentage. This is specific to gender, sport demands, and lean BMI. To figure out what a solid ideal weight is for an athlete, you have to assess the athlete globally. Having the correct amount of muscle can help an athlete perform better, not worse—*if* it is done correctly.

A scale does not tell how much muscle mass you have. It does not tell if your movement patterns are solid, or if they are broken and compensated for. It does not tell if you are efficient at burning fats for fuel or carbohydrates.

If you spend the time in resistance training, teaching your body the best movement patterns and position on the bike, you *will* perform better! Not only that, but the common issues of lower back pain and neck pain that seem to be inevitable for all cyclists, may be completely avoided or at least decreased in severity.

1. Eric R. Helms, et al. "RPE vs. Percentage 1RM Loading in Periodized Programs Matched for Sets and Repetitions." *Frontiers in Physiology* March 21, 2018. doi: 10.3389/fphys.2018.00247.

2. Eric R. Helms, et al. "Self-Rated Accuracy of Rating of Perceived Exertion-Based Load Prescription in Powerlifters." *Journal of Strength & Conditioning Research* 31,10 (2017): 2,938–2,943.

CHAPTER 14 SUMMARY

- Planning your strength training around your bike training, as well as factoring in recovery and adaptations, are key to programming.

- Intensity for strength training is based off of the speed of the movement, the load of the movement, and the level of recruitment of the nervous system for the movement.

- Because cyclists are not focused on moving a heavy weight so much as increasing the ability to get stronger and more powerful on the bike, we use perceived exertion (RPE) to measure the intensity of each set, each exercise, and each training session.

- The three types of riding workouts you'll be doing along with your strength training are recovery, stimulation, and development.

- The key to programming is to provide the correct training stimulus at the right time while not making it too complex.

- It is important to only go to technical failure and not repetition (muscular) failure (doing as many reps as you can). Repetition failure will lead to poor form and the possibility of injuries.

CHAPTER 15
PUTTING TOGETHER A TRAINING PLAN

As we get into the specifics of building a strength training program that will improve your on-bike performance, you need to understand the difference between something that is effective and something that is optimal. This difference will have a very deep impact on your strength training and the improvements you may (or may not) see in your riding.

Over the last 10 years or so, much of the strength training in the world of cycling has been made up of the leg press, hamstring curls, leg extensions, squats, perhaps some deadlifts, and lots and lots of "core" (aka planks). While these strength exercises may be effective, they are incredibly far from optimal in the quest to improve your cycling performance. Certainly, those who go from doing zero strength training to adding a strength training program with these exercises will see some change in their abilities. But these exercises will not be nearly as impactful and performance-boosting as Pallof presses, kettlebell swings, and hands-on-hips jumps used in a more dialed-in, progression-based approach that lasts a full training year, like we have here in the Vortex Method.

As you progress through the training year—and remember that the Vortex Method is a full year-round approach to strength training—you'll go through at least four, if not five, stages of strength training development. Each stage builds on the previous stage, allowing you to build a solid foundation and see amazing progress in your strength *and* on-bike abilities from stage to stage, and from year to year.

While the FUNdamental 5+1 movements are the wire frame for everything you do, how you make use of each of them will change as you move through the training year:

- **Traditional strength** training exercises, such as the barbell deadlift from blocks, barbell bench press, and seated rows, will be used to develop your general strength.

- **Special strength** will be developed through exercises like the single-leg hip lift, hands-on-hips jumps, Heidens (lateral jumps), and slide board/sliders hamstring curls.

- **Specific strength** will be built by using on-bike specific intervals, cadences, and other sport-specific drills and skills, which the vast majority of riders skip out on because they find them difficult or scary.

Many riders are tempted to skip out on the order of progression from traditional strength to special strength to specific strength. These riders will always find that it catches up to them, nearly always at the worst possible time (i.e., three weeks before their big peak event), and it will cost them dearly.

Do not be this rider!

Those who follow the Vortex Method's carefully thought-out and planned progressions will be handsomely rewarded, not only with improved power and performance on the bike, but with better off-bike quality of living and the confidence to take on new sports and adventures. This could look like an intense game of tag or Capture the Flag with your kids or grandkids without fear of hurting your back, hips, knees, or shoulders due to poor strength and movement patterns.

THE STRUCTURE OF YOUR STRENGTH TRAINING PLAN

How you set up and organize each strength training session is one of the most important aspects of building your program, as each exercise will set the table for the next, allowing you to get stronger and improve your balance at the joint, posture, and breathing patterns. It is important to know that when doing the strength training program, there are different focuses for each part of the year, which will determine how much time and effort you should put into each part.

As mentioned in earlier chapters, the 6 parts of the Vortex Method strength training program are:

1. Soft Tissue Work
2. Breath Work

3. Dynamic Warm-up
4. Explosiveness/Power/Jumps (low repetitions, high power)
5. Strength & Correctives
6. Postural Challenge/Rotary Stability

Walk into nearly any gym, and you will certainly see folks stroll in from the locker room, do 1–2 sets with a light weight, and consider themselves warmed up. While something is better than nothing, a good warm-up prepares the body and mind to get the maximum results possible out of a session, as well as ensures the tissues and structures of the body are prepared for the upcoming efforts.

A warm-up should always go from general to specific. This could look like going from walking or lightly riding the bike for 5–8 minutes to then doing strength movements that utilize the muscles that will be working during the day's strength training session.

For your strength training warm-up, there are a few considerations to take into account:

1. **Time of Day:** This is important, because *when* you choose to train can determine whether you need a longer or shorter warm-up, or a more specific or general warm-up.

2. **Mental State:** Depending on where your head is when you enter the weight room, you want to make sure you're focusing on the task at hand and are able to safely and effectively train. This doesn't mean that every time you enter the weight room you shouldn't be thinking about other things in your life, but rather, that when it comes time to do a set, you are able to push all distractions out of your mind and focus on the task at hand, executing it safely.

3. **Ambient Temperature:** Depending on the time of year, you may walk into the weight room sweating buckets or shivering in your sweats. It is important to keep temperature and climate in mind, as your body will respond differently when you ask it to perform. Cold weather may take you longer to get warmed up and get things moving. With hot and humid weather, you may have trouble bringing your heart rate back down in between sets and may need longer rest periods.

Keep these items in mind as you head into your strength training session, as they can have a significant impact on your training.

WHY TIME OF DAY MATTERS

When it comes to strength training, time of day matters! While there is no best time of day to strength train, so long as you're consistent, there are special considerations that need to be made for morning vs. evening training sessions. Here are a few of the major considerations for morning and evening sessions:

Morning

- Intervertebral discs overfill while you sleep, requiring 1–2 hours to come back down to "normal" height. If you must strength train first thing in the morning, perform the Cow-Camel exercise for a set of 8–10 easy repetitions, as well as the McGill Big 3 (McGill Crunch, Side Plank with Top Leg Forward, and Bird-Dog) before each strength training session, and aim to be up and moving for at least 30 minutes before beginning, if possible.

- Your nervous system needs some time to get going. If possible, perform a dynamic warm-up that slowly ramps you up and has you feeling and moving well by the end.

Evening

- After sitting all day at the computer, your intervertebral discs have pushed the nucleus (center) towards the back. Take 1 minute to help set yourself up for strength and power, not pain, by standing tall, chin tucked, with your hands overhead. Take 3 deep breaths in through your nose, while reaching your hands straight up and keeping your chin tucked. Lift your chest with each breath by filling the ribs.

- Your nervous system and brain are a bit tired after sitting and working most of the day. Take an extra set of 5–10 repetitions (for Push-reach, Pull, Squat, and Hinge) with light to no weight to get a feel for the movement and to help you focus in on the task at hand, while learning what your body is or is not up for today.

GENERAL GUIDELINES FOR YOUR WARM-UP

If you are strength training first thing in the morning, it is a good idea to do a bit of a "general" warm-up: walking, elliptical, or bike riding for 5–10 minutes, at an easy to moderate pace, just enough to break a light sweat. This allows the body's core temperature to rise, and gives your mind and nervous system time to wake up.

Another very important consideration in the morning is to ensure that you are decreasing your risk of back injury, by taking the time to warm up the spinal muscles and encourage the decrease of the extra fluids that accumulate in the spine during sleep.[1]

There are some things you can do to help ensure your back is primed for exercise, not injury:

1. Try to get out of bed as soon as your alarm goes off.
2. Park a little farther away from the gym door, and walk a little more around the house.
3. Perform a slightly longer general warm-up before beginning strength training.
4. Move through cow-camels as part of your warm-up.

It is incredibly important to warm up the spine prior to loading it with any type of force, be it strength training, cycling, or rowing. You see, while we are sleeping, the body is replenishing the fluids contained in the discs of our spine—another reason to pay attention to your hydration—and due to the long day ahead that we have up and moving around, the body overfills the discs with more fluids than they may need. For the first hour or so after we get out of bed, the forces of gravity and our movements will slowly push out the excess fluids. This mechanism is one of the major contributing factors as to why rowers tend to have disc herniation, and why herniation of the spinal discs are referred to as "rowers disease."

Since many cyclists head out first thing in the morning, it is important to ensure that we gently encourage the fluids of the spine to drop down to "normal" levels. This can be accomplished by performing the cow-camel movement (demonstrated with a video in the bonus content section of the Human Vortex Training Website) 6–8 times though the full range of (pain-free) motion. There is no need to hold the end range of motion as you would for a stretch. You just need to gently go through the full range of motion of flexion and extension.

You'll notice in the workouts section in this chapter that the first 2–3 exercises tend to take more focus, starting with the breathing exercises, and then the progressive exercises that target "hot spots" within the body and muscles you may not use as much in your sport, but still need to work.

These intro exercises serve two purposes: 1) to wake up the nervous system and establish the mind-muscle connection, and 2) to allow you to activate the deeper and more supportive muscles so that you can begin to understand your body and how it works.

BEFORE YOU BEGIN

Now, before you dive into the programming, there are two final areas that we absolutely *must* address:

1. Make sure you are genuinely and generally healthy.
2. Understand the latest research in strength training and sports science.

GENUINE HEALTH: REGULAR PHYSICAL EXAMS

I often hear endurance athletes say that they don't need to see their physician for an annual physical (or even every other year). They think that just because they work out and train regularly, they don't need a routine checkup. A regular visit to the doctor is incredibly important, especially for the blood work and lipid profiles. Just because you *seem* fit, it doesn't mean that you are healthy in all areas.

An example of this involves a long-time rider who was in her 70s and who rode for over 20 years. She was seen by the cycling community as a prime example of what eating right, training well, and taking care of yourself should look like. Even though she was a healthy person and active, she had a heart attack and ended up having an emergency triple bypass. She has shared her journey publicly and warns athletes to not assume that participating in regular and consistent training means that you can or should skip out on annual checkups or stress tests. Just because an athlete can ride long or strong does not mean that they are healthy.

We all can fall into the trap of thinking there is nothing wrong with us because we look good for our age/sex/height or because we train and compete. But I'll let you in on a little secret: We're not invincible.

We joke about the teens and 20-somethings thinking they are invincible, but, truth be told, I think that the biggest offenders are the 30-, 40-, and 50-somethings who compete in endurance events and think they're healthy and ignore signs and symptoms happening to them because they exercise regularly and watch what they eat. Please, don't become obstinate and think that just because you finished an Ironman or an MS 150 ride at the front of the group, you are immune to the health demons.

You're an endurance athlete! You have chosen to spend long hours out on the road or trail, learning and pushing your body's limits. I urge you to take the time that you're on your bike and *listen* to your body. Feel your heart beating, hear your breathing, and pay attention to the incredible machine that is your body as you propel yourself through the seas of asphalt and trails.

And treat your body right. Everything you eat, the air you breathe, the hours you sleep, and the stressors in your life, *all* have an impact on your body. If you sense something is off, or even just for an annual exam, make sure that you see your physician for regular checkups.

THE GOOD AND BAD OF RESEARCH

We are still learning so much about the human body, how it performs and responds, how it interacts with its environment, and how we can influence these factors to progress performance. And in the last decade, we've been seeing some big knowledge gains in Strength & Conditioning coaches, which reflects in the performance of our athletes. Every single one of us is different. Research doesn't always account for our differences. It's heavily biased, there are very small homogenous samples, and there's not a lot of long-term research actually being done.

Now, this is not to say that the research being done is not important; it's vital to increase our understanding and progress our abilities as coaches and athletes. But research has its limitations.

When it comes to research articles, consider the population the studies are looking at and who is being used as test subjects. Usually, in sport performance, the research is done on college-aged male students (the easiest population to get to do testing), and non-elite cyclists. In order to truly understand the importance and the relevance of a research article, you must take a look at all of the information and determine if the research is strong enough to take seriously and incorporate into performance, recovery, or whatever realm it relates to. You'll also want to be able to understand if all, some, or only a handful of the participants had the desired outcome, or some kind of other outcome.

If you'd like to learn how to read and break down research articles to determine if their findings are actually useful, take a listen to episode 30 of my podcast *The Strong Savvy Cyclist & Triathlete*.

PROGRAMMING: IT'S EASY ... RIGHT?!

As we move into the programming section, keep in mind two important things:

1. **Functional training is relative.** What's functional for a gymnast (e.g., handstand push-ups) is not even *close* to being functional for a cyclist. After all, at what point in a cycling race or ride of any kind, would you need to be inverted and push yourself up away from the floor, face down? As far as I know, if you're in that position, you've done something *very* wrong!

2. **You need to train what's not being trained!** Meaning, you're already getting thousands of repetitions of some form of "lunges" or "squats" on the bike ... so instead of doing more of those, let's train you on moving side to side, pulling and pressing, to help keep your joints in great positions so that the muscle can work as designed.

This is exactly why practicing the skill of riding, cornering, braking, climbing, and sprinting are so absolutely integral in making the most out of your strength training. Yes, you need to get more stable, stronger, and able to control and produce forces. But developing the ability to stiffen the entire body to pick up a heavy bar or squat a lot of weight does next to no good if you don't learn how to turn that over into usable strength on the bike.

Addressing these two issues will help guide you through the programming section and set you up for successful training.

Now, a word of warning, per Murphy's Laws of Combat: "No plan survives the first contact intact."[2] Meaning, you can plan out a fantastic strength program on paper, only to find that either it's too much for you to handle or the logistics of the gym or limitations of your home equipment make it hard or impossible to perform.

The best strength training program is the one that gets done consistently. Should it address your weaknesses and deficits? Absolutely. But if it doesn't get done consistently, it doesn't matter.

As you move through this section, realize that just as with everything in life and especially with training, we tend to do the things that we like and are good at, and we neglect the areas that we are weakest in or that need the most work. Embrace your weak areas. These are your areas of prime growth!

Some of the exercises look extremely easy, but they may be near impossible to execute *properly*, if at all. Don't give up. Recognize that there is something limiting you, and work to figure it out. The areas you need to grow in are the ones in which you will experience the most resistance.

As we get into each part of the strength training program and the different exercises, know that every single exercise written below, or in the sample training plans in the back of the book, has a video available for you to watch at www.HumanVortextraining.com. If you go to the "Book Bonus Content" section and enter the password "THEVORTEXTRIBE" you will have access to dozens of instructional videos.

HOW TO READ THE SAMPLE TRAINING PLANS

Understanding how to read your training plan is just as important as performing the exercises correctly. Here is an example of the first four weeks of a plan:

	WEEK 1	WEEK 2	WEEK 3	WEEK 4
A1. 3-1-3-1 Tempo Goblet Squats	2*8	3*8	3*10	3*10-12
A2. Hip Lifts	2*15	2*15	2*18	2*20
B1. KB Deadlift from Box	3*8	3*8	3*10-12	3*10-15
B2. Side-Lying Windmills	3*5 ea	3*5 ea	3*5 ea	3*5 ea
C1. TRX Rows	2*8	2*10	3*10	3*10-15
C2. Wall Scapular Slides	2*6-8	2*6-8	3*6-8	3*8-10
D1. Side Planks	3*20" ea	3*20" ea	3*30" ea	3*40" ea
D2. Max Effort Front Planks	3*(3*5" on, 3" off)	3*(3*5" on, 3" off)	3*(4*5" on, 3" off)	3*(5*5" on, 3" off)
D3. Bird Dogs, Level 1	2*5-7 ea	2*5-7 ea	2*6-8 ea	2*8-10 ea

For this workout's main segment, which comes after soft tissue work and the dynamic warm-up, we have three pairs of exercises (A1/A2, B1/B2, C1/C2), and one trio (D1/D2/D3). The letters A, B, C, and D indicate the order of the workout. The A pair is to be done first, B next, etc.

Next to each letter is a number. This indicates which exercise should be done first, which second, and which third. When you're performing the exercises, for example "A1. 3-1-3-1 Tempo Goblet Squats" and "A2. Hip Lifts," there should be as little time between exercises as possible. You should finish one set of the A1 exercise, and then move immediately to A2 and complete one set.

In the week columns, you'll see the number of sets and repetitions, which tells you how many sets of each exercise to perform, and how many repetitions per set. For example, "2*8" means you would do 2 sets of the exercise, with 8 repetitions per set.

Rest for the appropriate amount of time between sets. For example, during the hypertrophy phase, you would wait 2–4 minutes between sets. Once the appropriate time has passed, return to A1 and complete one set, then move immediately to A2, and complete another set there. Then rest the appropriate amount of time between sets.

Repeat until all sets are completed for A1 and A2, then move on to the B exercises, completing in the same fashion, and continue in this way for the entire workout.

HOW TO READ TEMPO

Some exercises include tempo instructions, for example, "A1. 3-1-3-1 Tempo Goblet Squats."

In this case you would lower over 3 seconds, hold the bottom position for 1 second (keeping tension), then slowly raise over 3 seconds, and then rest at the top for 1 second. That is one repetition. For more details on tempo, refer to Chapter 11.

HOW TO READ ONE-SIDED EXERCISES

Some exercises require you to work one side of the body and then the other side. For example, "B2. Side-Lying Windmills" has 3 sets of 5 repetitions each (3*5 ea). This means that for one set you'll complete 5 repetitions on one side of the body, and then switch to the other side where you'll do another 5 repetitions. Do this for all 3 sets.

HOW TO READ EXERCISES WITH HOLD AND RELAX

Some exercises require you to hold a position and then relax. In the sample above, exercise "D2. Max Effort Front Planks" has these instructions: 3*(3*5" on, 3" off).

This means that you'll do 3 sets of the exercise, with each set having 3 repetitions of a 5-second hold ("on") and 3 seconds relaxed ("off").

1. Soft Tissue Work

Whether you use a foam roller, a lacrosse ball, or other trigger point therapy for your soft tissue work, be sure to spend 3–5 minutes on the high target areas.

Foam Roller

Foam Roll (20–30 seconds each)

TFL / Lateral side of thigh

How to do it: Start with the foam roller on one hip, with the bone of the front of the hip being on top of the roller. Place your elbow on the floor to help you keep stable. Roll up and down, keeping the roller on the front-outside of your hip, only on the upper third of your upper leg.

Quads

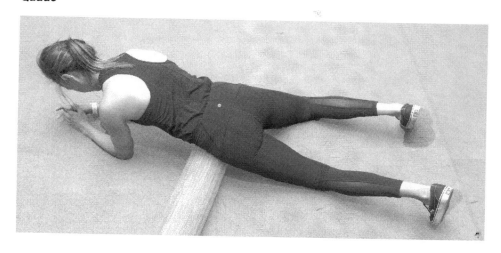

How to do it: This is a one-leg drill. Start with the inside end of the foam roller just under your crotch, with the roller perpendicular to your leg (90-degree angle). Place both elbows under your shoulders and set up in a plank position, with your opposite knee supporting some weight on the floor. Keeping a perfect plank position, pull yourself up towards your head, keeping your spine and hips straight. Do not lift your hips up in the air. Instead roll in 3–5 inch segments, and then walk your elbows further forward, allowing the foam roller to move lower down your upper leg.

Adductors / Medial side of thigh

How to do it: Set up in a front plank position. Take one foot out to the side, and turn the foot so the toes are pointing out. Place the foam roller at a 90-degree angle on the inner thigh, just below your crotch. Support your upper body with your elbows in a plank position, and use the opposite foot to help you roll up and down the inner thigh, keeping the leg at a 30–45 degree angle out to the side of your body.

See how to do it on the Human Vortex YouTube channel.

Thoracic Spine Extension

How to do it: Start with the foam roller perpendicular to your torso on the floor. Place the foam roller at the bottom of your shoulder blades. Lace your fingers together, and place your hands on the back of your head, allowing your chin to tuck and the hands to support the weight of your head. Gently squeeze your ears with your upper arms, pointing your elbows forward. Keeping your butt on the ground, take a deep breath in through your nose, filling your ribs completely. Slowly let air out through your mouth, slowly relaxing your upper body backwards, using the weight of your head in your hands. Keep your butt on the floor.

Pecs

How to do it: Lie on the floor on your stomach. Take the foam roller and place it at a 45-degree angle under the front of your shoulder. Keep your arm relaxed, and hand on the floor, with your elbow straight. Use your opposite hand to slowly move your body backwards and forwards in 2–4 inch movements, allowing the chest (front of your shoulder) to be released.

Lats

How to do it: Place the foam roller on the floor perpendicular to your upper body. Lie on your side over the foam roller, with the middle of the foam roller right in your armpit. While keeping the arm straight, use your feet or other hand to gently roll up on the foam roller, keeping it on your side. You may need to roll your upper body forward and backwards to get the correct spot.

See how to do it on the Human Vortex YouTube channel.

Lacrosse or Tennis Ball

Foot

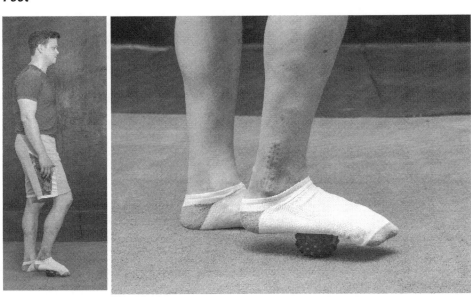

How to do it: Stand barefoot with a tennis ball or lacrosse ball in between your feet. Lift one leg up, and stop on top of the ball so that the ball is at the base of your big toe, just barely in the arch of your foot. Push down on the ball with about 5–10 pounds (2.5–5kg) of pressure, or until you feel a *gentle* pressure on the arch where the ball is. Gently roll the ball back towards your heel, and then forwards. Do not cause any pain. These muscles are small and relatively sensitive!

Calves

How to do it: Sit on the floor with your feet straight ahead. Place the lacrosse ball on the upper outside part of your calf, just below the knee. Push down into the ground with 5–10 pounds (2.5–5kg) of force from your glutes, while using your arms to support your upper body, and roll side to side, as well as forward and back. Work your way down your calf muscle for over 20 seconds on each side, and then return to any hot spots for 10 seconds.

Buttock

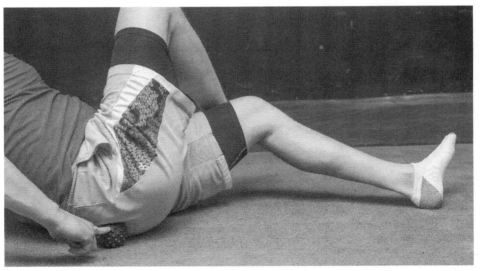

How to do it: Sit on the floor with your legs straight in front of you. Place the lacrosse ball just behind the bone on one buttock. Take the same side ankle, and place it on the opposite knee, keeping both hands behind you on the floor with elbows straight. Place as little weight as you need on the ball to feel the trigger point. Slowly move your hips right to left to hit the piriformis.

2. Breath Work

For breath work, remember the rib cage and pelvis need to be stacked up. You don't want to have them positioned like scissors. The diaphragm is directly over the pelvic floor, which will allow you to create great intra-abdominal pressure. This will allow the pelvic floor and the muscles to work together as they need to, and you'll have more muscles available to put power on the bike, as well as to squat, hinge, push, pull, press, and provide rotary stability.

Breathing patterns should not be skipped. They are an incredibly important part of the strength training regimen. Their power comes from doing them consistently and tapping you into the different positions and postures that you tend to carry. They also teach you how to bring your heart rate down and relax the body as you prepare for or recover from a hard effort.

We begin each session with a single breathing exercise, focused on getting 360-degree breaths. This means breathing in deeply through the nose and getting the air to enter into the mid-back and lower back. These areas are often tight and closed down, and simply getting air into these regions (or thinking about it) can help activate and open muscles that have become shortened and shut down.

- Each breath should take between 3–5 seconds.
- Inhale through the nose.
- Hold for 2–4 seconds.
- Exhale through your mouth (and from the bottom of your stomach up) 4–6 seconds, pushing all the air out.

BREATH WORK

Crocodile Breathing

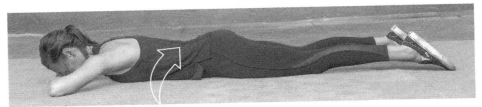

Belly and low back sinking into floor, shoulders relaxed

Breathing into mid and lower back, low back expanding, shoulders relaxed

Muscle Focus: Diaphragm, intercostals

Equipment: None

How to do it: Lie down on your stomach with your toes pointed behind you, ankles resting on the ground. Place your hands flat, one on top of the other, underneath your forehead, making sure to keep your neck neutral. Your eyes should be looking straight down at the ground. Relax your shoulders, and let your elbows come out to the side, away from your ears. Keep your shoulder blades relaxed, but back and down. Take a long, slow inhale through your nose for 3–5 seconds, while thinking about relaxing your hips and bringing that air into the area between your shoulder blades, into your lower back, and your sides. Hold your breath for 2–4 seconds, feeling the middle of your back and lower back open up, and your neck and shoulder relax. Breathe out through your mouth for 5 seconds.

Sphynx Breathing

BREATH WORK

Muscle Focus: Diaphragm, intercostals

Equipment: None

How to do it: This exercise is covered in Chapter 9 in full detail, including the 3 levels.

For level 3: Lie on your stomach on the floor, with your upper body supported on your forearms, as though you are riding a bike, except now think about keeping your shoulder blades back and down, but relaxed. While breathing in through your nose, think about the shoulder blades as floating on the rib cage, relaxed and able to move forward and back as your ribs inflate up and out with air. Breathe in, trying to fill the sides of your ribs, as well as the area right in between your shoulder blades, with air.

Level 3 of the Sphynx Breathing exercise should be pain free. If it is not, move back to level 1 or 2, as discussed in the breathing chapter.

3. Dynamic Warm-up

While each part of the workout has a role in your development, the dynamic warm-up is especially important, since it is where you will be addressing your muscular imbalances and movement challenges on a consistent basis.

When putting together your dynamic warm up, keep it relatively short and focused, with a total of 4–6 exercises.

- If you are doing 2 strength training days a week, you will use 1 dynamic warm-up routine on both days, as both days will be full-body workouts of some kind.

- If you are doing 3–5 strength training sessions a week, not including movement sessions, you will want to build 2 dynamic warm-ups: 1 warm-up for the upper-body focused days, and 1 for the lower-body focused days.

Dynamic warm-ups will change much less frequently than strength training programs. In the dynamic warm-ups, you are trying to get better mind-muscle connection, as well as build up the muscles, movements, and postures for strength-endurance.

If you struggle with a specific exercise, start off with 1–2 sets of 3–5 repetitions. This will allow you to focus on building high-quality repetitions. Then, as you gain better strength and control, you can move up to 1 set of 8–12 repetitions, and then up to a single set of 15–20 repetitions.

This progression should happen over the course of 2–4 months and should be done slowly. There is little to nothing to be gained by rushing to get your reps in. Mind-muscle connection and correct movement with appropriate stability and stiffness are what we are after here.

When moving through your dynamic warm-up, give it your full attention. These exercises should be done with focus and intent, allowing you to quickly build strength, stiffness, and stability appropriately. If you are moving through the exercises and barely breaking a sweat, you're not doing them properly.

Professional athletes and riders who go through these warm-ups with me in 1-on-1 sessions are often "getting into the zone," and they find that by the time they are done with the dynamic warm-up they've broken a light sweat and are aware of that day's capabilities.

Sample Dynamic Warm-up

Crocodile Breathing: 5 breaths

Side-Lying Windmill: 5 each side

Sofa Stretch: 20 sec. each

Side-Lying Straight Leg Lift: 10 each side

Hip Lifts: 20

McGill Crunches: 1*6 hold 3–5 sec. each

Side Planks, top leg forward: 30 sec. each side

Bird Dog (variation): 8 each side

DYNAMIC WARM-UP

HIP EXERCISES

Side-Lying Straight Leg Lifts

Muscle Focus: Gluteus medius/minimus complex, obliques, transverse abdominis

Equipment: None

How to do it: Lie on your side, with your bottom arm supporting your head in a neutral position. Bend your bottom knee and bring the leg forward so that you are balanced. Straighten the top leg, and brace your midsection, making sure your hips are vertical. Use *only* your glute medius (you can feel it on the back outside of your butt) to lift the top leg. Only go as high as you can while maintaining zero movement from the midsection. Slowly lower the leg and repeat until all repetitions are done, and then switch sides.

Hip Lifts

Muscle Focus: Gluteus maximus, obliques, transverse abdominis, quadratus lumborum

Equipment: None

How to do it: Lie on your back, bending your knees and bringing your feet about halfway towards your butt, where your feet can be flat on the floor. Relax your head and neck back onto the floor, keeping your eyes straight ahead. Brace your midsection slightly. Then use *only* the glutes to slowly hinge your hips off the floor, going only as high as you can get the movement from your glutes without the hamstrings. Squeeze the glutes at the top for 2–3 seconds, and then slowly lower the hips back to the ground, keeping an appropriate brace in your midsection.

Clamshells

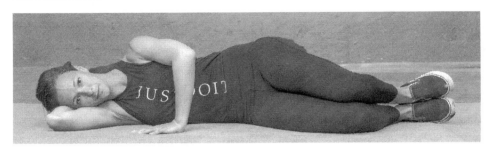

Muscle Focus: Gluteus medius/minimus complex, obliques, transverse abdominis

Equipment: None

How to do it: Lie on your side, with your bottom arm supporting your head in a neutral position. Bend both knees and bring the legs forward so that you are balanced. This is called the "side-lying hook position." Brace your midsection, making sure your hips are vertical. Use *only* your glute medius to lift the top knee away from the bottom knee. Only go as high as you can while maintaining zero movement from the midsection. Slowly lower the leg and repeat until all repetitions are done, and then switch sides.

DYNAMIC WARM-UP

Bird Dog

Muscle Focus: Gluteus maximus, obliques, transverse abdominis, quadratus lumborum, lats, serratus anterior, pectoralis major

Equipment: None

How to do it: The Bird Dog, or "All-4's Arm Opposite Leg" exercise is one of the most poorly taught and poorly performed exercises out there. The focus of this exercise is to maintain a stable spine in line with the hips, while getting movement from the shoulder and hips only.

Begin by putting the hands directly under the shoulders (90-degree angle), and the knees directly under the hips (90-degree angle). Keep your chin tucked and spine neutral. Brace your midsection, and carefully lift your hand and opposite knee off the floor. Moving from only the hip and shoulder, bring the hand overhead, and extend the leg back (glute only). Pause at the end of your range of motion, squeezing the glute and mid-back of the working arm and leg. Slowly return the hand and knee to their starting point, keeping your abs appropriately braced, and not letting anything else move. Repeat until all repetitions on that side are finished, and then rest and switch sides.

There are 3 levels to the Bird Dog, each needing to be mastered before moving on to the top level.

To see a complete tutorial on this exercise and its different levels of progression, visit the HVTraining YouTube Channel.

Half Clamshells

Muscle Focus: Gluteus medius/minimus complex, obliques, transverse abdominis

Equipment: None

How to do it: Lie on your side, with your bottom arm supporting your head in a neutral position. Bend your top knee and bring the leg forward so that you are balanced. Roll the whole body forward until the top knee is touching the ground. Brace your midsection, making sure your hips and ribs stay at a 45-degree angle to the ground. Use *only* your glute medius to lift the top knee off the ground, as you work to brace your midsection. Only go as high as you can while maintaining zero movement from the midsection. Slowly lower the knee while keeping the midsection braced, and repeat until all repetitions are done, and then switch sides.

Statue of Liberty

Front View   Side View

Muscle Focus: Rectus abdominis, glutes, rhomboids, lower and mid trapezius, deltoid

Equipment: None

How to do it: This dynamic warm-up exercise tends to be very challenging for cyclists. Take your time, and if it is difficult to hold your opposite foot, move to the Sofa Stretch instead.

Start by taking 3 regular steps forward. On the fourth step, reach back with your right arm while you bring your left foot up and across behind you. Once you have the foot in hand, brace your midsection, keep your eyes looking forward and slightly up, and stand as tall as you can, while keeping the abs braced, ribs down, and chin tucked. If you have the balance to, reach the opposite hand up overhead, using your mid-back muscles. Hold the top position while maintaining balance for 2–3 seconds and while firing your glutes. Let go of the foot, walk forward 3 steps, and continue until you've completed all the repetitions.

Lion King

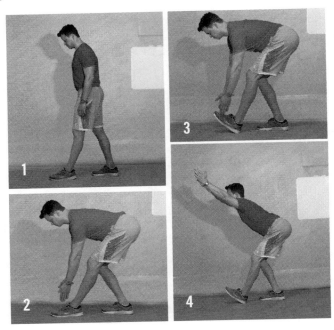

Muscle Focus: Active lengthening of hamstring, active firing of erector spinae, mid and lower trapezius

Equipment: None

How to do it: While hamstring stretching can decrease your performance, taking the hamstrings through an active range of motion while firing other muscles on the back of your body can help ready your body for performance.

Take 3 normal steps forward. On the third step, stop, push your hips back in a hinge while straightening your front knee. Your thighs should be even as you hinge. Lift the front foot's toes up, as you hinge and reach down towards your foot. Use both hands and brush your fingertips from both fingers on your front shoe. (If you cannot reach that far, just go through the range of motion you have.) Take a deep breath in while in this position, then as you breathe out, lift your arms up in front of you, lifting your shoulders up and back from your mid-back, until your upper body is in a "riding position." Hold the hands high overhead as you finish your breath out, feeling your mid-back working. Relax your hands down to your sides and continue until all repetitions are done.

Side Lunge Hands Overhead

Front View

Side View

Muscle Focus: Active lengthening of adductors, active firing of glutes, erector spinae, mid and lower trapezius

Equipment: None

How to do it: Start from a standing position. Take a medium-size step to your left side. As you plant your foot into the ground, slowly begin to push your left hip *out* and away from your right leg. You want to get your hip behind the outside knee, as pictured below. Keeping your abs braced, and feeling your inner thigh gently stretch and your left glute firing, slowly raise your hands in front and then overhead, using your mid-back muscles. Hold in this position for 1 deep breath in through your nose. As you begin to breathe out through your mouth, push hard off of your left foot to return to the starting position. Alternate sides until all repetitions are finished.

DYNAMIC WARM-UP

Sofa Stretch

Front View

Side View

Muscle Focus: Active lengthening of quadriceps, active firing of glutes, erector spinae, transverse abdominis, rectus abdominis, internal and external obliques

Equipment: A bench or seat. You may want a cushion or towel for under your knee.

How to do it: Find a seat, bench, or sofa that is at a height that you can rest your foot on and still rest your knee on the ground. You may want a pillow or towel for under your back knee. Resting the top of your foot on the sofa, take your opposite leg forward, and slowly lunge down, until your rear knee is resting on the floor. Brace your midsection, tuck your chin back, and fire the glute on the back leg. Slowly bring your hips forward until you feel a very light stretch while you are able to fire your glute. Hold this position for 3 deep breaths in through your nose, out through your mouth. You want to be in a straight line from your ear to your hip to your back shoulder. For many cyclists this will take time! Do not push into this stretch to really feel it. You want a gentle stretch along with glute activation and your whole abdominal hoop working, with your chin tucked, and great breathing patterns.

CORE STABILITY/BRACING EXERCISES

Side Planks, Top Leg Forward

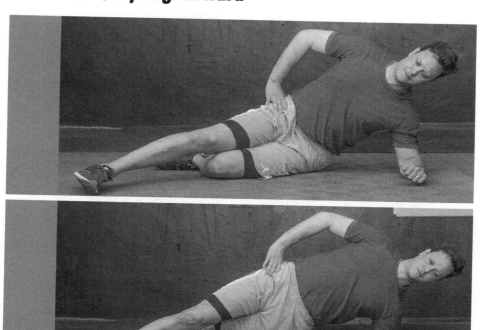

Muscle Focus: Obliques, quadratus lumborum, transverse abdominis, adductors, gluteus medius/minimus, rhomboids, serratus anterior

Equipment: None

How to do it: Start on the floor on your side, with the same side's forearm resting on the floor. Take your shoulder blade down away from your ear and forward just a little. Brace your midsection, and take your top foot forward around 12 inches (~30cm). Lift your hips up and away from the ground, and push your hips slightly forward until you feel that you have a straight line from your back leg's ankle, knee, hip, shoulder, to your ear. Make sure you're keeping your ribs down and abs braced. Hold this position for the prescribed amount of time.

McGill Crunch

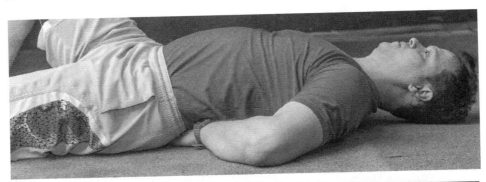

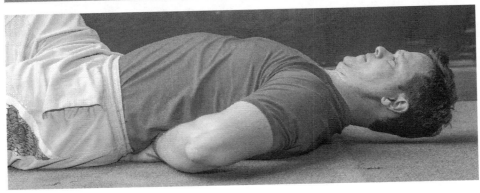

Muscle Focus: Transverse abdominis, obliques (internal and external)

Equipment: None

How to do it: This exercise is very detail-oriented. Please visit the Human Vortex Training YouTube Channel "HVTraining" to see and hear the instructions.

SHOULDER/UPPER TORSO EXERCISES

Reach, Roll, Lift

Muscle Focus: Transverse abdominis, obliques (internal and external), quadratus lumborum, mid and lower trapezius, rotator cuff

Equipment: None

How to do it: Begin on the floor in a squatting position, with your knees, elbows, and forearms resting on the floor. Tuck your chin back, with your eyes down, and brace your midsection lightly. Your back should be straight. With your palms facing down, slowly slide your left hand forward and slightly out to the side, pushing the hand on the ground using your middle back. When the hand is as far out as you can go while keeping your shoulders relaxed and back straight, turn the hand over, while keeping the outside of the pinky finger touching the ground the whole time. When the palm is facing up as far as you can manage while keeping the shoulder relaxed, brace your midsection a little more, and lift the hand off the ground using the muscles in your mid and lower back *only*. Slowly lower the hand back to the ground, turn the hand back palm down, and slowly return the arm to the starting position. Alternate sides until all repetitions are done.

DYNAMIC WARM-UP

Side-Lying Windmill

Muscle Focus: Latissimus dorsi, pectoralis major and minor, intercostals, breathing

Equipment: None

How to do it: This exercise is used to connect breathing with the release of the lats, glutes, and lower back, while opening the chest. This movement is extremely challenging for many cyclists. If you feel any sharp pain or stabbing, stop this movement immediately and move on to something else, such as the Foam Roller Y stretch.

Begin by lying on the floor in the side-lying hook position, with your arms straight, hands together in front of you. Begin by slowly sliding the top hand forward on the ground, keeping your hips vertical and getting the movement from your rib cage. Take a deep breath in through your nose. As you begin to slowly exhale, drag your fingertips on the ground up and overhead, keeping your eyes on the hand that is moving the whole time. Most riders will "get stuck" at step #3 as pictured below. Reach your hand up as far as you can, and take another deep breath in through your nose. As you begin to slowly breathe out, try to continue moving the hand overhead and behind you, rotating open from your midsection, until the arm is opened opposite of where you started. Take a deep breath in through your nose, and as you breathe out, bring the hand back to the starting position by lifting it off the ground and clapping your hands together. Finish all repetitions on one side, then switch sides.

Foam Roller Y

Muscle Focus: Pectoralis major and minor, latissimus dorsi, intercostals, breathing

Equipment: 1-meter or 3-foot long foam roller

How to do it: Start by lying on your back on the foam roller, with the roller parallel to your spine. Put your feet flat on the ground, with a soft bend in your knees. Brace your abs until you get all of your spine touching the

foam roller (or as much of it as you can, including your lower back) by using only your abs. Put your hands out straight in front of you, elbows straight. Take a deep breath in through your nose, and slowly lower the arms up and out slightly overhead in a "Y" position. Go as far down as you can, keeping your chest and arms relaxed.

Many cyclists find this very challenging and even painful in their shoulders. If this happens to you, use something like a sofa, chair, bed, or even a pillow above your head, to allow you to relax the arms overhead through the range of motion you have. Hold for either the number of breaths or length of time as prescribed, then return to the starting position the same way you came.

Wall Scapular Slides

Muscle Focus: Rhomboids, mid and lower trapezius, posterior deltoid, transverse abdominis, rectus abdominis, adductors

Equipment: None

Front View   Side View

How to do it: Stand with your feet together and heels around 6–8 inches (15–20cm) away from a wall. Lean back against the wall with your hips, with your shoulders touching the wall. Bend your knees slightly until you feel your weight a little more in your heels than your midfoot. Slightly brace your abs to bring your ribs down and pelvis forward, so that the space between the wall and your lower back doesn't exist. This is difficult for many cyclists, so just do the best you can. Put your arms up and back against the wall in a 90-degree angle at the shoulder and hip. Keep your abs braced, and try to keep your whole spine and the back of your head against the wall, as you slide your forearms up the wall. Take your time, and do not let any of your back come away from the wall. When you get to the point where you cannot keep your back flat, or it wants to pop away from the wall, pause, push the forearms, spine, and head against the wall for 2 seconds. Then slowly return to the starting position.

DYNAMIC MOVEMENT FOR JUMPING & EXPLOSIVENESS

A-March

Focus: Improve foot speed

Equipment: None

How to do it: Standing tall, take your right knee up and forward, bringing your left arm forward at the same time. Keep perfect posture, and be sure to move the opposite side arm along with the leg. Bring your knee high, keeping the knee fully flexed, at least to 90 degrees with great posture, and keeping the toes up and angle-flexed. When the front knee is at the highest point, your standing leg should be straight, glute fired. March using great posture and arm movement.

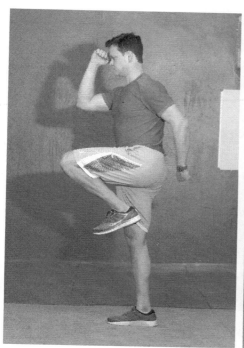 

Super Marios

Focus: Improve hip extension, learn appropriate stiffness in ankle, gain strength in hip flexion with better posture and head position

Equipment: None

How to do it: This exercise uses the same movements as the A-March above, but for Super Marios, you are skipping. Keep the same positions and postures as the A-March, with your foot strike being quiet but with explosive power. Focus on keeping the ankle firm but still, and use the glutes to get hip extension.

Agility Ladder

Focus: Mind-muscle connection, better timing and position for leg turnover

Equipment: Agility ladder, or chalk on the ground

How to do it: Run down an agility ladder (spacing of 46cm or 18 inches apart) as quickly as possible, making sure both feet touch down in between each rung. Focus on high knees and short, quick contact with the ground. These are very challenging for cyclists, but they allow you to really get a better connection with your posture, feet, and knees for more powerful pedaling.

There are a number of variations you can do. A few of them are available to watch in the bonus section for the book on the HVT website. Use the password THEVOR-TEXTRIBE to log in.

Cone Figure 8

Focus: Improve reaction time, train lateral coordinated movement you don't get in your sport, develop more balanced hip movements

Equipment: Cones

How to do it: Put two cones 5 yards (4.5m) apart. Start in the middle of the cones in a quarter-squat position (aka "ready" position) with your feet shoulder-width apart. Keeping your eyes looking forward and your shoulders facing forward, laterally shuffle your way behind and around the first cone, taking a big step forward. Then shuffle from in front of that cone to behind the second cone.

Please visit the Human Vortex Training YouTube Channel to see and hear the instructions.

Jump Rope

Focus: Increase quickness and elastic energy storage usage in lower limbs, low level plyometric

Equipment: Jumping rope

How to do it: Mark a spot on the floor. Skip the rope at a speed of roughly 2–3 small, quick jumps per second, keeping your chin tucked, ribs down, eyes forward, and with a very slight bend in your knees at the bottom.

4. Explosiveness/Power/Jumps

HOW TO PROGRAM JUMPS AND EXPLOSIVE EXERCISES

During the transition, base, and build 1 phases, jumps, power, and explosive work should be done right after your dynamic warm-up. You want to get the best possible training effect, which is immediately after your warm-up when you're moving well and your nervous system and muscles are fired up—not fried.

Ideally, here at HVT, I want my riders (and triathletes) finishing their last set of Olympic lifts, jumps, or explosive work with their best or second best speed (for the overall set) of the day. This tells me they are moving better and improving as they go through their sets—and that they can get some maximal movement strength as they go through the rest of that day's lifting program.

There are definitely times in the late Base and Build periods when you will want the last set to be right smack in the middle of your average for the day, but you ideally want to avoid having the last set, or last rep, be the slowest. Depending on where you are in the program, you are either not recovering well enough, or you are carrying over some fatigue.

EXPLOSIVENESS

BODY WEIGHT EXERCISES

Hands on Hips Jumps

Focus: Improve lower body power and mind-muscle connection

Equipment: None

How to do it: Start by standing on your toes, keeping your head, shoulders, hips, knees, and ankles in a straight line, with your ribs down, chin tucked, and hands on your hips. Quickly drop your heels down to the ground, getting into a ¼ squat position, and then explode up as quickly and as high as you can. At the top of your jump, your ears, shoulders, hips, knees, and ankles should all be in a straight line (#3), with your hands still on your hips. Absorb the landing with your glutes, hamstrings, quads, and abs. This will usually bring you back into the ¼ squat position. Freeze and hold this landing position for a count of "1-Mississippi, 2-Mississippi, 3-Mississippi" before resetting and preparing for the next repetition.

EXPLOSIVENESS

Hands on Hips Jumps to Box

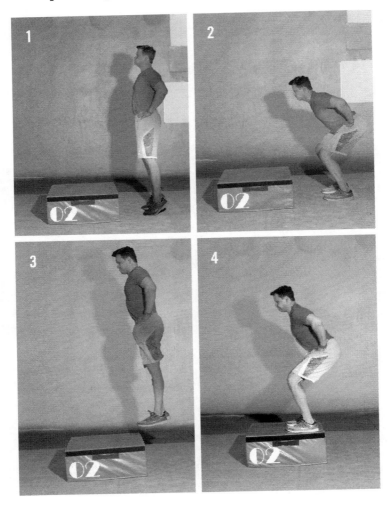

Focus: Improve lower body power and mind-muscle connection with lower landing forces, going easy on your joints as you learn how to produce power and explosiveness

Equipment: Box or step

How to do it: Find a soft plyo box or an aerobic step, making sure it is on a non-slip surface. Start with a step or box 4–6 inches (9–14cm) in height. It does *not* need to be high. Start with your feet shoulder-width apart, on your toes, with your ears, shoulders, knees, and ankles all in a straight line, ribs down, chin tucked, and hands on your hips. Quickly drop down into a ¼ squat position (just like hands on hips jumps) and then EXPLODE up to get full extension of your hips and knees (middle picture), called triple extension. Your power and explosiveness should carry you up over the box, where you'll land and absorb the landing with your glutes, hamstrings, quads, and abs. Hold the landing position for 3 seconds, and then stand up and step back down carefully.

Step-Off Absorb

Focus: Absorb the landing with your glutes, hamstrings, quads, and abs in great positions

Equipment: Box or step

How to do it: Stand on top of a 6–8 inch (14–18cm) box. Step off the box with one leg, dropping straight down to the ground, aiming to get your back foot off the box quickly so you hit the ground with both feet at the same time. Land with slightly bent knees and hips, using your glutes, hamstrings, quads, and abs to absorb the impact. Hold this position for 3 seconds before standing tall, turning around, and setting up for the next repetition.

EXPLOSIVENESS

Heidens

Focus: Develop balance and strength at the hips, improve stability, and develop core control and explosiveness

Equipment: None

How to do it: Start with both feet together on the ground. Lift the inside foot up, taking your arms out and away from the direction you want to jump, and push off the outside leg to jump sideways, using your arms to help. Land with the outside foot touching the ground first, and then set the trailing (back) leg down on the floor to help you absorb the landing. Land in a ¼ squat position, absorbing the landing with your glutes, hamstrings, quads, and abs. Stand tall and relax before the next repetition. Be careful when you first begin these, as cyclists tend to have weak and tight inner and outer thigh muscles.

Watch how to do it on the Human Vortex Training YouTube Channel.

TRX Assisted Vertical

Focus: Learn how to jump vertically while holding the TRX, which allows for more proprioceptive feedback and allows you to feel if your upper body is moving too far forward or back.

Equipment: TRX

How to do it: Start by getting into a ¼ squat "ready position," keeping your chin tucked, with ribs down. Your hips should be down and back a little so that you feel a bit of muscle tension in your glutes and your hamstrings. Lightly hold the TRX handles with your elbows bent as if you're doing a goblet squat.

Explode up as quickly and as high as you can. At the highest point of your jump, your ears, shoulders, hips, knees, and ankles should all be in a straight line (middle picture), with your hands still holding the TRX down near your hips. Absorb the landing with your glutes, hamstrings, quads, and abs. This will usually bring you back into the ¼ squat position. Freeze and hold this landing position for the count of "1-Mississippi, 2-Mississippi, 3-Mississippi" before resetting and preparing for the next repetition.

EXPLOSIVENESS

Broad Jumps

EXPLOSIVENESS

Focus: Improve lower body power and hip extension for power production

Equipment: None

How to do it: Due to the need for a strong core and the ability to get healthy hip extension into great landing postures and positions, the broad jump is a great movement to capitalize on all the work you've done in the training year to this point.

Stand with your feet parallel, shoulder-width apart (or close to it, as you feel comfortable). Drop down, taking your hips behind you and keeping your chest down, just like a kettlebell swing. Explode forward as far as you can, getting full hip extension. Land softly on your heels to midfoot, absorbing the landing with your midsection, glutes, hamstrings, and quads. Stand tall between repetitions.

WEIGHTED EXERCISES

Ball Slams

Focus: Improve lower body power and hip speed for explosiveness and power

Equipment: 2–6 lb. (1–3kg) slam ball*

How to do it: Start by standing on your toes, keeping your head, shoulders, hips, knees, and ankles in a straight line, with your ribs down, chin tucked. Hold a light 1–3kg (2–6 lb.) slam ball in your hands, directly overhead (but don't lose your "ribs down" position!).

Quickly drop your heels to the ground, and drop your hips as you *slam* the ball into the ground right in between your big toes. (It's okay if your feet leave the ground for a split second.) This should quickly get you into a full to half squat position, keeping your back straight.

Freeze and hold this bottom position (do not try to catch the ball!) with your hands down inside your legs for a count of "1-Mississippi, 2-Mississippi, 3-Mississippi" before resetting and preparing for the next repetition.

WARNING: Use only a slam ball for this exercise! Otherwise you run the chance of the ball bouncing and injuring you or those around you.

Russian Kettlebell Swings

Start   Back Swing   Top Swing

Focus: Glute, hamstrings, and midsection strength, timing for power production

Equipment: 20–30 lb. (8–12kg) kettlebell

How to do it: The Russian kettlebell swing is a challenging movement for many people to learn, as it taps into the hip hinge, a movement many of us have lost touch with, perhaps due to the amount of sitting we now do in our daily lives. In order to ensure you are learning how to do this properly, it is best for you to watch and listen to it being taught, instead of reading words on a page and seeing some static photos.

Watch how to do it on the Human Vortex Training YouTube Channel.

Note that kettlebell swings are used relatively widely through the sample programs here, ranging from A1 to A2 to B2. (When an exercise is written as "A1, A2," this means you are to perform one set of A1, and then *immediately* move to exercise A2, with no rest in between the exercises, if possible.) In the Vortex Method, kettlebells are used for both neuromuscular development and metabolic development. You can usually figure out what their purpose is based on where they are in the program, as well as the weight and number of repetitions per set.

OLYMPIC LIFTS

Learning and using different parts of the Olympic lifts, especially the clean, can prove to have very good results for your riding power, and overall strength and co-ordination. However, because of the complexity of these movements, no pictures or tutorials are provided here.

If you'd like to learn how to use the *parts* of the Olympic lifts that will help you as a cyclist, you should seek out an experienced strength or Olympic lifting coach who understands that you are not looking to excel at Olympic lifts, but rather are looking to learn what will improve your riding abilities. You do not need to learn the full Olympic lifts—especially the deep squat position or the positions in which the bar is overhead—unless or until you have great stability, strength, positions, and postures.

That being said, a few parts of the clean are useful in learning the coordination, skills, power, quickness, and explosiveness that can easily transfer over to the bike. Bear in mind that these movements are incredibly technical and *must not* be loaded heavy until your technique is beyond proficient.

- Hang Power Clean
- High Hang Pull
- Drop Clean
- Power Clean (from blocks)
- Push-Jerk (advanced)

EXPLOSIVENESS

When building up to the Olympic lifts, keep in mind two things:

1. You are *not* an Olympic weight lifter. You have very different movement patterns and abilities than those who are training for that sport.
2. Technique, technique, technique! This matters more than the amount of weight you pull. If your technique is bad or off, lower the weight to where you can get great technique and power, and work from there.

Be smart when programming Olympic lifts in—less is more! For even advanced weightlifting cyclists, 50–65% of e1rm for the Clean Pull is more than ample. Again, the key here is technique. Having great technique will help you get more power, which will help you get your body into powerful positions on the bike, which will lead you to more success!

If you cannot find, or do not have easy access to an Olympic lifting coach or a strength coach who can properly teach you the lifts, stick with the kettlebell swing, kettlebell clean, and their variations.

High Hang Pull with Wooden Dowel

High Hang Shrug with Wooden Dowel

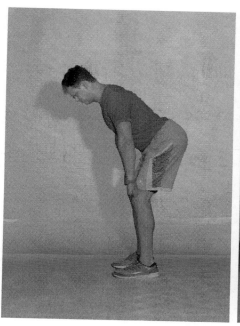
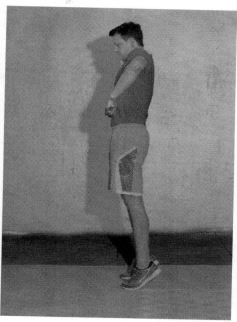

Drop Clean with Wooden Dowel

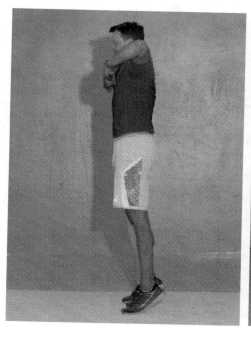

EXPLOSIVENESS

Drop Snatch with Wooden Dowel

5. Strength & Correctives

This is the part of the workout that nearly everyone thinks of as strength training, the "meat" of the program, if you will. It's very important to notice that by the time you've gotten to strength and correctives, you have already accomplished a *lot* to help you move better, breathe better, and to have your body primed for performance.

The soft tissue work, breath work, dynamic warm-up, and explosives/jumps allow you to create an environment, physically and mentally, that will get you far more out of your strength training than if you just jumped right in at this point.

While many cyclists are short on time and looking to get the most out of their strength training, skipping the first four parts of the workout will significantly decrease the benefits you gain. By sticking with the Vortex Method's six-part program, you'll actually save yourself more time in the long run as your improvements will be so significant and lasting and you will be less likely to be set back by injuries. You will get far more out of your strength training this way.

STRENGTH

Goblet Squat

Front View

Side View

Muscle Focus: Glutes, abdominal hoop, lats, quads

Equipment: 10–50 lb. (4–20kg) kettlebell or dumbbell

How to do it: Holding the kettlebell upside down by the horns of the handle at chest height, with your shoulders slightly forward of your chest and keeping them back and down, brace your midsection just enough to keep your ribs down and midsection active. Sink straight down, keeping your back straight, elbows close to your sides, and feet flat on the floor. The bottom of the movement will depend on where you begin to feel that you are either losing the gentle brace in your abs, your heels are coming off the floor, or your back is starting to round. Hold the bottom position for a count of "1-Mississippi," keeping everything braced and active. Fire your glutes to rise up out of the bottom position.

Barbell Front Squat

Muscle Focus: Glutes, abdominal hoop, lats, quads

Equipment: Barbell, bumper or normal weight plates, weight clips

How to do it: There are two grips one can use for the Barbell Front Squat. The first is pictured here and is called the "Clean Grip" due to its origin from the Olympic Clean Lift. However, many people, especially cyclists and triathletes, find this grip to be too challenging to execute because of the extreme range of motion. I would recommend using what is called the Crossed Grip.

You can watch a short YouTube video on the HVTraining channel to help set up for it correctly.

Start by ensuring you have a sound grip on the bar before unracking the weight, making sure to begin with the bar slightly lower than your tall standing position. Brace your abs, keep your ribs down, and get your feet under the bar to stand up and take the weight onto your upper chest. Keeping your elbows parallel to the floor, ribs down, and abs active, sink straight down, keeping your feet flat, abs braced, chin tucked, and back straight.

You've reached the bottom of your range of motion when you feel either the elbows drop down, your midsection getting harder to keep braced, or you feel like your heels want to start to come off the floor. Keeping your elbows up, chin tucked, and chest up, fire the glutes to stand up. Keep the elbows parallel to the floor the whole time. Reset in between repetitions. If you need to, you can re-rack the weight and adjust your grip, although we want to try to avoid that by selecting the right grip and a weight you can keep great technique with for the entirety of the set.

Barbell Back Squat to Bench/Box

Muscle Focus: Glutes, abdominal hoop, lats, quads

Equipment: Barbell, bumper or normal weight plates, weight clips; bench or box that is knee height, or high enough to meet you where you end your great posture/ position for barbell back squatting

How to do it: Begin by setting the bar up in the rack at a position slightly higher than the middle of your chest, with either a box or a bench that is slightly higher than your bottom of the squat movement. Walk under the bar, and hold the bar with both hands with a firm but relaxed grip, with your hands slightly wider than elbow width. Place the bar on your upper back.

Take one small step backwards out of the rack towards the bench behind you with each leg, and with the barbell resting on your upper back. Place your feet on either side of the bench so that you are 100% guaranteed to touch the bench as you squat.

Keeping your midsection braced, abs active, and gently pulling down on the bar with your lats, sink straight down, *gently* touching the bench with your glutes. Fire your glutes to stand straight up and return to the starting position. The bar should travel in a straight line up and down during this motion.

You can watch how to do it on the HVTraining YouTube channel.

Hex Bar Deadlift

Muscle Focus: Glutes, hamstrings, abdominal hoop, lats, erector spinae

Equipment: Hexagonal deadlift bar, bumper plates (or regular plates with blocks under them or on a rack to bring the bar up high enough to meet you where you need to start), clips

How to do it: Start with the hex bar elevated to meet you where your end of motion is. There is no added benefit of deadlifting off the floor! In fact, most cyclists put themselves at risk of injury by deadlifting off the floor.

Stand in the middle of the hex bar, with your ankle even with the middle of the handles. Brace your abs, tuck your chin, and hinge down to the bar by taking your hips back, keeping your back straight, and feeling your hamstrings and glutes engaging a little. Start by gripping one handle and *squeezing* it as you bring that shoulder blade back and down, engaging your lat. Do the same on the opposite side and make sure your ribs are down, abs active.

Slowly raise your hips up to where you feel your hamstrings engage and your back is flat. *Push the floor away*, as you use your hamstrings and glutes to raise your shoulders and hips at the same time. Squeeze the glutes and brace your midsection again at the top of the motion. Slowly lower the bar back down in reverse, taking two seconds or longer.

You can watch how to set up on the HVTraining YouTube channel.

KB Deadlift

Muscle Focus: Glutes, hamstrings, abdominal hoop, lats, erector spinae

Equipment: 20–110 lb. (8–48kg) kettlebell or dumbbell (standing on its side), box or step

How to do it: Start with the kettlebell or dumbbell on an aerobic step or box so that it is only as low as you can go with great technique. Keeping your back straight, chin tucked, and abs appropriately braced, bring your shoulder blades down, feeling your

STRENGTH

ribs and hips lock together. Grab the kettlebell, which should be directly in between your big toes, with a firm grip, then use your hamstrings and glutes to stand straight up, squeezing your glutes and bracing your midsection a bit harder at the top. Slowly lower the kettlebell in reverse, keeping the handle even with your shins as you lower it down. This will help you keep your lats, hamstrings, and abdominal hoop active.

Dumbbell Incline Bench Press

Muscle Focus: Abdominal hoop, lats, chest, shoulders, triceps, glutes

Equipment: Dumbbells of appropriate weight for you, incline bench press

How to do it: Start with a bench that is angled at 45 degrees, with the seat up (this keeps you from sliding down). Begin with the dumbbells resting lengthwise on your knees, with a firm but relaxed grip. Brace your midsection, lean back onto the bench, using your legs to push the dumbbells up towards your chest and into the starting position. Start by placing your feet flat on the ground, in a position where you can fire your glutes. Engage your abs, aiming to keep your ribs down.

Take your elbows out to the side at a 45-degree angle (about halfway between shoulder height and at your sides). Keeping a slight brace in your abs, press the weights up to around equal to where your eyes are (straight ahead), touch-

ing the weights together at the top, creating an "A" shape at the top of the movement. Keeping your midsection braced and feet pressed into the floor with glutes active, slowly lower the weights back to the starting position, taking 1–2 seconds to do so.

Barbell Bench Press

Muscle Focus: Abdominal hoop, lats, chest, shoulders, triceps, glutes

Equipment: Barbell, weight plates or bumper plates, flat bench, rack, clips

How to do it: Begin by lying under the bar, with the bar on the rack, preferably at a height that you need a slight bend in your elbows to take the bar. Brace your midsection, using your legs to push into the floor as you take the bar off the rack and into the starting position above your chest at arm's length.

Slowly lower the bar (1–2 seconds), bringing your elbows out to the side at a 45-degree angle (about halfway between shoulder height and at your sides). Keeping a slight brace in your abs, lower the bar towards the chest and think about meeting the bar with your chest. This will help you keep the elbows in good position and maintain a good back and spine position.

When the barbell touches your chest, your feet should be firmly on the ground, elbows at 45 degrees to your side, with your forearms vertical and wrists straight. Press the bar up away from your chest, and think about bending the bar into an upside down "U" until you reach the top of the movement.

Half Kneeling Landmine Press

Muscle Focus: Abdominal hoop, lats, chest, shoulders, triceps, glutes

Equipment: 30–45 lb. (15–20kg) barbell, landmine apparatus or 25 lb. (10kg) plate on its side, an exercise mat or folded towel for under the back knee

How to do it: Start with the barbell resting on the floor. Take your right knee and place it just inside the end of the barbell on the exercise mat or folded-up towel. Pick the bar up with *both* hands, bringing it up to your right shoulder. You should be able to rest the end of the barbell on your right shoulder. Take the barbell in your right hand with your thumb pointing behind you, elbows slightly away from your ribs.

Dig the ball of your right foot into the ground as if you are about to start a running sprint. Tuck your chin, bring your ribs slightly down by bracing your midsection, and fire your glute to really dig those back toes into the ground. Keeping a neutral wrist, push the barbell up overhead, hinging from the knee that is down, and keeping your ear, shoulder, hip, and back knee in a straight line. Stop when you've reached the highest point that you can keep your shoulder blade on your ribs, with some space between your upper arm and ear.

The barbell should travel in a straight line.

Landmine Deadlift

Muscle Focus: Glutes, hamstrings, abdominal hoop, lats

Equipment: 30–45 lb. (15–20kg) barbell, landmine apparatus or 25 lb. (10kg) plate on its side, additional small weight plates (in 1.25–25 lb. increments)

How to do it: Keeping your back straight, chin tucked, and abs appropriately braced, bring your shoulder blades down, feeling your ribs and hips lock together. Grab the barbell at the last 4–6 inches (10–14cm) of the bar. The end of the bar should be directly in between your big toes, with your elbows straight, and the bar end around

2–3 inches (5–8cm) in front of your crotch. Slowly hinge backwards, keeping your hips high and shins vertical, until you feel you've reached the point where you can no longer take your hips backwards while keeping your back straight and midsection braced.

Use your hamstrings and glutes to stand straight up, squeezing your glutes and bracing your midsection a bit harder at the top. Slowly lower the barbell in reverse, keeping the handle even with your shins as you lower it down. This will help you keep your lats, hamstrings, and abdominal hoop active.

Landmine Low Grip Squat

Note the difference in the hips and upper body position for the Landmine Low Grip Squat vs. the Landmine Deadlift.

Muscle Focus: Glutes, quadriceps, hamstrings, abdominal hoop, lats

Equipment: 30–45 lb. (15–20kg) barbell, landmine apparatus or 25 lb. (10kg) plate on its side, additional small weight plates (in 1.25–45 lb. increments). You may also need an aerobic step, box, blocks, or something to rest the weight on for when you bring it up to your bottom position.

How to do it: This is a great exercise to teach how to brace and move from the bottom of the squat position. Due to where and how the weight is loaded (straight arms at a low position), this is a great beginner exercise.

Keeping your back straight, chin tucked, and abs appropriately braced, bring your shoulder blades down, feeling your ribs and hips lock together. Grab the barbell at the last 4–6 inches (10–14cm) of the bar. The end of the bar should be directly in between your shins, with your elbows straight, and arms in between your legs. Interlock your fingers to grip the bar with an underhand grip.

Start by tucking the chin, bracing the midsection, and engaging your glutes. Fire the glutes to stand straight up, keeping your feet flat on the ground and pushing the ground away from you. Brace your midsection at the top, where the end of the bar should be 2–3 inches (5–8cm) away from your crotch, with your elbows straight or softly bent.

One-Arm Bench Rows

Muscle Focus: Abdominal hoop, lats, rhomboids, pec major, serratus anterior

Equipment: 20–110 lb. (8–48kg) kettlebell or dumbbell, flat bench or wooden box

How to do it: Begin with the kettlebell or dumbbell on the floor next to the bench. Place your right knee on the bench directly under your right hip, and place your right hand on the bench directly under your right shoulder. Gently push your right hand into the bench while you brace your midsection to lock your ribs and hips together as you take your left foot out away from the bench until you find a position where the knee is straight and your hips are parallel to the floor. (Think about someone putting a glass full of water on your lower back; your back should be straight and the water shouldn't spill.)

Tuck your chin, looking straight ahead as you pick up the kettlebell. Start with your left arm straight, keeping your midsection fired, ribs down, as you row the kettlebell up using the muscles in the middle of your back. Pull the kettlebell until your upper arm is even with your upper body, making sure to keep your shoulder back. Slowly lower the weight down, keeping your chin tucked, ribs down, and abdominal hoop active.

Seated Neutral Grip Rows

Muscle Focus: Abdominal hoop, lats, rhomboids, pec major, glutes

Equipment: Seated cable row machine with neutral grip attachment, or bench with band anchored

How to do it: Start by taking the handle in both hands while your feet are flat on the floor, with good, upright posture. Place both feet on the footrests and push yourself back, until you have a soft bend in your knees, with your midsection braced, ribs down, and chin tucked. Keeping good posture, with your glutes active, pull the handle back towards your chest, and think about using the muscles in the mid-back. Stop the movement before you feel your shoulders rolling forward. Slowly reverse, returning to the beginning position as you maintain control of the weight.

Seated Lat Pulldowns

Muscle Focus: Abdominal hoop, lats, rhomboids, rear deltoids

Equipment: Seated lat pulldown machine, or chair with band anchored

How to do it: Before sitting, make sure that the pad allows you to have your feet flat on the ground. Sitting at the lat pulldown machine, grab the bar with your hands at a comfortable distance from one another. Tuck your chin, and brace your abdominal hoop so that your ribs are down. Pull the bar down towards the very top of your chest. Focus on pulling down from the lats (the muscles under your armpits that run down your sides), and pulling your shoulder blades back and down, not letting your shoulders roll forward.

Some may find that in order to keep your shoulders from rolling forward, you can only do part of this motion, around half to two-thirds of the way down. That is *your* range of motion. Focus on getting better muscle activation through great postures and positions.

STRENGTH

TRX Rows

Muscle Focus: Abdominal hoop, lats, rhomboids, rear deltoids, glutes

Equipment: TRX

How to do it: After grabbing the TRX handles, walk backwards about 1 meter (3 feet) from where the TRX is anchored. Keep your feet together, and slowly lean backwards, keeping a firm grip on the TRX handles, slowly extending your arms. You want to have your glutes fired, ribs down, and chin tucked, while keeping your toes flexed up towards your face and your heels firmly on the ground.

Begin the movement by pulling from your mid-back and your lats. Fire your abdominal hoop and glutes together to help you keep your body in a straight line as you row. Stop the movement when your upper arms are parallel to your upper body, and keep your shoulders back. Slowly reverse to the starting position, keeping tension the whole time so that you do not lose your posture or any of the positions.

If this exercise is too difficult, move your feet backwards so that you have less of a lean. If it is too easy, walk your feet forward so that you are at more of an angle.

6. Postural Challenge/Rotary Stability

At the end of your session, tie everything together by producing rotary stability and maintaining great posture when you're fatigued. By putting these postural challenge and rotary stability movements at the end of the workout, you can accomplish much more than if they were earlier in the program. Here's why:

1. They keep you from using unnecessarily heavy weights.

2. They help you learn where and how you break down first, allowing you to be more tuned in on the bike when it matters most—when you're tired but the pace is picking up!

3. They teach you how to use the muscles of your true core—everything between your neck, your elbows, and your knees—to be able to provide great postures, breathing patterns, and strength.

The rotary stability/postural challenge exercises are to be done with resistance or a weight just heavy enough for you to have to work to properly do the movement. In order for the rotary stability/postural exercises to have the biggest positive impact, stick with 2–3 sets of only as many repetitions as you can do with *great* technique.

Suitcase Carries

Muscle Focus: Obliques, abdominal hoop, lats, glute medius/minimus complex, some grip strength

Equipment: Kettlebell or dumbbell

How to do it: Start with the kettlebell either on an aerobic step or on the floor (if you hinge from the floor with great technique), with the middle of the kettlebell even with your pinky toe, on the outside of your right foot. Grab the kettlebell with a firm grip, making sure your abdominal hoop is braced, your shoulder blade is back and down, your lat on that side is fired, and your chin tucked. Brace hard with your abdominal hoop, and use your glutes and hamstrings to stand tall, squeezing your glutes and abs. Then either march in place or walk for the

prescribed distance (10–75 feet) or length of time (15–60 seconds). At the end, slowly lower the kettlebell back to the beginning position, fighting to keep the weight from pulling you out of alignment. You may feel that your grip is your limiting factor here. Be sure to keep great posture throughout, and use a weight that you can manage.

Farmer Carries

Muscle Focus: Obliques, abdominal hoop, lats, glute medius/minimus complex, grip strength

Equipment: 2 kettlebells or dumbbells of equal weight, aerobic step (optional)

How to do it: Similar to the Suitcase Carries, but with 2 kettlebells or dumbbells, one in each hand. Start with the kettlebells either on an aerobic step or on the floor (if you can hinge from the floor with great technique), with the middle of each kettlebell even with your pinky toes, on the outside of your feet. Grab the kettlebells with a firm grip, making sure your abdominal hoop is braced, your shoulder blades are back and down, your lats are fired, and your chin tucked. Brace hard with your abdominal hoop, and use your glutes and hamstrings to stand tall, squeezing your glutes and abs. Then either march in place or walk for the prescribed distance

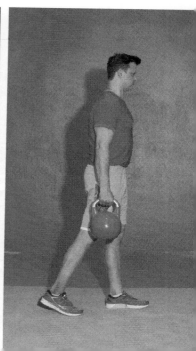

(30–100 feet) or length of time (10–60 seconds). At the end, slowly lower the kettlebells back to the beginning position, fighting to keep the weight from pulling you out of alignment. You may feel that your grip is your limiting factor here. Be sure to keep great posture throughout, and use a weight that you can manage.

Front Plank Reach

Muscle Focus: Abdominal hoop, glutes, lats, quadriceps

Equipment: None

How to do it: Start off on the floor with your feet shoulder-width apart, elbows directly under your shoulders, forearms flat. Squeeze your glutes to bring your "belt buckle" up towards your chin. Brace your abdominal hoop and glutes hard as you lift one elbow off the floor. If you can maintain your position, take the arm forward as if you're Superman, using your mid-back muscles to lift the arm. Return to the starting position, rebrace, and lift the other arm. That is one repetition.

You can watch how to do this on the HVTraining YouTube channel.

TRX Row with Knee Lift

Muscle Focus: Abdominal hoop, lats, rhomboids, rear deltoids, glutes

Equipment: TRX

How to do it: After grabbing the TRX handles, walk backwards about 1 meter (3 feet) from where the TRX is anchored. With your feet together, slowly lean backwards, keeping a firm grip on the TRX handles and slowly extending your arms. You want to have your glutes fired, ribs down, and chin tucked, while keeping your toes flexed up towards your face and your heels firmly on the ground.

Begin the movement by pulling from your mid-back and your lats. Fire your abdominal hoop and glutes together to help keep your body in a straight line as you row. Stop the movement when your upper arms are parallel to your upper body and your shoulders are back. Lift your right leg off the floor into a high-knee position as pictured, pushing the bottom of your opposite foot into the floor, and using *all* of your muscles to keep your balance. Try to hold this position for 1 second, before lowering the leg down.

Slowly reverse to the starting position, keeping tension the whole time so that you do not lose your posture or any positioning. Repeat for the other leg, continuing to alternate which leg you raise.

If this exercise is too difficult, move your feet backwards so that you have less of a lean. If it is too easy, walk your feet forward so that you are at more of an angle.

Bird Dog

Muscle Focus: Glute max, obliques, transverse abdominis, quadratus lumborum, lats, serratus anterior, pectoralis major

Equipment: None

How to do it: The bird dog, or "All-4's Arm Opposite Leg" exercise is one of the most commonly mistaught and poorly performed exercises out there. It can be used both as part of the dynamic warmup, and as part of the correctives, or even trunk work. It all depends on how you program it.

The focus of this exercise is to maintain a stable spine in line with the hips, while getting movement from *only* the shoulder and hips.

Begin by putting the hands directly under the shoulder (90-degree angle), and the knees directly under the hips (90-degree angle). Keep your chin tucked and spine neutral. Brace your midsection, and carefully lift your hand and opposite knee off the floor. Moving from only the hip and shoulder, bring the hand overhead, and extend the leg back (glute only). Pause at the end of your range of motion, squeezing the glute and mid-back of the working arm and leg. Slowly return the hand and knee to their starting point, keeping your abs appropriately braced and not letting anything else move. Repeat until all repetitions on that side are finished, and then rest and switch sides. Take a short rest period in between sides if you need.

To see a complete tutorial on this exercise, and its different levels for progression, visit the HVTraining YouTube Channel.

Start

Level 1

Level 2

Level 3

End

Pallof Press

Muscle Focus: Glutes, obliques, chest, shoulders, abdominal hoop

Equipment: 1–2 inch band (2.5–5cm)

How to do it: Start with the band anchored at the same height as the bottom of your ribs. Move a half step behind the anchor point so that the band will be straight when your arms are halfway straight in front of you. Take the band in both hands with your fingers interlaced, and step away from the anchor point until you have medium tension on the band. Lower down into a ¼ squat position with your hands at your heart. Make sure your weight is shifted slightly backwards and you can feel your glutes firing. Take a deep breath in through your nose as you press the band away from your chest in a straight line. Brace your abdominal hoop and glutes as you press, and keep the hands in a straight line with your heart. When your arms are fully straight, take a breath in through your nose. As you return the band to the starting position, keep your hands in a straight line with your heart.

Start

End

1. Dr. Stuart McGill, *Low Back Disorders: Evidence-Based Prevention and Rehabilitation*, 3rd ed. (Human Kinetics, 2015).

2. Murphy's Laws of War: http://www.military-info.com/freebies/murphy.htm.

CHAPTER 15 SUMMARY

- During the strength training year, you will go through four or five stages of strength development, each stage building on the previous one.

- For each session's warm-up, always take into account the time of day, your mental state, and the ambient temperature.

- Before you begin a strength training program, make sure you are genuinely and generally healthy and understand the latest research and how to discern good from bad research.

- Functional training is relative to the individual and the sport, and you need to train what's not being trained.

CHAPTER 16
CONVERTING TO SPORT-SPECIFIC STRENGTH

While it's really important to know how to properly strength train, any book on strength training for a sport is incomplete without helping you figure out how to convert your newly developed strength to in-sport (or in our case, on-bike) performance. By skipping out on the strength side of things, or mismatching the following on-bike efforts with the wrong phase of the strength training program, you will likely lessen the results you get from your program.

That is not to say that you won't see any results. You will; however, they will not be as good had you followed the pairings as written here. Your results will depend on who you are, where you are in your training year, and what your own strengths and weaknesses are. What I've put together in this chapter are the best practices to help you tie together your on-bike training and your strength training, in order to help you see far better results.

Note that these on-bike training sessions are based off of your *strength training program year*, not your on-bike program.

A NOTE ABOUT DIFFERENT KINDS OF CYCLING

Before we get into the specific on-bike intervals, note that there are six different sports within cycling: mountain bike (enduro), road cycling, track cycling, time trialing, cyclocross, and gravel cycling.

Of course, within each of these sports there are a number of different disciplines, each with their own unique demands. The recommendations that follow are geared towards road cyclists and because they fit most riders' abilities. However, with careful thought and consideration, as well as power profile testing, you should be able to determine what your needs are for your specific sport and style of riding or racing.

In the Vortex Method and the sample plans that follow, the recommendations for sets, reps, and frequency are built for a rider who:

- is male aged 43 or female aged 34 in her follicular phase*
- is riding 8–10 hours a week
- has an indoor trainer to use during inclement weather
- has a power meter that has been properly calibrated
- is strength training as per the recommendations and programming here

*For special considerations for women, please refer to Chapter 4.

ON-BIKE METABOLIC INTERVAL WORK

Anaerobic Power Stomps (APS)

Anaerobic Power Stomps (APS) are a unique and innovative way to increase aerobic abilities. They do so by increasing the endurance of your fast-twitch muscle fibers by increasing the mitochondria present. These efforts recruit your motor units at the highest threshold level, and thus improve their abilities by increasing their oxidative capabilities through supplying them with constant oxygen.

This is also another way to convert strength gains from weight training to power and strength on the bike. As you get stronger/better at these, you can increase the resistance by starting at a slower speed, or in a bigger gear.

Intensity: Max

Volume: 1–3 sets of 8–10 reps per set/workout, 1–2x a week

Allow 2–4 minutes in between efforts. Start off with more recovery (4 min.) in between efforts, and decrease as your abilities improve.

Phase of Strength Training: Hypertrophy, Conversion to Sport-Specific Strength, Maintenance

How to do it: Gearing should be large 52-53x 12-16, depending on your level of development. While seated, starting at 15–20 mph, stay seated and start to stomp on the pedals as hard as you can, concentrating on pulling through the bottom of the pedal stroke. Keep your upper body as still as possible while using your legs to drive the pedals. Your midsection should be braced, and you should have great breathing throughout.

Big Ring Over-Geared Climbs (BROC)

These climbs are designed to help stimulate higher levels of endurance of the fast-twitch muscle fibers by way of greater oxygen utilization. This interval set will challenge your aerobic system with a unique combination of high intensity and high volume, accomplished through the use of extremely high tension. Stop the efforts if you feel like you're bobbing and weaving. Standing is okay.

Intensity: High, heart rate should stay in the 150–160s

Volume: 4–20 min. per set, 1–2x per week

Rest is 5–10 min. in between efforts, pedaling at a cadence of 80–100 with very little tension/power (true recovery is 20–40% FTP).

Terrain: Uphill

Phase of Strength Training: Max Strength

How to do it: Start off by getting into your big ring x, as hard of a gear as you can push for 50–60 rpm up the climb, or as low a cadence as you can without falling over or bobbing side to side. If you can manage it without falling over or dangerously weaving, your cadence can drop as low as 40 rpm (usually these cadences are done on the indoor trainer with resistance). Keep your upper body and hips as solid as you can, and keep your shoulders relaxed. With a firm but relaxed grip on the hoods or bars, climb the hill in the big gear, keeping constant high tension on the pedals throughout the *entire* pedal stroke.

Explosive Sprinting Repeats (ESR)

Geared especially to improve your fast-twitch muscle fibers' abilities to produce power aerobically and test how quickly you can repeat an effort, these short, hard, and cluster-based movements are extremely taxing. Extra riding outside of what's prescribed is detrimental to your progress.

Intensity: Max

Volume: 1–2 sessions per week

1–3 sets per session

1 set = 1–3 clusters

1 cluster = 6–10 reps

Allow 30–60 sec. recovery in between efforts, 8–10 min. easy between clusters, and 8–12 min. easy between sets.

*Progress workload from week to week by increasing work time and decreasing recovery time:

Week 1: 8–10 sec. work: 60 sec. rest

Week 2: 10–12 sec. work: 40 sec. rest

Week 3: 12–14 sec. work: 30 sec. rest

Terrain: Flat, rolling, or uphill

Phase of Strength Training: Max Strength, Conversion to Sport-Specific Strength

How to do it: Gearing should be large 52-53x 12-16, depending on your level of development. While seated, starting at 15–20 mph, stay seated and start to stomp on the pedals as hard as you can, concentrating on pulling through the bottom of the pedal stroke. Keep your upper body as still as possible while using your legs to drive the pedals.

Attack Repeats (AR15s)

These repeats are designed to help stimulate higher levels of enzymes used in anaerobic glycolysis, thus making it so that you can produce more energy faster for these kinds of efforts. These are called AR15s due to this interval series giving you the ability to attack repeatedly with high power.

Intensity: Max

Volume: 1–2x per week

2–4 sets per workout

3 reps per set

Rest is 8–15 min. easy in between sets, and 1–3 min. in between repetitions.

Terrain: Flat, rolling, or uphill

Phase of Strength Training: Anatomical Adaptation, Max Strength, Conversion to Sport-Specific Strength

How to do it: Starting from a tempo pace effort of about 15–20 seconds in length, drop the hammer (pedal cadence 90+) for 20–40 seconds. In your mind you are attacking the small group that you are with at the head of the race, trying to get away for the solo win.

Short Power Intervals (SPI)

Designed to help increase your anaerobic capacity, or *how long* you can sustain high power outputs. By following harder and longer efforts with shorter rest periods, you are forcing the energy system to focus more on capacity (length of time) than allowing it to recover fully and produce more power. These efforts come at a cost to aerobic capacity, however, and so must be used very carefully within the training cycle.

Intensity: Max

Volume: 1–2x per week

> 2–4 sets per workout
>
> 3 reps per set
>
> 90–120 seconds per effort

Allow for 4–6 minutes rest between sets, 1–2 minutes recovery in between reps.

Terrain: Flat, rolling, or uphill

Phase of Strength Training: Hypertrophy, Max Strength, Conversion to Sport-Specific Strength

How to do it: Starting from a tempo pace effort of about 15–20 seconds in length, drop the hammer (pedal cadence 90+) for 90–120 seconds. In your mind you are attacking the small group that you are with at the head of the race, trying to get away for the solo win.

Small Ring Sprints (SRS)

Designed to help increase your maximal power output and acceleration, the goal of these intervals is *not* to become fatigued, but rather to generate the greatest amount of power on each rep as is possible. *Quality trumps quantity in the workout.* If you cannot accelerate all the way through to the end, or you see a drastic drop in power, stop the efforts and ride 8–15 min. easy before moving on to the next part of your ride or workout.

Intensity: Max

Volume: 1–3 sessions a week

> 1–2 sets per workout
>
> 5–6 reps per set (total of 10–12 reps)

Recover 2–5 min. between efforts with easy riding, and get your heart rate back down below 120bpm before your next effort. Recovery intervals may increase (up to 5 min. total) as the workout progresses in order to meet this requirement. Allow 8–15 min. easy before the next exercise.

Terrain: Flat to rolling

Phase of Strength Training: Max Strength, Conversion to Sport-Specific Strength

How to do it: Starting from 3–5 miles per hour, and in the small ring x 14-16, start with one pedal parallel to the downtube (you should feel tension in your calf muscle and glutes on that side). Sprint in the small gear for 7–10 seconds, focusing on MAX acceleration and MAX power for the *entire* effort. (A change of gears is okay once upper level cadence (130+) is reached in your starting gear.)

Power Starts (PStart)

These are used to tap into the neuromuscular systems' abilities to provide MAX power. PStart efforts are short, MAX efforts of 8–12 seconds with *full* (5–10 min.) recovery in between so the nervous system has time to reboot. These are explosive efforts, much like jumps and Olympic lifts, and so we need long rest periods.

Pick a gear that is a bit on the bigger side for you (big ring 52-53x 12-16), depending on your level of abilities on the bike. But keep in mind that if the gear is too big, you won't be able to put down enough power to get what you need from the efforts. Because the efforts are so short and require MAX power, there are no ranges for power or HR.

Intensity: Max

Volume: 1–3 sets of 4–6 efforts. Efforts should be 8–12 seconds each, with *full* recovery in between. 1–2x per week

Pedal Cadence: NA

Terrain: Flat to slightly uphill road

Phase of Strength Training: Hypertrophy, Max Strength

How to do it: Gearing should be on the big (harder) side, based on your level of abilities. Ideally you want a gear that is within 10–14 pedal strokes, where you feel you are getting "on top of" the gear (meaning it's moving fast!).

As is safe, slowly bring your speed down to a near-standstill stop, gearing into your gear choice as you roll down to 3–5 miles per hour. As you hit 3–5 miles per hour, jump out of the saddle and drive the pedals down as hard as possible. Stay out of the saddle and use your rotary stability strength to keep your upper body still, as you work the bike side to side in a *straight* line and finish the effort.

Small Ring Endurance (Small Ring Endur)

Not all endurance rides are created equal! Making use of cadences, as well as restricting what gears you can use, will allow you to get different results from your endurance rides. The small ring endurance ride is geared towards allowing you to get neuromuscular fatigue well before your cardiorespiratory system gets tired. This kind of riding allows you to work on your pedal speed, your speed-endurance, and your ability to spin to win when the road tilts up.

Intensity: 69–83% of threshold HR, 56–75% threshold Power

Volume: 1–2 longer endurance rides a week

Frequency: At least 18–20 hours in between sessions

Terrain: Flat to rolling (some may be prescribed with hills!)

Cadence: 95+ for beginners, 85–95 for advanced

Phase of Strength Training: Anatomical Adaptation, Hypertrophy, Max Strength

How to do it: These workouts will be used primarily in the base and transition periods of your training year, as the endurance miles will be done at a moderately faster cadence. Try your best to stay seated on the hills, using smooth, perfectly circular pedal strokes to get you up the hill. Some riders living in hilly to moun-tainous terrain may find it very beneficial to use a triple chainring up front to help them stay within the parameters of the small ring endurance rides.

Be smart! If you are going to do endurance in a group, be sure to stick to your ranges, and if the group is going a little harder, stay out of the wind and work on keeping your power in the endurance range, following wheels and getting to the front in the mile leading up to the climbs. This will allow you to control the pace and conserve your energy up and over the climb! Cadence trumps all, and you'll want to keep your cadence 5–15 rpm over your normally comfortable endurance range, or within the prescribed cadence ranges.

Big Ring Endurance (Big Ring Endur)

The big ring endurance ride is geared towards allowing you to get neuromuscular fatigue well before your cardiorespiratory system gets tired, and putting more focus and stress onto the connective tissues. While many make the mistake of calling this "strength training on the bike," you want to take the rotary stability, better positions and postures, as well as improved breathing patterns, and use the big ring endurance rides to help solidify those changes on the bike. This will allow you to expose any existing weaknesses (especially in your upper body) or ability to maintain a locked-together rib cage and hips.

Intensity: 69–83% of threshold HR, 56–75% threshold Power

Volume: 1–2 longer endurance rides a week

Frequency: At least 24–36 hours in between sessions

Terrain: Flat to rolling (some may be prescribed with hills!)

Cadence: -10 rpm below normal self-selected cadence (lowest cadence allowed is 75)

Phase of Strength Training: Hypertrophy, Max Strength, Maintenance

How to do it: These workouts will be used primarily in the base and build periods of your training year, as the endurance miles will be done at a moderately slower, more focused cadence. When doing the big ring endurance rides, ride with focus on a firm but loose grip on the handlebars, great positioning on the bike, and a nice, solid hip and upper body connection while pedaling perfect circles.

Be smart! Cadence trumps all, and you'll want to keep your cadence 10 to 15 rpm below your normally comfortable endurance cadence range.

Low Cadence Tempo (CTemp)

These intervals are used to help improve neuromuscular unit recruitment, build up strength of the connective tissues, help smooth out pedal stroke mechanics, and give you a tool to "steam roll" rolling terrain. Cadence is the most important aspect here and will help you develop the abilities to handle subtle changes in the road without having to change gears. As a result, improving your pedaling economy on slightly rolling terrain can tap into more muscle motor unit fibers to help develop your strength through the entire pedal stroke. Make note that HR should not climb into the lactate threshold. It is important to remain seated on any climbs and focus on proper pedal stroke mechanics.

Intensity: HR: 88%, Power: N/A

Volume: 10–120min. 1–3x per week

Terrain: Steady climbs, hills, flat, or rolling

Cadence: 70–75 rpm

Phase of Strength Training: Year-round

How to do it: You *must* stay seated at all times and have as few interruptions as possible (stop signs, etc.). Focus on keeping a smooth pedal stroke, pushing over the top of the pedals, and pulling through the bottom. Effort should be moderate, keeping a steady and strong posture on the bike, with a firm but relaxed grip on the hoods/bars, and keeping constant pressure on the pedals.

Fast Pedals (FastP)

Fast Pedals intervals increase your ability to recruit more of the motor unit, gaining a wider range of comfortable cadences that you can pedal and put power down with, helping you develop a smooth, well-rounded pedal stroke. Make sure to do these correctly, as you want to keep a consistent, smooth pedal stroke, pushing over the top and pulling through the bottom without bouncing in the saddle.

Fast is loose, and loose is fast. It's simple, but not easy!

Intensity: N/A. HR will increase, but you are not worried about intensity, as these are done with no focus on power, just pedal smoothness and quickness.

Volume: 30 seconds -10 min with equal amounts of work to rest (1 min. of work = 1 min. of rest), unless written otherwise. 3–5x per week

Terrain: Flat to slightly downhill, or trainer/rollers

Cadence: Beginners: 85–100 rpm, intermediate and above: 105–130+ rpm

Phase of Strength Training: Year-round

How to do it: These workouts should be performed on a relatively flat section of road. The gearing should be light with low resistance. Begin by *slowly* ramping up your cadence (pedal speed), while staying solid in the saddle. (TIP: If you do not have a cadence meter, start out with roughly 15–16 pedal strokes on one leg per 10 seconds; this equals roughly 90–96 rpm.) Slowly increase your pedal speed, keeping your hips steady with no rocking or bouncing.

Concentrate on keeping a smooth pedal stroke, pulling through the bottom and pushing over the top. After 15–20 seconds, you should be maintaining about 18–22+ pedal strokes on one leg per 10 seconds (equaling about 108–130 rpm). Maintain this cadence for the remainder of the interval. Your heart rate will climb during this workout, but *don't* use it to judge intensity!

For best effect you should perform the fast pedal intervals without any interruptions (stop signs, traffic lights, etc.), since you need to maintain a continuous cadence while riding. If you are having difficulty doing this outdoors due to changes in terrain or finding a safe stretch, try them for the first 4–6 sessions on the trainer. If you do use a trainer to perform these, use a mirror (or two) to get instant visual feedback to help you maintain proper pedal stroke and body positioning.

Common poor habits during fast pedaling:

- bouncing in the saddle
- rocking on the saddle
- toes pointed down
- heels down
- arching the back to maintain cadence

It is imperative that you maintain *excellent* posture on the bike while performing these!

CHAPTER 16 SUMMARY

- Strength training must be paired with sport-specific training to get the best results out of both programs.

- Specific on-bike intervals can be paired with different phases of the strength training year.

- On-bike intervals should complement strength training, which means they are often something different than what you're doing in your strength. This is a part of the conjugate method of training.

- There are many training tools you can use each time of year. Pick one or two, and be consistent.

CHAPTER 17
METABOLIC TRAINING

NOTE: *This training approach is* only *for those who have gone through at least one appropriate cycle of Anatomical Adaptation, Hypertrophy, and Max Strength. Please take this word of caution very seriously, as failure to follow the minimal requirements for this programming can result in an injury or overtraining.*

After a rider has reached the level of having gone through the first three stages of strength training for a single training year (1. Anatomical Adaptations, 2. Hypertrophy, 3. Max Strength), they can begin to think about more non-traditional ways to boost training responses, increase training value, and get much more out of their time-crunched training schedule. To do this, they must have great tissue properties, good posture, and a relatively good balance of strength and range of motion at the joints.

When Chris Carmichael's book *The Time-Crunched Cyclist* came out in the mid-2000s, it led to a massive boom in fitness for those working full-time jobs and trying to gain fitness in what little time they had to train. The book brought to the forefront what those of us in the Exercise Physiology field had come to understand: When you develop training on structured interval work after building the necessary energy systems and developing neuromuscular resiliency, you *can* get great results for sports of moderate endurance, with much less time than had been traditionally prescribed or used (with the caveat of limitations on the length of the event and training age of the athlete).

Of course, if you wanted to tackle these massive 3+ day events of (road mileage) greater than 80 miles per day (~130km), you would indeed need at least a handful of carefully built-in long endurance rides in your training schedule. But even just over 10 years after its publication, up until the Vortex Method, no one had spoken about the highly effective way in which you can use a metabolic strength training circuit pre-ride to pre-fatigue the rider before doing some mid-length training rides in order to increase and even (carefully) maximize the training effect for super sport-specific results.

Before I get into the "how" and give an example of what this training would look like, I must stress again that this approach is only appropriate for and to be used by riders who have gone through at least the first three stages of strength development (anatomical adaptation, hypertrophy, and max strength). The tissue adaptations, mastery of the technique, and ability to maintain great posture and breathing patterns under fatigue are must-haves before you attempt this approach.

When used appropriately, for the right athlete, these pre-fatigue metabolic workouts can prove to be incredibly powerful. If you have not yet gone through a continuous proper build of these three stages, there are other means you can use to increase the impact of your time on the bike, including specific riding protocols, as well as some of the pre- or post-ride strength circuits here in this book.

The pre-fatigue metabolic workouts may not be complex, and may look simple, but you must be capable of dealing with the forces you will be producing in order to avoid injury.

PRE-FATIGUE METABOLIC STRENGTH WORKOUTS

When the right athlete comes along (or, more often than not, is developed in the Vortex Training system), we can begin to sprinkle in some pre-fatigue metabolic strength workouts in the mid- to late-wintertime, when the rider is finishing up their base and beginning to head to their build period. While these pre-fatigue metabolic rides need to be carefully planned so as to ensure proper recovery, when done right, they can have a supercharger effect on the rider's fitness!

These workouts are incredibly stressful on the localized energy systems, muscle tissues, and even the nervous system—which allows us to add more training load to a rider with much shorter endurance, tempo, or somewhat zippy (prescribed) group rides.

As with any strength training session, the pre-fatigue metabolic workouts will begin with 1 breathing exercise (1 set of 5–8 breaths); a core activation series such as side planks (top foot forward), straight-leg kickbacks, and McGill crunches; and 1–2 corrective exercises that hit the athlete's major focal points.

After this nice little warm-up (no longer than 8–10 minutes), you'll move into your PFMC (Pre-Fatigue Metabolic Circuit), which will need to be done after you are kitted up, but with tennis shoes and regular socks. If it's wintertime, you'll do these in gym shorts and a T-shirt and kit up after, so as not to overheat. While this delays the transition over to the bike a bit, it's more important to have you not overheated and sweaty as you head out the door. You don't want to be freezing in your own sweat, which can completely derail a training ride—or even worse, make you sick.

A sample PFMC workout would look something like this:

1. Frog Hip Lifts x 30

2. Body Squat x 30

3. Hands-on-Hips Jumps x 15

4. Side Lunge Hands Overhead x 10 each side, alternate sides

20–30 seconds total per exercise (so you're moving at a nice clip through your full range of motion!)

1–3 rounds, no rest between rounds (beginners start with 1 round, and over the course of 3–6 weeks, work their way up to 2 rounds)

WHEN TO USE PRE-FATIGUE METABOLIC CONDITIONING

There are three prime instances for using the PFMC workouts. Each has its own fairly strict guidelines, as we need to be sure that we are only pre-fatiguing the neuromuscular and metabolic systems, not *totally* fatiguing them.

1. A busy 2–3 weeks at work or the holiday season

In the case of an impending deadline at work, or a demanding family/ life time period, you would add a single PFMC session to a Saturday long ride, subtracting the time necessary to perform the session immediately pre-ride, keeping the rest of the ride time as prescribed.

2. A rider is in need of increased training load, but can only give another 15–30 minutes for a single ride each week

In this instance, you would use that little bit of extra training time to perform the PFMC session before a Sunday long ride, allowing you to significantly push the body. There is a catch, however. Saturday's ride cannot leave you feeling sluggish or tired upon waking on Sunday. This means nutrition, sleep, and recovery need to be on point. Otherwise, you'll ditch the PFMC session, opting to add a little intensity in the ride and performing a 10-minute post-ride "movement quality under fatigue" session immediately after the ride.

3. **At the end of base or build, when you are preparing to make the leap up to a significantly more competitive level**

   Examples of this include going from Cat 3 to Cat 2 (USA), or domestic professional (USA Cat 1/Pro) to international professional (UCI Pro-Continental).

   In this scenario, you will hit the last 30–60 minutes of your ride with a higher level of neural fatigue, allowing you to work on end of race high-intensity scenarios, or to simply apply more neural and metabolic fatigue with fewer hours on the bike.

   This can be incredibly potent if you are looking at a big (>10%) increase in your to-date ride volume following more traditional "builds," as the PFMC approach significantly lowers the training volume and can decrease the development of overtraining injuries and other high-volume issues, such as saddle sores and neck/upper back pain due to too much time in the saddle.

When looked at from a traditional strength training perspective, Pre-Fatigue Metabolic Conditioning sessions are simply power-endurance training approaches, used very carefully, to help athletes who can handle the stresses placed on the body to increase the training effect of the time they have available to them or to continue along the desired training effect and training load guidelines, but with a significantly reduced recovery time in between training sessions.

The PFMC sessions should *only* be used by riders who have met or exceeded the requirements necessary to ensure they can handle these training sessions. Failure to do so may result in injuries or lost training time due to prolonged recovery times between training sessions.

If you have not done the three required phases in their appropriate lengths (for you and your needs), or if you have not completed these three phases in the previous 12–18 weeks, skip the PFMC sessions and opt to use on-bike training strategies combined with the strength training phase and programming most appropriate for your (strength) training age and on-bike abilities.

CHAPTER 17 SUMMARY

- If you have gone through the first three stages of strength training (Anatomical Adaptation, Hypertrophy, and Max Strength), metabolic training can boost your training responses.

- Metabolic strength training is done pre-ride to fatigue the neuromuscular and metabolic systems.

- Pre-fatigue metabolic conditioning is usually done in the late base / early build periods, during busy seasons, or when a rider is in need of increased training load.

- It is not to be used year-round, or if you have not completed the first three stages of strength training.

CHAPTER 18
RECOVERY & ADAPTATION

Showing up and doing the work consistently may be your #1 challenge, but supporting that training by doing a few other relatively simple things consistently, comes in at a close second. The problem is, if it's easy to do, it's easy not to do. People love to overcomplicate easy stuff, don't they?

If you're looking to get the most out of your training, following these guidelines will help you maximize your results and your recovery.

NUTRITION

Proper nutrition to support your training will vary based off of your age and sex, as well as the training intensities and amount of activity you perform in your everyday life. That being said, there are a few easy and simple things that you want to aim for on a consistent basis that will significantly boost your results and your health.

Vegetables and protein, specifically, are two foods that many of us don't get enough of.

VEGETABLES

For any serious athlete, one of the questions we hear thrown around is, "How big is their engine?" While you may first think about how many Watts per kilo the rider can average, or how strong her sprint is for a specific distance, you should take this question at its most basic level: You are an engine. In order for you to perform well, your engine needs to be efficient, strong, and able to put out loads of power for periods of time longer than your competition.

But in order for that engine to work at its best, you need high octane fuel and fuel injectors and spark plugs that are clean and firing correctly.

Vegetables contain the vitamins and minerals that are your spark plugs, as well as the fiber that can help you keep your fuel injectors (intestinal tract) clean, healthy, and full of good gut bacteria.

For every athlete, the kinds of vegetables they like and will eat is going to vary quite a bit. But there are specific vegetables that should serve as a basis for all athletes, and those are dark, leafy greens. These vegetables are packed with tons of vital micronutrients that you need in order to stay in top shape and keep illness at bay.

What you need: Each day aim for 5 servings of dark leafy greens + another 5–8 servings of a wide variety of colorful vegetables. Aim to eat seasonal and local. Throw in 4–5 servings of fresh fruits as well, although these are best eaten for dessert after a meal, or along with a protein at a main meal.

1 serving size = the size of your fist

PROTEIN

Endurance athletes can be absolutely awful about eating protein. It was once thought that if you ate more protein you would automatically turn into Arnold Schwarzenegger or Jay Cutler. If only.

In fact, protein provides you with the building blocks necessary to repair the damage done to the body's tissues, especially the muscles, during training. We're finally seeing sports nutrition catch up, and the current recommendations for endurance athletes now vary between 1.4g/kg to 2.4g/kg, depending on the research studies you look at.

As I mentioned in Ch. 4, the women-specific considerations chapter, women during their luteal phase will need 1.8–2.0g/kg per day of protein to help fight the catabolic effects of their high hormone phase. They will also need to ensure they are eating a meal with mixed-protein sources within 30 minutes of finishing their exercise.

For men, I tend to suggest 1.6–1.8g/kg per day of protein, as this really helps maintain lean muscle mass and ensures that you are aiming a bit high, so that when you fall short, you have more than enough protein to help repair and build muscle, not break down.

Nutrition is something that should be given careful thought and some focused attention. I strongly recommend that you find a local professional to help you with your nutrition and diet, and to dial in to your specific needs. However, the above recommendations are a great place to start while you seek out someone to work with you 1-on-1.

SLEEP

Not all sleep is equal!

When we talk about sleep for recovery, this doesn't mean the kind of sleep where you wake up in the morning feeling as though you need another hour or two to feel refreshed.

Sleep is often the area that many endurance athletes perform poorly in, as they are either cutting down hours of sleep so that they can head out for their training, or they are not developing and embracing proper sleep hygiene or routines.

STRESS MANAGEMENT

It is important to take active steps towards developing rituals and ways to help you recognize and deal with stress. For some, it's planning a vacation every 6 months, while for others, it's taking 15 minutes every evening to themselves in a quiet room without any screens.

Find what works for you, and make practicing stress management part of your daily routine. It has a big impact on your physical, emotional, and psychological health.

PUTTING IT ALL TOGETHER

Just showing up to the gym or to your on-bike training session is not enough to help you get the most out of the time and effort you put into training. If you truly want to "train smarter, not harder," you must take the steps to finding balance in your life—social, family, work, training, and time for yourself—to keep you balanced and healthy.

CHAPTER 18 SUMMARY

- In the hours when you are not training, you can support your training by eating well, sleeping enough, and managing stress.

- Proper nutrition that supports your training includes vegetables and protein.

- Getting enough sleep will give your body time to recover and adapt.

- By developing good stress management habits, you can greatly impact your physical, emotional, and psychological health.

SECTION 4:
SAMPLE TRAINING PLANS

SAMPLE TRAINING PLANS

Below you will find sample training plans for three different kinds of equipment setups:

1. Standard gym with barbells, bands, cable stack machines, etc.

2. Home setup with kettlebells (2), bands (2–3), and a door anchor for the bands

3. Home setup with kettlebells (2) and a TRX System

Each of these workouts shows you how a training program may be built throughout the training year. Videos on how to execute these exercises are available on the Human Vortex Training website (www.humanvortextraining.com), in the "Book Bonus Content" section. The password to access this content is: THEVORTEX-TRIBE. You'll have instant access as soon as you create a free account, and will then be able to access these videos at any time.

As you read the workouts, note that the exercises are grouped by letters A, B, C, and D. You'll do the exercises in A-B-C-D order, and each letter has 2 or 3 exercises to be done as a group, with no rest in between exercises.

When an exercise is written as "A1, A2," this means you are to perform one set of A1, and then *immediately* move to exercise A2, with no rest in between the exercises, if possible. Because you may be working out in a gym with other people, this may not always be possible, but you'll want as short of a rest in between exercises as possible. The start of your rest period should begin after you've finished the *second* (or last) exercise in that series.

In some cases, the number of sets for the paired exercises are different. When that happens you should finish all the rounds of the exercises that are paired together, and then continue with the other exercise (for which there are more sets). Continue to perform the exercise with the correct rest period in between your sets, until you've completed all the prescribed sets, before moving on.

The sets and reps are indicated with an asterisk (*) between two numbers. For instance, if an exercise calls for 2 sets of 8 reps, it will read "2*8" in the plan. If an exercise calls for work on each side of the body, that will be indicated with an "ea" at the end. For instance, if the instructions for side planks are "3*20 ea" you will do 3 sets of holding a side plank for 20 seconds on one side and then 20 seconds on the other.

Some exercises include tempos, which are explained at the end of Chapter 11. Please refer there for more details.

Isometric holds are noted in seconds, i.e., Front Plank 15" means "front plank 15 seconds."

Standard Gym with Barbells, Bands, Cable Stacks, etc.

Anatomical Adaptation, 4 weeks

	WEEK 1	WEEK 2	WEEK 3	WEEK 4
A1. 3-1-3-1 Tempo Goblet Squats	2*8	3*8	3*10	3*10-12
A2. Hip Lifts	2*15	2*15	2*18	2*20
B1. KB Deadlift from Box	3*8	3*8	3*10-12	3*10-15
B2. Side-Lying Windmills	3*5 ea	3*5 ea	3*5 ea	3*5 ea
C1. TRX Rows	2*8	2*10	3*10	3*10-15
C2. Wall Scapular Slides	2*6-8	2*6-8	3*6-8	3*8-10
D1. Side Planks	3*20" ea	3*20" ea	3*30" ea	3*40" ea
D2. Max Effort Front Planks	3*(3*5" on, 3" off)	3*(3*5" on, 3" off)	3*(4*5" on, 3" off)	3*(5*5" on, 3" off)
D3. Bird Dogs, Level 1	2*5-7 ea	2*5-7 ea	2*6-8 ea	2*8-10 ea

Hypertrophy, 12 weeks

HYPERTROPHY 1 (6 WEEKS)	WEEK 1	WEEK 2	WEEK 3	WEEK 4	WEEK 5	WEEK 6
A1. Hex Bar Deadlift off Blocks	3*8	3*8	3*10	3*10-12	3*12	3*12-15
A2. Half-Kneeling Banded Lat Stretch	3*5 breaths/ea	3*5 breaths/ea	3*5 breaths/ea	3*5 breaths/ea	3*5 breaths/ea	3*5 breaths/ea
B1. Seated Underhand Cable Rows	3*10	3*10	3*12	3*12	3*12-15	2*12-15
B2. Seated Dumbbell Shoulder Press	3*5-7 ea	3*5-7 ea	3*6-8 ea	3*8 ea	3*8 ea	2*6 ea
C1. Chest Supported Dumbbell Rows	3*8	3*8	3*10	3*10	3*10 (heavier)	2*8
C2. Dumbbell Incline Bench Press	3*10	3*10	3*8	3*8	3*5	2*5
D1. Side Planks on Knees (Hinge Pattern)	3*5 ea	3*5-7 ea	3*6-8 ea	3*8 ea	3*8-10 ea	3*10 ea
D2. Farmer Carries	3*30 sec	3*30 sec	3*30 sec (heavier)	3*40 sec	3*40 sec	3*45 sec

HYPERTROPHY 2 (6 WEEKS)	WEEK 1	WEEK 2	WEEK 3	WEEK 4	WEEK 5	WEEK 6
A1. Hex Bar Deadlift off Blocks	3*8	3*8	3*6	3*6	4*5	2*5
A2. Half-Kneeling Banded Lat Stretch	3*5 breaths/ea	3*5 breaths/ea	3*5 breaths/ea	3*5 breaths/ea	3*5 breaths/ea	3*5 breaths/ea
B1. Barbell Box Squats with Pause	3*8	3*8	3*5	4*5	4*4	2*5
B2. Brettzel	3*5 breaths/ea	3*5 breaths/ea	3*5 breaths/ea	3*5 breaths/ea	3*5 breaths/ea	3*5 breaths/ea
C1. Lat Pulldowns	3*12	3*12	3*10	3*10	3*8	2*6
C2. One-Arm KB Shoulder Press	3*6 ea	3*6 ea	3*8 ea	3*8 ea	3*10 ea	2*5 ea
D1. Pallof Press	3*5 ea	3*5 ea	3*5-7 ea	3*6-8 ea	3*8-10	3*8-10
D2. Inchworms	3*4	3*4	3*6-8	3*8	3*6 (longer)	3*6

Max Strength, 6 weeks

	WEEK 1	WEEK 2	WEEK 3	WEEK 4	WEEK 5	WEEK 6
A1. Barbell Front Squats to Box w/ Pause	3*8	3*8	3*6	3*4	3*3	4*3
A2. Med Ball Slams	3*4	3*4	3*5	3*5	4*4	4*4
B1. Hex Bar Deadlifts	1*10, 2*6	1*10, 2*6	1*10, 2*5	1*10, 2*5	1*8, 1*5, 2*4	1*8, 2*4
B2. Half-Kneeling Landmine Press	3*6	3*6	3*5	3*5	4*4	2*5
C1. Seated Neutral Grip Rows	3*8	3*8	3*6	3*6	3*8 (same weight)	2*5
C2. Suitcase Carries	3*15"	3*15"	3*15"	3*15" (heavier)	3*15"	3*15"

Conversion to Specific Strength, 10 weeks

CONVERSION TO SPECIFIC 1 (5 WEEKS)	WEEK 1	WEEK 2	WEEK 3	WEEK 4	WEEK 5
A1. 2-1-1-1 Tempo Barbell Squats	2*12	2*15	3*10	3*12	3*15
A2. Hands on Hips Jumps	2*5	2*5	3*5	3*5	3*4
B1. Landmine Deadlift	2*12	2*15	2*10	2*10	2*12
B2. Half-Kneeling Landmine Press	2*8 ea	2*8 ea	2*6 ea	2*6 ea	2*5 ea
C1. Seated Neutral Grip Rows w/ Pause	2*10	2*10	2*8	2*8	2*12
C2. Suitcase Carries (40m)	3*	3*	3* (heavier)	3*	3*

CONVERSION TO SPECIFIC 2 (5 WEEKS)	WEEK 1	WEEK 2	WEEK 3	WEEK 4	WEEK 5
A1. Landmine Low Grip Squats	3*12	3*12	3*15	3*15	3*15 (heavier)
A2. Heidens with Stick	2*5	2*5	3*5	3*5	3*4
B1. Russian Kettlebell Swings	5*8	5*8	4*12	4*12	5*10
B2. Pallof Press	2*8 ea	2*8 ea	2*10 ea	2*10 ea	2*12 ea
C1. Seated Neutral Grip Rows w/ Pause	3*5	3*5	2*6	2*6	2*8 (same)
C2. Suitcase Carries (40m)	3*	3*	3* (heavier)	3*	3*

Maintenance, 10 weeks

MAINTENANCE 1 (5 WEEKS)	WEEK 1	WEEK 2	WEEK 3	WEEK 4	WEEK 5
A1. Hex Bar Deadlift off Blocks	2*4	2*4	3*3	2*3	2*3
A2. Hands on Hips Jumps	2*3	2*3	3*3	2*3	2*3
B1. One-Arm KB Bench Rows	2*8 ea	2*8 ea	2*5 ea	2*5 ea	2*6 ea
B2. Half-Kneeling Landmine Press	2*8 ea	2*8 ea	2*10 ea	2*10 ea	2*10 ea
C1. Side Planks, Top Foot Forward	2*45-60"ea	2*45-60" ea	2*60" ea	2*60" ea	2*60" ea
C2. Farmer Carries	2*15"	2*15"	2*20"	2*20"	2*20"

MAINTENANCE 2 (5 WEEKS)	WEEK 1	WEEK 2	WEEK 3	WEEK 4	WEEK 5
A1. Landmine Deadlift	1*8, 1*5	1*8, 1*5	1*8, 1*4	1*8, 1*3	1*8, 1*3
A2. Hands on Hips Vertical	2*4	2*4	2*3	2*5	2*5
B1. One-Arm KB Bench Rows	1*8 ea	1*8 ea	1*6 ea	1*6 ea	1*5 ea
B2. Side Planks, Top Foot Forward	2*60" ea	2*60" ea	2*60" ea	2*60" ea	2*60" ea
B3. Bird Dogs, Level 2 or 3	2*8 ea	2*8 ea	2*8 ea	2*8 ea	2*8 ea

Home Gym with Kettlebells and Bands

Anatomical Adaptation, 4 weeks

	WEEK 1	WEEK 2	WEEK 3	WEEK 4
A1. 3-1-3-1 Tempo Goblet Squats	2*8	3*8	3*10	3*10-12
A2. Hip Lifts	2*15	2*15	2*18	2*20
B1. KB Deadlift from Block	3*8	3*8	3*10-12	3*10-15
B2. Side-Lying Windmills	3*5 ea	3*5 ea	3*5 ea	3*5 ea
C1. Band Rows w/ Pause	2*8	2*10	3*10	3*10-15
C2. Wall Scapular Slides	2*6-8	2*6-8	3*6-8	3*8-10
D1. Side Planks	3*20" ea	3*20" ea	3*30" ea	3*40" ea
D2. Max Effort Front Planks	3*(3*5" on, 3" off)	3*(3*5" on, 3" off)	3*(4*5" on, 3" off)	3*(5*5" on, 3" off)
D3. Bird Dogs, Level 1	2*5-7 ea	2*5-7 ea	2*6-8 ea	2*8-10 ea

Hypertrophy, 12 weeks

HYPERTROPHY 1 (6 WEEKS)	WEEK 1	WEEK 2	WEEK 3	WEEK 4	WEEK 5	WEEK 6
A1. Double KB Hover Deadlift	3*8	3*8	3*10	3*10-12	3*12	3*12-15
A2. Half-Kneeling Banded Lat Stretch	3*5 breaths/ea	3*5 breaths/ea	3*5 breaths/ea	3*5 breaths/ea	3*5 breaths/ea	3*5 breaths/ea
B1. Half-Squat Band Rows	3*10	3*10	3*12	3*12	3*12-15	2*12-15
B2. KB Around the Worlds	3*5 ea way	3*5 ea way	3*6-8 ea way	3*8 ea way	3*8 ea way	2*8 ea way
C1. Push-ups	3*10	3*10	3*8	3*8	3*5	2*5
C2. Banded Lat Pulldowns	3*12	3*12	3*15	3*15	3*10 (harder)	2*10 (harder)
D1. Side Planks on Knees (Hinge Pattern)	3*5 ea	3*5-7 ea	3*6-8 ea	3*8 ea	3*8-10 ea	3*10 ea
D2. Farmer Carries	3*30 sec	3*30 sec	3*30 sec (heavier)	3*40 sec	3*40 sec	3*45 sec

HYPERTROPHY 2 (6 WEEKS)	WEEK 1	WEEK 2	WEEK 3	WEEK 4	WEEK 5	WEEK 6
A1. KB Lunge	3*8 ea	3*8 ea	3*10 ea	3*10 ea	3*12 ea	2*15 ea
A2. Brettzel	3*5 breaths/ea	3*5 breaths/ea	3*5 breaths/ea	3*5 breaths/ea	3*5 breaths/ea	3*5 breaths/ea
A3. Side Lunge Reach w/ Weight	3*5 ea	3*5 ea	3*6-8 ea	3*6-8 ea	3*8-10 ea	2*10 ea
B1. Lat Pulldowns	3*12	3*12	3*10	3*10	3*8	2*6
B2.One-Arm KB Shoulder Press	3*6 ea	3*6 ea	3*8 ea	3*8 ea	3*10 ea	2*5 ea
C1. Pallof Press	3*5 ea	3*5 ea	3*5-7 ea	3*6-8 ea	3*8-10 ea	3*8-10 ea
C2. Inchworms	3*4	3*4	3*6-8	3*8	3*6 (longer)	3*6

Max Strength, 6 weeks

MAX STRENGTH (6 WEEKS)	WEEK 1	WEEK 2	WEEK 3	WEEK 4	WEEK 5	WEEK 6
A1. 2-1-1-1 Tempo Goblet Squats	3*10	3*10	3*12	3*12	3*15	2*18
A2. Hands on Hips Vertical	3*4	3*4	3*5	3*5	4*4	4*4
B1. Russian Kettlebell Swings	5*8	5*10	6*8	8*8	10*8	5*12
B2. Brettzel	3*5 breaths/ea	3*5 breaths/ea	3*5 breaths/ea	3*5 breaths/ea	3*5 breaths/ea	3*5 breaths/ea
C1. One-Arm Bench Rows	3*8 ea	3*8 ea	3*6 ea w/ 2-sec squeeze	3*6 ea w/ 2-sec squeeze	3*5 ea w/ 5-sec squeeze	2*5 ea w/ 5-sec squeeze
C2. Suitcase Carries	3*15"	3*15"	3*15"	3*15" (heavier)	3*15"	3*15"

Conversion to Specific Strength, 10 weeks

CONVERSION TO SPECIFIC 1 (5 WEEKS)	WEEK 1	WEEK 2	WEEK 3	WEEK 4	WEEK 5
A1. Goblet Lunge Isometric Hold	3*20" ea	3*20" ea	3*30" ea	3*30" ea	2*30" ea
A2. Broad Jump	2*3	2*3	3*3	3*4	2*3
B1. 3-1-3-1 Tempo KB Deadlifts NOT to Floor	3*10	3*10	3*12	3*12-15	2*18
B2. One-Arm KB Shoulder Press	2*8 ea	2*8 ea	3*6 ea	3*6 ea	2*8 ea
C1. Half-Squat Band Rows w/ Pause	2*10	2*10	2*8	2*8	2*12
C2. Suitcase Carries	3*60"	3*60"	3*60"	3*70"	3*75"

CONVERSION TO SPECIFIC 2 (5 WEEKS)	WEEK 1	WEEK 2	WEEK 3	WEEK 4	WEEK 5
A1. KB Goblet Squats	2*18	2*18	2*20	2*20	2*10
A2. Heidens with Stick	2*5	2*5	3*5	3*5	3*4
B1. Kettlebell Swings	5*8	5*8	4*12	4*12	5*10
B2. Pallof Press	3*8 ea	3*8 ea	3*10 ea	3*10 ea	3*12 ea
C1. Seated Band Rows w/ Pause	2*10	2*10	2*12	2*12	1*15
C2. Front Plank Reach	3*3 ea	3*3 ea	3*4 ea	3*4 ea	3*5 ea

Maintenance, 10 weeks

MAINTENANCE 1 (5 WEEKS)	WEEK 1	WEEK 2	WEEK 3	WEEK 4	WEEK 5
A1. 2-1-1-1- KB Deadlifts	2*10	2*10	2*12	2*12	2*10
A2. Can Crush	2*6 ea	2*6 ea	2*6 ea	2*6 ea	2*6 ea
B1. KB Around the Worlds	2*8 ea	2*8 ea	2*5 ea	2*5 ea	2*6 ea
B2. Side-Lying Windmill	2*6-8 ea	2*6-8 ea	2*6-8 ea	2*6-8 ea	2*6-8 ea
C1. Side Planks, Top Foot Forward	2*45-60"ea	2*45-60" ea	2*60" ea	2*60" ea	2*60" ea
C2. McGill Crunch	2*5 w/ 5" hold	2*5 w/ 8" hold	2*5 w/ 8" hold	2*5 w/ 10" hold	2*5 w/ 10" hold
C3. Bird Dogs, Level 1, 2, or 3	2*5-7 ea	2*5-7 ea	2*6-8 ea	2*8 ea	2*8-10 ea

MAINTENANCE 2 (5 WEEKS)	WEEK 1	WEEK 2	WEEK 3	WEEK 4	WEEK 5
A1. 2-1-1-1- KB Deadlifts	2*15	2*15	2*18	2*18	2*12-15
A2. Prisoner Vertical	2*6	2*8	2*8	2*10	2*10
B1. McGill Crunch	2*5 w/ 10" hold	2*5 w/ 10" hold	2*6-8 w/ 10" hold	2*6-8 w/ 10" hold	2*8-10 w/ 10" hold
B2. Side Planks, Top Foot Forward	2*60" ea	2*60" ea	2*60" ea	2*60" ea	2*60" ea
B3. Bird Dogs, Level 2 or 3	2*8 ea	2*8 ea	2*8 ea	2*8 ea	2*8 ea

Home Gym with Kettlebells and TRX

Anatomical Adaptation, 4 weeks

	WEEK 1	WEEK 2	WEEK 3	WEEK 4
A1. 3-1-3-1 Tempo Goblet Squats	2*8	3*8	3*10	3*10-12
A2. Hip Lifts	2*15	2*15	2*18	2*20
B1. KB Deadlift from Block	3*8	3*8	3*10-12	3*10-15
B2. Side-Lying Windmills	3*5 ea	3*5 ea	3*5 ea	3*5 ea
C1. TRX Rows w/ Pause	2*8	2*10	3*10	3*10-15
C2. Wall Scapular Slides	2*6-8	2*6-8	3*6-8	3*8-10
D1. Side Planks	3*20" ea	3*20" ea	3*30" ea	3*40" ea
D2. Max Effort Front Planks	3*(3*5" on, 3" off)	3*(3*5" on, 3" off)	3*(4*5" on, 3" off)	3*(5*5" on, 3" off)
D3. Bird Dogs, Level 1	2*5-7 ea	2*5-7 ea	2*6-8 ea	2*8-10 ea

Hypertrophy, 12 weeks

HYPERTROPHY 1 (6 WEEKS)	WEEK 1	WEEK 2	WEEK 3	WEEK 4	WEEK 5	WEEK 6
A1. Double KB Hover Deadlift	3*8	3*8	3*10	3*10-12	3*12	3*12-15
A2. One-Arm Deep Squat Lat Stretch w/ Breath	3*5 breaths/ea	3*5 breaths/ea	3*5 breaths/ea	3*5 breaths/ea	3*5 breaths/ea	3*5 breaths/ea
B1. One-Arm Bench Rows	3*10 ea	3*10 ea	3*8 ea (heavier)	3*8 ea	3*10 ea	2*10 ea
B2. KB Around the Worlds	3*5 ea way	3*5 ea way	3*6-8 ea way	3*8 ea way	3*8 ea way	2*8 ea way
C1. Push-ups	3*8	3*8	3*10	3*10	6*5	2*12
C2. TRX Supinated Rotating Grip Rows	3*12	3*12	3*15	3*15	3*10 (harder)	2*10 (harder)
D1. Side Planks on Knees (Hinge Pattern)	3*5 ea	3*5-7 ea	3*6-8 ea	3*8 ea	3*8-10 ea	3*10 ea
D2. Inchworms	3*4-6	3*4-6	3*6-8	3*6-8	3*8	2*10

HYPERTROPHY 2 (6 WEEKS)	WEEK 1	WEEK 2	WEEK 3	WEEK 4	WEEK 5	WEEK 6
A1. TRX Squat Press	3*10	3*10	3*12	3*12	3*15	2*15
A2. Side Lunge Reach w/ Weight	3*5 ea	3*5 ea	3*6-8 ea	3*6-8 ea	3*8-10 ea	2*10 ea
A3. Brettzel	3*5 breaths/ea	3*5 breaths/ea	3*5 breaths/ea	3*5 breaths/ea	3*5 breaths/ea	3*5 breaths/ea
B1. TRX Assisted Pull-ups	3*4-6	3*6	3*6	3*6-8	3*8	2*6
B2. One-Arm KB Shoulder Press	3*6 ea	3*6 ea	3*8 ea	3*8 ea	3*10 ea	2*5 ea
C1. TRX Overhead Side Crunch	3*5 ea	3*5 ea	3*5-7 ea	3*6-8 ea	3*8-10	3*8-10
C2. TRX Pikes	3*4	3*4	3*6-8	3*8	3*6 (longer)	3*6

Max Strength, 6 weeks

MAX STRENGTH (6 WEEKS)	WEEK 1	WEEK 2	WEEK 3	WEEK 4	WEEK 5	WEEK 6
A1. 2-1-1-1 Tempo Goblet Squats	3*10	3*10	3*12	3*12	3*15	2*18
A2. Hands on Hips Vertical	3*4	3*4	3*5	3*5	4*4	4*4
B1. Russian Kettlebell Swings	5*8	5*10	6*8	8*8	10*8	5*12
B2. Brettzel	3*5 breaths/ea	3*5 breaths/ea	3*5 breaths/ea	3*5 breaths/ea	3*5 breaths/ea	3*5 breaths/ea
C1. TRX Row w/ Knee Lift	3*5 ea	3*5 ea	3*6-8 ea	3*6-8 ea	3*8-10 ea	2*8 ea
C2. TRX Knee Tuck Slalom	3*15"	3*15"	3*15"	3*20"	3*20"	3*20"

Conversion to Specific Strength, 10 weeks

CONVERSION TO SPECIFIC 1 (5 WEEKS)	WEEK 1	WEEK 2	WEEK 3	WEEK 4	WEEK 5
A1. TRX Single-Leg Squats	3*6-8" ea	3*6-8" ea	3*8-10" ea	3*8-10" ea	2*12 ea
A2. Broad Jump	2*3	2*3	3*3	3*4	2*3

B1. 3-1-3-1 Tempo KB Deadlifts NOT to Floor	3*10	3*10	3*12	3*12-15	2*18
B2. One-Arm KB Shoulder Press	2*8 ea	2*8 ea	3*6 ea	3*6 ea	2*8 ea
C1. TRX Static Hip Lift Row	2*10	2*10	2*12	2*12	2*12
C2. Suitcase Carries	3*60"	3*60"	3*60"	3*70"	3*75"

CONVERSION TO SPECIFIC 2 (5 WEEKS)	WEEK 1	WEEK 2	WEEK 3	WEEK 4	WEEK 5
A1. TRX Single-Leg Squat to Skip	2*18	2*18	2*20	2*20	2*10
A2. Heidens with Stick	2*5	2*5	3*5	3*5	3*4
B1. Kettlebell Swings	5*8	5*8	4*12	4*12	5*10
B2. Brettzel	3*5 breaths/ea	3*5 breaths/ea	3*5 breaths/ea	3*5 breaths/ea	3*5 breaths/ea
C1. TRX Static Hip Lift Rows w/ Pause	2*10	2*10	2*12	2*12	1*15
C2. Front Plank Reach	3*3 ea	3*3 ea	3*4 ea	3*4 ea	3*5 ea

Maintenance, 10 weeks

MAINTENANCE 1 (5 WEEKS)	WEEK 1	WEEK 2	WEEK 3	WEEK 4	WEEK 5
A1. 2-1-1-1- KB Deadlifts	2*10	2*10	2*12	2*12	2*10
A2. Can Crush	2*6 ea	2*6 ea	2*6 ea	2*6 ea	2*6 ea
B1. KB Around the Worlds	2*8 ea	2*8 ea	2*5 ea	2*5 ea	2*6 ea
B2. Side-Lying Windmill	2*6-8 ea	2*6-8 ea	2*6-8 ea	2*6-8 ea	2*6-8 ea
C1. Side Planks, Top Foot Forward	2*45-60"ea	2*45-60" ea	2*60" ea	2*60" ea	2*60" ea
C2. McGill Crunch	2*5 w/ 5" hold	2*5 w/ 8" hold	2*5 w/ 8" hold	2*5 w/ 10" hold	2*5 w/ 10" hold
C3. Bird Dogs, Level 1, 2, or 3	2*5-7 ea	2*5-7 ea	2*6-8 ea	2*8 ea	2*8-10 ea

MAINTENANCE 2 (5 WEEKS)	WEEK 1	WEEK 2	WEEK 3	WEEK 4	WEEK 5
A1. 2-1-1-1- KB Deadlifts	2*15	2*15	2*18	2*18	2*12-15
A2. Prisoner Vertical	2*6	2*8	2*8	2*10	2*10
B1. McGill Crunch	2*5 w/ 10" hold	2*5 w/ 10" hold	2*6-8 w/ 10" hold	2*6-8 w/ 10" hold	2*810 w/ 10" hold
B2. Side Planks, Top Foot Forward	2*60" ea	2*60" ea	2*60" ea	2*60" ea	2*60" ea
B3. Bird Dogs, Level 2 or 3	2*8 ea	2*8 ea	2*8 ea	2*8 ea	2*8 ea

A SAMPLE TRAINING YEAR OVERVIEW

NOVEMBER 1–JANUARY 1

- Work on technique for Olympic movements.
- Work on trunk endurance (high reps, low weight, or positions held for time), spinal stability/strength.
- Coinciding with the above, do "normal" cadence work to recruit more type IIx muscle fibers (think long endurance rides at 95+ cadence on *all*).
- Strength exercises should focus on multi-joint movement with perfect technique.
- Focus on extension exercises for hips, shoulders/chest, rotator cuff, and mid-back musculature.
- ***Bike fit performed November 1st–15th*** to allow the bike fitter to give feedback about which muscles or movement chains are broken or not working well, and/or which muscles are tight.

JANUARY 1–MARCH 15

- Begin Hypertrophy phase.
- Lift to elicit strength response of musculature, specifically weak links in muscular chains.
- Do isolation work of weak muscles.
- On-bike workouts begin to include more muscular efforts, as well as pedaling and positioning technique on the bike.
- Movements focus on cycling-specific movements, with joint-balancing movements performed.
- Ascertain whether strength program has elicited proper response.
- Dial in rider to a more aggressive position as the body will tolerate. Some riders will have small or no adjustments to be made.
- Time trial (TT) fit—Optimal time, as athlete will have enough hours on the bike and a good foundation of strength for the fitter and coach to have a good idea of what the optimal TT fit will be for this athlete.
- TT fit may be revisited 4–6 weeks prior to goal event.

MARCH 15–APRIL 30

- *Bike fit check March 15–April 1*
- Do more cycling-specific movements.
- Introduce appropriate plyometrics and sprint work.
- Introduce yoga or Pilates as appropriate for specific athletes.
- Focus on higher end of strength repetitions.

APRIL 30–JUNE 15

- Focus on the trunk.
- Strength training time limited to 2–3 x 15–30 minute sessions a week.
- Improve abilities on the bike, including an increase in flexibility for more aggressive TT or RR position (as appropriate).
- Increase balance work.
- Increase on-bike strength work to 10–20% of structured ride time.
- Review training logs to ascertain weak/tight muscles on long/hard efforts and rides.

JUNE 15–JULY 1 (AND ONGOING THROUGH STAGE RACES)

- ***Bike fit tweaks***
- Focus on personal needs and desires for upcoming races. Bike fits should be performed 7–14 days out from competition, and for high level-athletes, these may need to be tweaked ongoing.

JUNE 16–SEPTEMBER 15

- Focus on trunk strength, balance, and stability (10–20 minutes 2–4x a week, as rider body indicates needed).
- Off-bike strength training limited to plyometrics (as appropriate) and moderate weights to keep joints in good balance.
- Strength training sessions take on a more "fun" approach, including safe but competitive "games" that also allow for team and/or coach and athlete bonding. These should be highly tailored to individual needs!
- Some athletes may need more yoga or Pilates, while others may need a highly focused 20–30 minute trunk program.

SEPTEMBER 15–OCTOBER 1 (OR AFTER LAST ROAD/ MTB RACE OF SEASON)

- Anatomical Adaptations *or* transition period with little formal/structured programming. Yoga, Pilates, or low weight/medium repetitions for target areas/problem areas.
- You may include swimming, hiking, or other fun activities.
- You may need this time off, but be encouraged to do some light strength training for target areas.

OCTOBER 1–NOVEMBER 1

- Do a movement assessment and begin strength program for next season.
- Some athletes may need to begin strength training two weeks after their season has finished, depending on their injury status and performance the year prior. Also, workout and structured free time is recommended to allow ample time to be with friends and family, and to decompress from the previous season.

FINAL THOUGHTS

Strength training for cycling performance entails far more than just heading into the gym or picking up some weights.

The Vortex Method is incredibly powerful when used properly. Riders of all abilities, levels, and training ages have used it with great success. I hope that you too will see impressive results as you use the Vortex Method as your strength training program, and that you'll begin to see that the weights you move don't matter as much as *how* you are moving and the positions, postures, and breathing patterns that you are using.

If you'd like to learn more about the Vortex Method, or if you'd like to use one of my programs, head over to www.HumanVortexTraining.com and check out my pre-made strength training programs, educational courses, or my Strength Training for Cyclists Certification.

If you prefer to learn in person, make sure to subscribe to my HVTraining Newsletter to be the first to know about my upcoming speaking engagements, workshops, and presentations around the world.

I'd love to hear from you and how the Vortex Method has helped you unleash your pain-free, lion-of-a-rider abilities! Feel free to email me at Brodie@HumanVortexTraining.com to share with me your transformation and growth as a rider.

Remember: Train Smarter, Not Harder, Because it's all about YOU!

EQUIPMENT

In this section I'll go over the different pieces of equipment that you may find in the weight room and help you understand their general uses and how to recognize them so that you can feel confident and comfortable in the weight room.

By no means is the list here exhaustive. There are plenty more pieces of equipment, "toys," and accessories that you may find in your local gym. Each tool has its place; some will become regulars in your strength training regimen, while others you may never touch or need.

BARBELLS

Spin Lock barbell: Often sold for home gyms, these can serve the purpose of keeping costs low, although the ability to load them up with weight will be limited, and they are *not* appropriate for Olympic lifts.

Standard barbell: Relatively cheap, not built to hold heavy weights or withstand beatings. Often found at low-end gyms and hotel gyms.

Powerlifting barbell: Stiffer than Olympic barbells, these can be longer in length to allow for more weight and may be thicker in diameter. Hash marks on bar are closer together (32 inches vs 36 inches on Olympic bar). Without bearings, these don't really spin. Center knurling to help keep barbell from sliding off back during back squat.

Olympic barbell: Solid sleeves, with bushings and sleeves with bearings that allow the bar to "spin" while loaded. 7.2 ft long (2.2m), standard bar diameter (28mm), 44 pounds (20kg). It has more flex (called "whip") than a powerlifting barbell and is built to take a beating from being dropped repeatedly.

Olympic barbell (women/beginners): Solid sleeves, with bushings and sleeves with bearings that allow the bar to "spin" while loaded. No center knurling, 6.9 ft long (2.1m), smaller bar diameter (25mm), 33 pounds (15kg). Has more flex (called "whip") than powerlifting barbell and is built to take a beating from being dropped repeatedly.

EZ Curl Bar: This bar has a slight W pattern to it. Usually used for bicep curls and tricep exercises, which the bar was originally designed for, it can also be used for hip thrusts, as the shorter bar length and mid-bar curvature make it easier to control and somewhat more comfortable.

Safety Squat Bar: Looking like a yoke, the Safety Squat Bar is a great tool for cyclists—if you have access to one—as it takes a lot of stress off of the shoulder, upper, and middle back, due to your being able to hold the bar with the handles in front of you.

Hex bar: A go-to choice for deadlifts, the hex bar allows you to not have to worry about "clearing the bar" over the knees, and gives you a more natural hand position, allowing you to better produce trunk stiffness and great positions to lift from. This small yet significant change is very often a game-changer for cyclists to be able to get the most out of their deadlifting. Be aware of the weight, as hex bars can come in a variety of weights, from 30 lb. (15kg) all the way up to 100 lb. (45+kg). If unsure, ask the staff.

Swiss bar: Also known as a "football bar" due to the shaping of the center-handled section, the Swiss bar is like the Swiss Army knife of pressing and rowing barbells due to the variety of handle positions it offers you. Much like the hex bar, the Swiss bar comes in a variety of weights, although most are usually 35–40 lb. (15–20kg) in weight.

PLATES & COLLARS

There is a *very* significant and important difference between the kinds of plates you use, especially for anything where you are lifting the barbell off the floor or from a lower position, as well as for Olympic lifts, where you need to drop the barbell. Many injuries have happened to riders because they do not know the differences here.

Bumper plates: The weights that are made for these activities are called bumper plates and are made of a synthetic material, usually plastic, or they are coated in a special plastic that is meant to take a beating. No matter the weight, all bumper plates, from 5 lb. up to 100 lb., will have the *same diameter*.

Standard plates: Standard plates are what most gyms have. If you are doing deadlifts or movements from the floor, you *must* be sure to put blocks or some-thing under the plates on the bar, so that the bar begins at least ⬜ up your shin. Standard plates are usually metal and are *not* made to be dropped.

Collars, also called "clips," are used to lock the weights onto the bar so that they do not move on the bar or fall off while you lift. Be aware that collars *do* add weight to the bar. Usually, but not always, spring collars and plastic collars will weigh around 0.25 pounds, while Olympic collars will vary. *Always use collars!* No matter if the weight is light or very heavy, always use collars to secure your weights.

Plastic collars: These have become more popular the last few years as they are rel-atively cheap and easy to use. They usually open and close like a latch, with a click.

Oly collars: The heavy-duty, rugged, "the weight isn't gonna move anywhere" collar, Olympic collars are used for Olympic weightlifting. They are super secure and keep the weights from moving at all. There are a variety of styles, but if pos-sible, these should be used for all Olympic lifts.

Spring collars: Always "fun" to get on and off the bar, spring collars can be a pain until you get the hand strength and angles correct. Be sure to use them, even if they're your only option!

KETTLEBELLS

A foundational piece to your home gym or training studio, start with 1–2 kettlebells (beginners: 8kg and 12kg, intermediate: 12kg and 16kg, advanced: 16kg and 24kg). Allowing you to perform a broad variety of strength and explosive strength exercises in a small space, kettlebells are extremely portable, and along with a suspension trainer and 2–3 bands, they will fill out your low-cost, high-impact home gym or studio.

Traditional & Non-Competition: Traditional kettlebells are all iron, with a slightly oversized handle. In the early 90s when kettlebells were just being introduced to western civilization, Dragon Door Publications were the sole producers and importers to the U.S. Nowadays there are a number of companies that produce kettlebells, but beware! Not all kettlebells are created equal. If you have the option, go with the traditional kettlebells or competition kettlebells, as they are the sturdy workhorses and have many years of development to their subtle shapes and smooth, single-cast handles.

While there are kettlebells with plastic coating, vinyl coating, filled with sand, etc., I do *not* advise using any of those, as the quality of the handles and the bells themselves is not high.

Competition: These are my preference for home gyms for cyclists and triathletes, as every single weight of the competition kettlebells are the exact same size and built exactly the same. While kettlebell purists will say learning to master the bigger kettlebell is part of the challenge and skill, I prefer to keep the instrument the same, as it decreases your learning curve and helps you progress in your main sport of cycling, getting what you need out of your strength training a bit faster.

One thing to note: Competition kettlebells are not as rough and tumble as their traditional cousins. Especially for the weights below 20kg, if dropped too many times, or on the wrong surface, the inner core can become loose and cause problems. However, in our program you won't be throwing or dropping the kettlebells. Competition kettlebells are my choice for beginner and intermediate strength training cyclists.

IMPORTANT NOTES FOR KETTLEBELLS

- Make sure the handle is completely smooth and does not have any bumps or ridges on it. While it may feel okay when just picking it up and putting it down, these small deformities on the handles can tear up your hands when doing swings, cleans, and other dynamic movements.

- If you have a high-quality wood, parquet, or tile floor, coated kettlebells might be a good choice after all . . . just make sure the handles are smooth.

Continued...

- When purchasing kettlebells, do *not* give in to the temptation for small weight differences. Kettlebells serve a great purpose by being made in 4kg increments, as this forces you to truly master a movement at a specific weight before thinking about moving on.

- For those living in the US, divide the weight of the kettlebell in pounds by 2.2 in order to determine how many kilograms it is.

DUMBBELLS

Standard (plastic-coated): Most modern gyms use plastic- or PVC-coated round or hexagonal dumbbells. Things to pay attention to are the shape of the handles, especially for those who have smaller hands.

Metal: Some gyms still have the old hexagonal metal dumbbells, while others have nicely machined and polished metal dumbbells up to 30 lb. (20kg). Pay attention to the size of the handles, and note that there will be more variation in how the weight balances and feels in your hands.

Adjustable (for in-home use): There are a number of these on the market, from "spinner" weights where the collars spin onto a machined bar, to PowerBlock and BowFlex brands, and many more. For those who are more advanced or require heavier weights for home use, these can be great choices. Bear in mind that adjustable dumbbells may have some limitations for explosive or power movements. Always read the owner's manual and know what is and is not safe.

BANDS

For all bands, you want to be aware of what you are anchoring them or tying them to and how. Sharp corners will compromise the bands and make them unsafe/unfit for use. Purchase a "door anchor" to help give you more options for what exercises you can perform.

Jump Stretch: These look like giant rubber bands and are made of one continuous piece. They are usually priced by the resistance level. Make sure you are purchasing the correct sizes for you.

Mini: These small, continuous loops are generally around 6–8 inches in length (15–18cm) and are used for smaller muscle groups by targeting movements at the hip and shoulder. Don't be fooled, they'll make you work!

Hip loop: Made of a more durable, cloth-like material, the hip loop has been growing in popularity since around 2012 when Bret Contreras started working with them for his glute workouts. These can serve a purpose in your strength training, but they are usually used for intermediate to advanced strength training athletes who have graduated from the mini band resistances.

Tubing & bungee cord: Popular in physical therapy clinics, tubing usually has handles at both ends, making it easier to use. Unlike Jump Stretch bands, your hands won't start to hurt with tubing, which makes it a good choice for upper body exercises. There are a number of varieties of tubing, including "bungee cords," which will offer you a slightly different length-tension curve than the standard tubing.

SUSPENSION TRAINERS

A foundational piece to your home gym or training studio, a suspension trainer will serve you extremely well. It also travels well for race weekends. Just remember where you put it in the car, and do not leave it hanging while you are out for your race or ride—someone *will* take it.

TRX: The "original" TRX is a highly compact and travel-friendly piece of equipment, and it offers two handles that are directly tied together in one continuous piece. Performing single-arm and single-leg versions of exercises may prove to be a little challenging, especially for those with small hands and feet, due to the handle and hook sizes.

Jungle Gym: The most popular follow-up to the TRX, this is my preferred choice, as the straps are completely independent and come with a built-in, heavy-duty rubber/plastic anchor to each strap, which can be used pretty much anywhere. Handles are made of plastic and rubber and are *not* one piece, but they do have a non-slip, built-in stirrup, which makes putting your feet in far easier.

BENCHES

Don't go cheap on benches. Ever. I've seen cheap benches in clients' houses and at commercial gyms that nearly kill or maim people due to poor construction, poor stability, or just being used in ways they are not built for. Your safety and well-being are worth the extra $100 to pay for a sturdy, well-built bench.

Heavy-duty: The only kind of bench to buy, in my opinion, as they come in a variety of weight limits, adjustability, and prices. Your bench should have feet at least as wide as the bench itself, with rubber "ends" that help it keep non-slip contact with the floor.

Adjustable: Heavy-duty benches come in a variety of styles, usually flat or adjustable. If you're going to go adjustable for your home gym (I suggest heavy-duty benches rated for *at least* 400 lb.), go with the one that allows you to adjust the incline from 0 to 165 degrees. Being able to decline is nice, but you don't need it.

CABLE STACKS

Adjustable: Usually, but not always, in commercial gyms as a "cable cross." There will be a weight stack with a pin to change the weight selection, oftentimes with one weight stack on the right and another on the left. Sometimes the pulleys will have a slight 20–30 degree angle, in an effort to make chest flies easier to execute. The adjustable cable stacks will have a pulley that can be moved up and down and locked in at a variety of heights in order to execute a number of exercises, at a number of angles.

Non-adjustable: The less useful version of the adjustable cable stack, these will have a fixed pulley either at the floor level, at the top of the machine, or both.

FreeMotion: The super cool, adaptable, and useful cousin of the cable stack is the FreeMotion machine. This machine will have the weights for both sides located in the middle, with arms that come out at either side, some at set angles and others with a number of angles that you can adjust the arms to, and at a variety of heights. This is a fantastically useful, yet often under-utilized, piece of equipment in the gym.

CABLE STACK HANDLES

D-Grip: Single-hand grip that looks like the letter "D."

Soft Grip: Single-hand grip with a plastic handle set on a nylon loop.

V-Grip: Looking like the letter "V," this grip is most often used for rowing exercises.

EZ Grip: An attachment for the cable stacks that is shaped just like its barbell cousin, the EZ Curl Bar, in the shape of a "W."

Straight Bar: Clip-on attachment about the length of your forearm that is perfectly straight.

Neutral Grip: Clip-on attachment that looks almost like a handlebar on the road bike or a handlebar mustache. At both ends there are handles that are parallel to each other.

Wide Neutral Grip: Clip-on attachment similar to the neutral grip, except the parallel handles are wider than your shoulder width.

Lat Bar: Clip-on attachment where the ends slant down at about a 30-degree angle. This is most often found on the Latissimus Dorsi pulldown machine.

No-Grip Ankle/Wrist Attachment: Clip-on attachment, usually Velcro, that you can attach to your ankle, forearm, or wrist, so you can do grip-free upper body work or hip work.

Rotational Grip: Clip-on attachment that usually looks like the wide neutral grip bar, except the ends spin and move as you go through the exercise of choice.

SQUAT RACK

Moveable/Storable: The movable squat rack requires you to add 20kg (45 lb.) plates on the bottom to stabilize it (this version is common in CrossFit gyms), and can be adjusted to heights ranging from 1m (~3 ft) tall up to almost 2m (~6 ft).

Basic: This squat rack tends to have multiple levels for you to rack the bar on. Usually used for squatting, although it's also useful for overhead pressing and some top-down hinge variations, like the Romanian Deadlift. It often has storage pins for weights on the side or front, helping to weight the rack down so you don't tip it over.

Cages: These enclosed "cages" can be used for a broad number of exercises. Called cages due to there being no way to get the bar out unless you move it on its side, cages often come with "pins," which can be used for self-spotting, safety for bench press, or a number of other uses.

Olympic platforms: Not just squat racks! Olympic platforms are very specifically designed to allow an athlete to perform explosive power movements such as the clean and the snatch. Noted for its center wooden platform and hard but absorbent black (or other colored) flooring on either side of the wooden center, Olympic platforms are often incredibly well-built and sturdy. Keep in mind that these are incredibly rare to find in non-athletic facilities, and often facilities that do have them will most likely also have an Olympic weightlifting club or coach.

Gym etiquette tip: If you have the choice between a cage/squat rack or an Olympic platform, and you are doing squats, *don't* take the Olympic platform.

Smith Machine: Special racks that are made for benching, squatting, and a number of other exercises, the Smith Machine is a barbell that is permanently connected to a pair (or quartet) of metal rails. The user will have some safety—they can turn the bar and lock the weight onto the rack at any point, as there are multiple levels, and the machine allows you to work with different angles.

***Important Note:** Smith Machine bars are *not* all the same weight! Be careful and mindful if you are using these in your program and are at a new gym. *Always* do a warm-up set with just a barbell/bar to see how you're feeling for a given movement. This will allow you to get a feel for what the bar weighs on that specific Smith Machine.

OLYMPIC EQUIPMENT

Blocks (and substitutes): While not technically only for Olympic lifting, blocks, pins, and other pieces designed to help dial in the starting height of the bar are usually very easy to find at gyms that have Olympic platforms. However, a growing number of commercial gyms also offer these.

Wrist wraps: Elastic cloth with a small loop for the thumb and with strong Velcro on the outside, wrist wraps are made to help support the wrists through flexion (bending the hand backwards). While designed for Olympic lifting, they are also useful for those starting to do kettlebell cleans and a number of other exercises. However, as with all assistive equipment, aim to work up to not needing wrist wraps to perform the lifts, or use them only for heavier or more challenging sets.

Shoes: Olympic shoes are specially designed shoes that offer a hard, non-move-able sole, much like that of the high-end road cycling shoe. These shoes put the wearer in a slightly elevated heel position, which helps in getting to the different hip angles needed for Olympic lifting.

Chalk: More and more commercial gyms are banning chalk, as it is messy and hard to clean up. However, chalk is used to help keep a firm grip on the barbell/kettlebell/dumbbell. There are liquid versions of chalk you can get, which I always try to travel with, as the liquid chalk is not messy and it gives you the same grip-assurance as its powdery cousin. Just be sure to thoroughly wash your hands, and don't rub your eyes (or cough or sneeze into your freshly chalked hands!).

BELTS

As discussed in Chapter 5, "Foundations of a Healthy Spine," you want to build up your "natural" weight belt's abilities to protect your spine and produce stiffness when and where you need it.

Most beginners, unless they have been instructed by a physical therapist or doctor, should first work with weights that do not require support, and through movements that are low-risk of injury that will teach them *how* to brace properly.

Simply slapping on a belt and having at it only drastically slows your strength in the long run, as well as keeps you from learning the strategies, skills, and approaches you need in order to see results out on the bike.

If you're unsure about whether or not to use a weight belt, talk with your physical therapist or see a skilled and reputable strength coach or personal trainer for guidance on this issue.

Olympic: These belts tend to be slimmer than their powerlifting cousins, as greater movement is needed for the Olympic movements.

Powerlifting: Sturdier and wider than Olympic belts, powerlifting belts are meant for handling big, heavy weights in the movements of a bench press, squat, and deadlift, but they are not too useful for much else.

PLYO BOXES

When doing plyometrics or jumps, as a whole, *never* land hard or "stomp down!" This is incredibly bad for the joints and for the movement patterns you're teaching your body. Learn how to use the muscles to decrease the impact of landing as much as possible.

Wood: Probably the most common, especially at CrossFit gyms, it's important to note that many of these boxes do *not* lock together to keep them from sliding around. While most people won't need to stack two boxes on top of each other for anything in our program, perhaps you will get to that level in the future. If you're using these, beware of the fact that they can, and probably will, slip at some point if you're not careful.

Soft: Coming in just a few varieties, "soft" plyo boxes are usually some kind of nylon or other grippy but soft material. These boxes, while soft, are not squishy! Most often they come with long Velcro flaps that allow you to connect the boxes together so they do not slip or move. With the combination of a firm but soft surface and the ability to lock the boxes together, use these (as long as the heights are appropriate for you).

Aerobic step: For many beginners, an aerobic step will do more than fine for step-ups, step-downs, jumps, and much more. Just be careful on the stability of the step (those square plastic risers are not as sturdy as you think, especially if you are doing jumps and explosive work!).

BALLS & BAGS

Medicine ball: These are harder weighted balls, usually ranging from 1kg (2.2 lb.) to 5kg (12 lb.). These are usually intended to be held in your hand and are not made to be bounced. You may also find some "old school" med balls that are made of leather, but these are still not to be bounced.

Slam ball: Soft-shell weighted balls, these are made to be slammed and will absorb the impact and will not bounce much.

Wall ball: These are usually around 1 foot (30cm) in diameter and often have a weighted core, with a cotton stuffing around the outside of the core. They are generally made to be thrown and caught, as they are big, soft on the hands, and don't bounce far.

Sandbag: These are made to be carried in some fashion, with a number of handles attached. While some versions are evenly weighted, others have sand in an open compartment inside, which will flow freely.

Ankle weights: Usually weighted with sand and having some kind of Velcro fastener, ankle weights can be put around the ankles or forearms for added resistance.

IMPORTANT PIECES

GHD: The Glute Ham Raise (GHR), also called the Glute Ham Device (GHD), is an incredibly useful piece of equipment if you know how to use it and have built up the strength necessary to use it properly. Usually found in professional sports teams' weight rooms and gyms that serve serious athletes.

45-degree back extension (adjustable): This can be a very useful tool when used properly, to help hit the glutes, hamstrings, and spinal extensors. Proper setup is very important, so be sure to ask a staff member or knowledgeable coach to help you learn how.

Assisted pull-up machine: This is a useful piece of equipment, as it often allows better body position, as compared to the seated lat pulldown.

Hip Thruster bench: This bench is made to be at the correct height to set up properly for the Hip Thruster movement in a way that you don't have to worry about getting under the bar or about the bench moving under you during your set.

ADDITIONAL RESOURCES

COURSES

Human Vortex Training's Strength Training for Cyclists Certification Course:

https://www.humanvortextraining.com/courses-strength-training-for-cyclists-and-triathletes/

Strength Training for Cycling Success, TrainingPeaks University:

https://trainingpeaks-university.thinkific.com/courses/strength-training-for-cycling-success

Strength Training for Triathlon Success, TrainingPeaks University: https://training-peaks-university.thinkific.com/courses/strength-training-for-triathlon-success

Menopause for Athletes, Dr. Stacy Sims: https://www.drstacysims.com/meno-pause

PODCASTS

The Strong Savvy Cyclist & Triathlete Podcast: https://www.humanvortextraining.com/podcast/

VIDEOS

HVTraining YouTube channel: https://www.youtube.com/user/HVTraining

WEBSITES

Human Vortex Training: https://www.humanvortextraining.com/

BackFitPro: www.BackFitPro.com

REFERENCES

INTRODUCTION

Carmichael, Chris. *The Time-Crunched Cyclist: Race-Winning Fitness in 6 Hours a Week*, 3ʳᵈ ed. Boulder: VeloPress, 2017.

Rountree, Sage. *The Athlete's Guide to Recovery: Rest, Relax, and Restore for Peak Performance*. Boulder, VeloPress, 2011.

CHAPTER 1: THE IMPORTANCE OF STRENGTH TRAINING FOR CYCLISTS

Baechle, Thomas R., and Roger W. Earle, eds. *Essentials of Strength Training and Conditioning*, 3ʳᵈ ed. Champaign, IL: Human Kinetics, 2008.

Jamieson, Joel. *Ultimate MMA Conditioning*, 2009.

CHAPTER 2: STRENGTH TRAINING BASICS

Myslinski, Tom. "The Development of the Russian Conjugate Sequence System" Elite FTS. December 19, 2016. https://www.elitefts.com/education/the-development-of-the-russian-conjugate-sequence-system/.

CHAPTER 3: PERFORMANCE LIMITERS & RESPONSES TO TRAINING

Bassham, Lanny. *With Winning in Mind*, 3rd ed. Mental Management Systems, 2012.

Bothe, Kathrin, Franziska Hirschauer, Hans-Peter Wiesinger, et al. "Gross Motor Adaptation Benefits from Sleep After Training." Wiley Online Library, December 23, 2019. https://doi.org/10.1111/jsr.12961.

Jamieson, Joel. *Ultimate MMA Conditioning*, 2009.

CHAPTER 4: SPECIAL CONSIDERATIONS FOR WOMEN

American College of Sports Medicine. *ACSM's Resources for the Exercise Physiologist*, 2nd Ed. LWW, 2017.

Aragon, Alan Albert and Brad Jon Schoenfeld. "Nutrient Timing Revisited: Is There a Post-Exercise Anabolic Window?" *Journal of the International Society of Sports Nutrition* 10, 5 (2013). doi: 10.1186/1550-2783-10-5.

John, Dan. *Intervention: Course Corrections for the Athlete and Trainer.* On Target Publications, 2012.

Rinaldi, Dr. Nicola J. *No Period, Now What?: A Guide to Regaining Your Cycles and Improving Your Fertility.* Antica Press, 2016.

Sims, Dr. Stacy. *ROAR: How to Match Your Food and Fitness to Your Unique Female Physiology for Optimum Performance, Great Health, and a Strong, Lean Body for Life.* Rodale, 2016.

Wikström-Frisén, Lisbeth, Carl J. Boraxbekk, and Karin Henriksson-Larsén. "Effects on Power, Strength and Lean Body Mass of Menstrual/Oral Contraceptive Cycle Based Resistance Training." *Journal of Sports Medicine and Physical Fitness* 57, 1-2 (2017): 43–52. doi: 10.23736/S0022-4707.16.05848-5.

CHAPTER 5: FOUNDATIONS OF A HEALTHY SPINE

McGill, Dr. Stuart. *Low Back Disorders: Evidence-Based Prevention and Rehabilitation*, 3rd Ed. Human Kinetics, 2015.

CHAPTER 6: THE FUNDAMENTAL 5+1 MOVEMENTS

Huseynov, Alik, Christoph P. E. Zollikofer, Walter Coudyzer, Dominic Gascho, Christian Kellenberger, Ricarda Hinzpeter, and Marcia S. Ponce de León. "Developmental Evidence for Obstetric Adaptation of the Human Female Pelvis." *Proceedings of the National Academy of Sciences of the United States of America* 113, 19 (2016): 5227–5232.

Somerset, Dean and Tony Gentilcore. "The Even More Complete Shoulder & Hip Blueprint." https://www.completeshoulderandhipblueprint.com.

CHAPTER 7: COMPONENTS OF AN INTELLIGENT STRENGTH TRAINING PROGRAM

Duhigg, Charles. *The Power of Habit: Why We Do What We Do in Life and Business.* Random House, 2014.

CHAPTER 14: PROGRAMMING: WHAT'S THE BIG IDEA?

Friel, Joe. *Fast After 50: How to Race Strong for the Rest of Your Life.* Boulder: VeloPress, 2015.

Helms, Eric R. et al., "RPE vs. Percentage 1RM Loading in Periodized Programs Matched for Sets and Repetitions." *Frontiers in Physiology* March 21, 2018. doi: 10.3389/fphys.2018.00247.

Helms, Eric R. et al., "Self-Rated Accuracy of Rating of Perceived Exertion-Based Load Prescription in Powerlifters." *Journal of Strength & Conditioning Research* 31,10 (2017): 2,938–2,943.

Hutchinson, Alex. *Endure: Mind, Body, and the Curiously Elastic Limits of Human Performance.* William Morrow, 2018.

CHAPTER 15: PUTTING TOGETHER A TRAINING PLAN

McGill, Dr. Stuart. *Low Back Disorders: Evidence-Based Prevention and Rehabilitation*, 3rd Ed. Human Kinetics, 2015.

Murphy's Laws of War: http://www.military-info.com/freebies/murphy.htm.

CHAPTER 17: METABOLIC TRAINING

Carmichael, Chris. *The Time-Crunched Cyclist: Race-Winning Fitness in 6 Hours a Week*, 3rd ed. Boulder: VeloPress, 2017.

Note: Page citations appearing in **boldface** indicate figures and photos.

A

A-march, 248–49, **249**

abdominal hoop, 266, 267, 268, 270, 271, 272, 273, 274, 275, 276, 278, 279, 280, 281, 283, 284, 285, 288

abdominals, 34, 255

aches, 29, 75, 85, 86, 205

Acute Training Load (ATL), 126

adaptation, 10, 11, 14, 158, 186, 198, 199; attention for, 194; breathing patterns and, 129; cardio-respiratory, 191; hormonal, 191; metabolic, 23, 157, 170, 191; neuromuscular, 23, 191; recovery and, 50–51, 185, 195, 311–13; sport-oriented, 172; strength-training and, 92; stress on, 194; tissue, 51, 306; weeks, 36. *See also* anatomical adaptation

adductors, 241, 243, 247

adductors/medial side of thigh, foam roller and, 223–24, **223**

agility ladder, 250

anaerobic power stomps (APS), 292–93

anatomical adaptation, 175, 182, 305, 306, 321, 325; described, 176–77

ankle, appropriate stiffness for, 249

arms, 93; power/speed and, 79, 81–82

assisted pull-up machine, 344

attack repeats (AR15s), 294

B

back: healthy/pain-free, 87–89, 106; lower, 88; rounding, 105

back body expansion, 134–35

back on corner shoulder "no money," 148

balance, 256, 313; strength training and, 29

ball slams, 259–60, **259**

ballerinas, 145

balls and bags: ankle weights, 343; medicine ball, 343; sandbag, 343; slam ball, 343; wall ball, 343

bands, 187, 188; anchoring, 317; described, 336–37; hip loop, 337; jump stretch, 336; mini, 337; training with, 33, 318–21, 321–24; tubing/bungee cord, 337

barbell back squat to bench box, 268–69, **269**

barbells, 27, 40, 188, 317; described, 332–33; Olympic, 332–33; powerlifting, 332; Spin Lock, 332; training with, 318–21

bars, 187; EZ curl, 333; hex, 333; holding, 161, 162; lifting, 162; pulling, 162; safety squat, 333; Swiss, 333

basal caloric needs, 60

basal metabolic needs, 59, 61

Base period, 196, 198, 199, 202, 308

battle ropes, 9

bedrock foundation, described, 152

belts: described, 341–42; Olympic, 342; powerlifting, 342

bench presses, 96, 161, 193; barbell, 97, **273, 273–74**; dumbbell incline, 272–73, **272**

benches, 338

biceps curls, 79, 96, 154

big ring endurance (Big Ring Endur), 299–300

big ring over-geared climbs (BROC), 293

bike fit, 75, 82, 328, 329; importance of, 131; issues with, 25; movement and, 85; performing, 84; quality, 16; spine and, 84

bike fitters, role of, 85

bike handling, 16, 171

biomechanical chain work, 28

bird dog, 110, 147, 194, 201, 214, 237–38, **237**, 286, 287, **287**

Blackburns, 147

blood plasma volume, loss of, 65

blood pressure, changes in, 118

blood sugar, controlling, 72

BMR, calculating, 59, 60, 61

body, 213; composition, 58, 72, 208; understanding, 122

body temperature, 65, 213. *See also* core temperature

body weight: strength and, 33

bodybuilder approach, 8, 12, 34

bodyweight movement, dynamic warm-up, 143

bone health, deterioration of, 62

bones, 41; broken, 24; density, 61, 72; weakening, 106; weight training and, 37

BOSU balls, 9, 91

braking, 16, 171, 180

breath work, 115, 116, 118, 152, 212; described, 229–31; soft tissue work and, 142; thoughts on, 138–39

breathing, 3, 53–55, 59, 96, 104, 107, 141, 158, 178, 217, 246, 247; attention for, 194; deep, 214; as foundation, 129; impact of, 55; improving, 55, 131; movement and, 55; power of, 54; recovery and, 54; warm-up and, 132, 133

ABOUT THE AUTHOR

Menachem Brodie has been an athletic performance specialist since 2007 and has been coaching since 2000. He has worked with athletes from a number of sports, including cycling, triathlon, basketball, rugby, Brazilian jiu-jitsu, running, swimming, and many more. In 2007, Menachem started Human Vortex Training to help endurance athletes experience and explore the performance gains offered by an intelligently de-signed strength training program that complements their in-sport training programs.

Menachem is recognized as a leader in strength training for cyclists and triath-letes. He is an NSCA-Certified Strength & Conditioning Specialist, a USA Cycling Expert Coach, & Serotta Certified Bike Fitter. A strong believer in reducing low back pain and injury, Brodie is also the world's first and only McGill Method Certified Practitioner who focuses on cyclists and triathletes. To help cycling coaches teach his methods, he has developed a Strength Training for Cycling Certification pro-gram, which can be found at the Human Vortex Training website. He presents na-tionally and internationally for organizations and conferences in the sports perfor-mance and fitness industries and is often hired as a consultant for cutting-edge technologies and approaches in the health, fitness, and performance fields.

Menachem is the author of the best-selling courses "Strength Training for Cy-cling Success" and "Strength Training for Triathlon Success" on TrainingPeaks University. He writes a regular column on PezCycling News and is a regular con-tributor to the TrainingPeaks Coach Blog. He has appeared numerous times in sports and health publications including *Bicycling* magazine, *VeloNews, Triath-lete* magazine, *Runner's World, Shape, Men's Health, Women's Health,* as well as on TonyGentilcore.com, Dr. Sarah Duvall's "Pregnancy and Postpartum Corrective Exercise Specialist Course," Global Cycling Network (GCN), That Triathlon Show, *VeloNews* Fast Talk podcast, The Strength Running Podcast, and many more.

In his downtime, Menachem enjoys good coffee, reading and learning about training, traveling, making podcasts and videos, and time with his family.

Menachem is available for seminars, workshops, and consulting and can be con-tacted via email at Brodie@HumanVortexTraining.com.

ACKNOWLEDGMENTS

As with all great accomplishments, this book would not have happened if not for the help and support of many people:

First and foremost, The Creator/God/Lord/Universe/Gaia or whatever your chosen terminology is. Without my own physical challenges and the athletes who have found their way into my little corner of the world, none of this would have happened.

Thank you to my wife and my parents, for their support and gentle nudges. To my sisters, who constantly challenge me and share new knowledge and insights through our discussions and arguments on training, treatment, and medical needs of the human body.

Thank you to my mentors, friends, and colleagues who have shared their time and knowledge with me for this book and beyond: Eric Malzone, Dr. Sarah Duvall, Dr. Stuart McGill, Tony Gentilcore, Joel Jamieson, and countless others.

Thank you to Asher Frank and Andrew Seitz. You are both lifelong friends who came into my world as athletes and have given your friendship, time, effort, and honest feedback on this book and so much more.

Thank you to Ari & Yoni Reinfeld for introducing me to the sport of cycling and for the push to go into Exercise Physiology instead of Physical Therapy. You literally changed the trajectory of my life.

Thank you to Glenn Pawlak for bringing me into the world of cycling. I am forever grateful that you saw potential in a college kid and gave him a chance.

Thank you to Tim Beltz for keeping it real and pushing me to be better, to think outside the box, and for grounding me. You've no idea the positive impact you've had.

A massive thank you to Kara Mannix, my editor, for your guidance and help in making this a coherent and easy-to-follow book. Your abilities to refine and simplify things into usable take-home points has made this an even more powerful book. There are many others who have helped or contributed to this book in a variety of ways, and for that I am incredibly grateful.

I'd also like to thank YOU, the readers of this book for investing your time and your hard-earned money. Thank you for the opportunity to help you along your journey of becoming fitter, faster, and stronger. I hope the information and knowledge in this book give you what you need to Train Smarter, Not Harder. I look forward to hearing how you have used this book to improve your riding, and how you look, feel, and move in your everyday life. I wish you health, happiness, and much success in your endeavors.

Finally, this book is dedicated to Dr. Joel Alcoff, my powerlifting coach, who passed away after a hard-fought battle with leukemia while I was in college. He was an exceptional coach, always there to give me a pat on the back, a kick in the pants, or to teach me to question things and find the truth that aligned with my experiences. You are sorely missed.

Made in the USA
Las Vegas, NV
21 June 2024

91279234R00203